Egmont Key

University Press of Florida

Florida A&M University, Tallahassee

Florida Atlantic University, Boca Raton

Florida Gulf Coast University, Ft. Myers

Florida International University, Miami

Florida State University, Tallahassee

New College of Florida, Sarasota

University of Central Florida, Orlando

University of Florida, Gainesville

University of North Florida, Jacksonville

University of South Florida, Tampa

University of West Florida, Pensacola

Edited by Laura K. Harrison and Brooke Hansen

Egmont Key

Digital Heritage and Engagement on the Disappearing Island

University Press of Florida Gainesville / Tallahassee / Tampa / Boca Raton
Pensacola / Orlando / Miami / Jacksonville / Ft. Myers / Sarasota

Cover: Aerial photo of the Egmont Key lighthouse, showing the 1858 structure at the north end of the island surrounded by foliage and the sea. A research team stands at the base of the lighthouse. The photo was taken in May 2019. Photo by Mel Rodgers. Design by Mindy Basinger Hill.

Published in the United States of America

31 30 29 28 27 26 6 5 4 3 2 1

DOI: https://doi.org/10.5744/9780813079660

Library of Congress Cataloging-in-Publication Data

Names: Harrison, Laura K., 1985– editor | Hansen, Brooke editor
Title: Egmont Key : digital heritage and engagement on the disappearing island / edited by Laura K. Harrison, Brooke Hansen.
Description: Gainesville : University Press of Florida, 2026. | Includes bibliographical references and index.
Identifiers: LCCN 2026021854 (print) | LCCN 2026021855 (ebook) | ISBN 9780813079660 hardback | ISBN 9780813081700 paperback | ISBN 9780813075587 ebook | ISBN 9780813074351 pdf
Subjects: LCSH: Cultural property—Protection—Florida—Egmont Key | Coast changes—Florida—Egmont Key | Sea level—Environmental aspects—Florida—Egmont Key | Historic sites—Conservation and restoration—Florida—Egmont Key | Digital preservation—Florida—Egmont Key | Cultural property—Florida—Egmont Key—Management | Seminole Indians—Florida—Egmont Key—History | Egmont Key (Fla.)—History | BISAC: SOCIAL SCIENCE / Archaeology | HISTORY / United States / State & Local / South (AL, AR, FL, GA, KY, LA, MS, NC, SC, TN, VA, WV)
Classification: LCC F317 .E36 2026 (print) | LCC F317 (ebook) | DDC 363.6/90975965—dc23/eng/20260507
LC record available at https://lccn.loc.gov/2026021854
LC ebook record available at https://lccn.loc.gov/2026021855

The University Press of Florida is the scholarly publishing agency for the State University System of Florida, comprising Florida A&M University, Florida Atlantic University, Florida Gulf Coast University, Florida International University, Florida State University, New College of Florida, University of Central Florida, University of Florida, University of North Florida, University of South Florida, and University of West Florida.

University Press of Florida
PO Box 140239
Gainesville, FL 32614
floridapress.org

GPSR EU Authorized Representative: Mare Nostrum Group B.V, Doelen 72, 4831 GR Breda, The Netherlands, gpsr@mare-nostrum.co.uk

Contents

Illustrations

Charts

Figures

Tables

Acknowledgments

There are many people and organizations who can be considered contributors to this book. The journey for us started on a trip to Big Cypress to meet with Paul Backhouse, then part of the Seminole Tribe of Florida's Tribal Historic Preservation Office (THPO). Many members of the Tribe followed and provided generous guidance on how to bring histories to light where they can be seen and reflected on, including Quenton Cypress, Tina Osceola, Aaron Tommie, and others. The THPO has been a partner on this book since its inception and much gratitude is due to Dave Scheidecker, Juan Cancel, the rest of the THPO staff and also the Ah-Tah-Thi-Ki Museum.

We are also deeply indebted to the many land managers and community partners who helped along the way from US Fish and Wildlife to Florida State Parks. We are especially grateful to Richard Sanchez, who dedicated many years as president of the Egmont Key Alliance, for his enlightening tours of the island and for sharing his deep historical knowledge and friendship. The Tampa Bay Pilots Association has been integral to the island's heritage for many years, and we thank John Timmel and Jack Timmel for helping to educate us and ferrying us to the island to learn about the Pilots and scan the village after Hurricane Helene. Carrie Caignet also provided deep insights into the history of the Pilots and the Lighthouse Keepers at Egmont Key that added depth to our understanding of the island's past.

There were so many strands to pull together to understand the complex histories of the island, and we could not have done that without the help of April Min, Neil Hurley, and Bruce McCall. Their generosity and expertise helped us appreciate just how much history is truly contained within—and beyond—the island's shores.

None of the work of the Egmont Key Project would have happened without the dozens of students, interns, and workshop participants who spent many a hot day on the island scanning, inventorying signs, picking up trash, and documenting hurricane damage. In particular, integral members of our team have included Sophie Annis, Sam Vorce, and Cassidy Bazley. We thank Hubbard's Ferry for the many swift and safe voyages back and forth to the island that enabled our research team to visit the island in wildly varying weather conditions over the years.

We extend a sincere thanks to the many granting organizations that have provided funding and support to our project over the years, including the National Parks Service, Florida Humanities Council, Archaeological Institute of America, and the University of South Florida.

On a personal level, Laura Harrison thanks her partner Sean Kernan for unwavering support and patience throughout the years researching and working on this volume. Brooke Hansen must acknowledge her family, especially Sierra and Darrius, who spent much time caretaking the household while she was off to the island.

Finally, we thank Mel Rodgers for the iconic cover picture, which captured the essence of the island and also included our research group standing by the lighthouse.

Egmont Key

1

Hidden Histories and Changing Landscapes

BROOKE HANSEN AND LAURA K. HARRISON

Encountering the Disappearing Island

The long and winding car ride led us east across Alligator Alley, a highway that bisected the Everglades and strangled the flow of water when it was built in the mid-twentieth century. It was a place of reflection on the many changes wrought upon land and cultures over the centuries. We were headed to Big Cypress, home of the Seminole Tribe of Florida, to learn more about a disappearing island at the mouth of Tampa Bay where Seminole people were incarcerated in the mid-nineteenth century. As we approached the Ah-Tah-Thi-Ki Museum, we were greeted by the sweet smell of smoldering logs at the Seminole Campfire, a continuously burning fire that welcomes guests and signals entry into a cultural space.

In speaking to members of the Seminole Tribal Historical Preservation Office (THPO), we learned of the Tribe's painful and largely unknown history on Egmont Key. We asked if or how we could be of assistance, and they responded by expressing their wish for people to know about the Egmont Key story and what happened to the Seminole people there. As academics that work in the fields of digital heritage and tourism interpretation, we knew that we had some useful tools. They recommended that we get in touch with the Egmont Key Alliance, a nonprofit group that had been working to protect and preserve the island for many years, so we quickly reached out. This initial encounter with Egmont Key would set us on a transformative journey, unraveling layers of hidden histories, remarkable events, and immediate threats surrounding this mysterious and vanishing island.

Figure 1.1. Map of Egmont Key showing key research sites, erosion, and land ownership. Map created by Alex Fawbush, Access 3D Lab, University of South Florida.

After our initial meeting with the Seminole THPO, we embarked on a ferry to Egmont Key to explore the island, a long and narrow landmass about 1.3 km^2 that is both a Florida State Park and a National Wildlife Refuge (1.1). The island is located where the Gulf of Mexico meets Tampa Bay and is only accessible by boat. The 45-minute ride through the swirling waters and strong currents of the Egmont Channel left us reflecting on what we might encounter within its shores. As we set foot on the island, we were immediately captivated by its natural beauty, with sparkling turquoise waters and pristine white sand beaches. The striking lighthouse acted as a beacon of several kinds—leading us to explore the many ruins scattered across the island's interior, while also serving as a notable visual landmark. Near the lighthouse, we encountered a simple cemetery, adorned with white crosses—a visual reminder of the lives lived and lost on this island that is now predominantly frequented by beachgoers. Brick roads extended behind the cemetery into an area called Ghost Town, where crumbled foundations of military buildings have been overtaken by thick foliage with nearby signs providing visual evidence of what was once there.

As we crested the dune and approached the western shoreline of the island, we were confronted with the sight of a decaying historic power plant, its remains crumbling into the sea as waves crashed against the rubble. We learned that this structure was once at the center of the island, and that several similar buildings were already completely underwater. Egmont Key is rapidly eroding into the sea, having lost about half of its landmass in the last 150 years. This loss of land in turn endangers and destroys cultural heritage sites—a process that continues as strong storms, sea-level rise, and the effects of currents continue to exacerbate the erosion.

As we traversed the pathways toward the north of the island, we were struck by the ruins of military structures, now nearly engulfed by dense brush. Along the way, we encountered charming gopher tortoises, throngs of tourists bathing in the sun, numerous boats anchored off the island's picturesque shoreline, and flocks of birds. We were also surprised by some things we did not see—such as bathrooms and trash receptacles. Throughout our visit, the stories shared by the Seminoles remained invisible to us, save for a mere mention of a few Seminole burials on a sign near the Lighthouse Cemetery.

Taking Action

Inspired by our first encounter with Egmont Key, a sense of urgency propelled us to learn more about the disappearing island. What might be lost if we didn't take action? Together, we started formulating plans to better understand and document the island's endangered natural and cultural heritage. Little did we know, this tiny island at the mouth of Tampa Bay was to become a living learning laboratory and guide our research, teaching, and community engagement for years to come. One of our first projects was a University of South Florida (USF) digital heritage and sustainable tourism workshop for students geared toward creating 3D scans of built heritage sites on the island (the lighthouse, cemetery, and Spanish-American War forts), while also exploring tourists' understandings of the island and whether digital heritage experiences (like virtual reality tours) might transform those understandings. The professional development workshops became a centerpiece of the research project, as we enlisted students from USF and beyond, professionals, and interested community members in engaging with Egmont Key.

Over the years, the Egmont Key Project has come to include a multitude of interconnected initiatives, all related to better stewarding the island through documentation, reflection, and collaboration. We partnered with the Egmont Key Alliance and other organizations to engage in public outreach and interpretation at events such as Discover the Island. We obtained research permits, took on interns, delivered public presentations, and won research grants. Our network grew and our research directions crystallized. We were guided by the wealth of archival documents related to the many histories of Egmont Key. We set to work poring over these records, which contained everything from military documents and poems written by lighthouse keepers to firsthand accounts of hurricanes. Some of these materials started to shed light on elements of the Seminole story—one of the most inaccessible parts of the island's history. We also examined the erosion problem, investigating its natural and human causes as well as the many proposed solutions to the accelerating loss of land. The disappearing island became an overarching framework that guided our ever-expanding research.

While writing the book, these themes and motifs took on additional meaning, and a sense of urgency, as two major 2024 hurricanes destroyed entire parts of the island and caused massive destruction. The Tampa Bay Pilots Association village, a base of operations for over a century, was inundated by Hurricane Helene and then further wrecked by Hurricane Milton's strong winds, leaving the buildings strewn about the village. One building was lifted from its foundations and swept out to sea—literally disappearing into the Gulf of Mexico. The land managers' base, docks, and the Florida Park Ranger's residence were left in ruins, uninhabitable, which created a staffing crisis for the island. The land itself was also heavily impacted: the southern end of the island, within the National Wildlife Refuge, sustained heavy losses, its width reduced as a result of the storm surge and the winds. Although the 2024 hurricane season was highly destructive, neither Hurricane Helene nor Milton was a direct hit or a Category 5 storm at landfall. If this scenario materializes in the coming years as predicted, the island could be permanently destroyed.

Egmont Key: Digital Heritage and Engagement on the Disappearing Island provides valuable insights into Egmont Key's historical significance, the complexities of sustainable tourism, and the role of technology in understanding and communicating cultural heritage. The chapters explore the island's role in shaping US history, its connection to the Seminole Tribe, and the challenges and lessons of managing heritage at risk. We introduce sustainable tourism perspectives, the use of digital tools in preserving cultural heritage, and the application of lidar and Geographic Information Systems (GIS) technologies in monitoring coastal dynamics. This book is unique in synthesizing historical records, environmental data, Indigenous perspectives, and community collaboration in a Participatory Action Research (PAR) framework.

Key Directions in Heritage and Sustainability Research

Our research on Egmont Key is embedded with global issues and scholarship on digital heritage and storytelling, sustainable tourism, and climate change. In recent years, the field of digital heritage has become increasingly focused on using technology to democratize and increase access to cultural heritage resources to benefit communities, stakeholders, and students (Díaz-Andreu 2017; Munday et al. 2024; Stephan et al. 2025). This goal manifests in many directions, such as publishing online resources and virtual tours that democratize access to cultural heritage resources (Burkey 2022; Kidd 2018); digitally preserving heritage sites that are at-risk due to industrialization, climate change, or armed conflict (Lercari et al. 2016; Stylianidis and Remondino 2016); and incorporating crowdsourcing and citizen participation to engage the public and descendant communities who are connected to cultural heritage (Giglitto et al. 2021; Shiri et al. 2022).

The future of digital heritage is tasked with ensuring that digitization and virtualization of heritage sites and artifacts is not an end in itself, but rather an important milestone on the road to an applied digital heritage that serves multiple stakeholder communities. Recent scholarship in digital heritage also intersects with sustainable tourism themes of climate preparedness, protection of cultural sites, public engagement, and upholding the triple bottom line of people, planet. and prosperity (Buragohain et al. 2024; El Archi et al. 2023).

Egmont Key provides an ideal setting to examine the intersections of sustainable tourism and digital heritage. The United Nations Sustainable Development Goals (SDGs), ongoing debates about tourism in the wake of the COVID-19 pandemic, and industry-wide efforts to promote sustainability all inform this work (Legrand et al. 2023; Spenceley 2021; Wood 2017). From the outset, SDG 11.4—which calls for strengthening efforts to protect and safeguard cultural and natural heritage—aligns directly with our objectives for the island (United Nations n.d.). SDG 13, Climate Action, proves equally relevant, as National Oceanic and Atmospheric Administration (NOAA) sea-level-rise prediction data enable more precise mapping of projected impacts on heritage structures. Additional SDGs also shaped the research: SDG 12, Responsible Consumption and Production, addressed the significant accumulation of marine debris; SDG 15, Life on Land, focused attention on biodiversity and vulnerable nesting bird and turtle populations; and SDG 17, Partnerships for the Goals, reflected the collaborative nature of the project. SDG 14, Life Below Water, became especially salient as recurrent outbreaks of red tide (*Karenia brevis*) devastated marine life at Egmont Key, leaving thousands of sea creatures dead along its shores. Beyond ecological impacts, red tide also disrupted tourism by posing health risks for visitors in coastal environments (Bechard 2019).

Our work is informed by scholarship that weaves together themes of conservation, the UN SDGs, sustainable tourism, and virtualization technologies (also referred to as geoinformatics) (Hansen et al. 2022; Harrison 2019). In particular, the research by Xiao and colleagues (2018) has been influential for how geoinformatics within the SDG framework are applied to support SDG 11.4 for the protection of cultural and natural heritage and SDG 8.9 for the promotion of sustainable tourism. This informative article provides an overview of the threats to heritage that can be addressed with this approach, including environmental degradation, tourism pressures, and land management issues, all of which are at play on Egmont Key. This volume will add to this growing literature that unites these interrelated themes.

Navigating this Book: Four Key Themes

Egmont Key: Digital Heritage and Engagement on the Disappearing Island is organized around four interrelated themes: (1) illuminating invisible histories; (2) managing sustainable tourism; (3) applying digital heritage; and (4) reflecting on Egmont Key. Each theme uses multiple lenses to deepen understanding of Egmont Key from diverse perspectives. This work is driven by the island's impending loss, which forces us to confront not only how to "preserve" a disappearing heritage site, but also why preservation matters if further loss is inevitable. How do we preserve something that is dynamic, unfolding, and ever-changing? The islands of Tampa Bay have never been static—they have always ebbed and flowed, reflecting the many cultures that have passed along their shores. Within this context, preservation raises critical questions: Should we focus on conserving natural species and replenishing land? On maintaining built heritage that will eventually wash away? Or on intangible elements, such as stories, memories, and cultural practices tied to lands that are already lost or washing away? While we cannot fully preserve a disappearing landmass, we can take action to protect elements important for future generations. We can document historic buildings and landscapes using digital scanning technologies, record and share memories to highlight invisible histories, develop sustainable tourism frameworks that minimize degradation, and use digital modeling to anticipate when and how the island will be inundated.

ILLUMINATING INVISIBLE HISTORIES: CHAPTERS 2 AND 3

In Chapter 2, "History Happened Here: A Tiny Island's Remarkable Role in US History," volume editors Harrison and Hansen, along with colleagues Scheidecker, Min, and Sanchez, discuss Egmont Key as an enigmatic historical site, emblematic of the history of the United States, from ancient times to the present day. The island's story begins with early Indigenous presence, followed by Spanish and British explorers who mapped its strategic location and tried to claim it for colonial empires. Throughout the eighteenth and nineteenth centuries, renowned historical figures including Robert E. Lee, Paul Revere, and Clara Barton were associated with the island. During the 1800s, Egmont Key played a role in the Civil War, as it was held by the Union and served as a refuge for enslaved people. From 1856 to 1858, members of the Seminole Tribe were incarcerated there, during the last gasp of Indian Removal in the United States. The outbreak of the Spanish-American War in 1898 spurred militarization on the island and led to the construction of Fort Dade and a system of seacoast defenses. Throughout the twentieth century, Egmont Key transformed from a site of rum-running and military target practice to a popular tourism destination. By interweaving these historical narratives, this chapter reveals Egmont Key's significant role in US history and highlights its enduring significance. While some of these histories are known, others have been rendered invisible, and with each passing day they recede further into obscurity. This chapter aims to ensure these stories don't disappear, even if the sands of Egmont Key wash away.

In Chapter 3, "Seminole Perspectives on Egmont Key," chapter authors Osceola and Scheidecker of the Seminole Tribal Historic Preservation Office (THPO) present a compelling overview of the involvement of Native Americans at Egmont Key, specifically the Seminole Tribe of Florida. During the Seminole War (1816–1858), the US Army was engaged in trying to forcibly remove all Seminoles from the state of Florida. Egmont Key was chosen as a site of internment, as Native people were being transported west to Oklahoma. From 1856 to 1858, Seminoles were held on Egmont Key in a wooden stockade. They refer to this period as their "Alcatraz" or a "dark place." One of the most powerful stories of Seminole resistance and resilience is the story of Polly Parker (Ematcloye), who was imprisoned on the island but later escaped in St. Marks and made her way back to the Okeechobee area on foot through hostile territory. This chapter recounts this little-known history and explores how the Seminoles today view this event.

MANAGING SUSTAINABLE TOURISM: CHAPTERS 4 AND 5

Hansen and Harrison frame sustainability at Egmont Key around managing people and place for biodiversity, heritage preservation, and visitor use. Chapter 4, "Key Lessons for Managing Heritage at Risk," addresses the problems of endangered cultural heritage in the context of multiple pressures from natural and anthropogenic threats that include erosion, climate change, overtourism, and the willful destruction of heritage sites. Managing Egmont Key's heritage is profoundly complex, with many federal, state, private, and nonprofit entities involved. The intentional entanglement of multiple interests was designed to safeguard the island from development pressures, but it has also had some unintended consequences. Each year, these problems become more urgent as the waters of the Gulf of Mexico erode the fragile shoreline and the number of visitors rises, endangering habitats and heritage sites. This chapter details how academics and university partners can enhance heritage management plans by conducting collaborative research with land managers and stakeholders on interpretation, preservation, and virtualization. Such approaches are especially valuable at endangered sites that often lack the resources to pursue this research independently and are plagued by immediate problems of site management rather than long-term comprehensive planning. Incorporating partnerships into heritage conservation and public engagement aligns with international frameworks, including the UN Sustainable Development Goals that champion the protection of cultural and natural heritage.

In Chapter 5, "Footprints in the Sand: Building a Sustainable Tourism Future for Egmont Key," Hansen and Harrison delve into how the sustainable tourism paradigm applies to Egmont Key, revealing how this popular tourist destination is a microcosm of challenges for enacting sustainable tourism globally. Issues plaguing the island include overtourism, inadequate signage, ineffective interpretation, vandalism, and infrastructural issues including waste management and the lack of Wi-Fi connectivity. Land managers report frequent incidences of visitors trespassing in the restricted National Wildlife Refuge area. Wildlife harassment has been an ongoing struggle during the nesting season, especially when people bring their dogs to the island, which is prohibited. With increased tourism pressures, these species may disappear from the island. This is compounded by more frequent outbreaks of red tide that severely impact wildlife and is attributed to a number of anthropogenic causes. Many of these issues were exacerbated after the 2024 hurricanes that left the island with little intact signage and only sporadic land managers on-site after docks and buildings were destroyed.

Dedicated community and volunteer groups are essential in efforts to promote and protect the island by hosting public outreach, monitoring birds and turtles, and sponsoring island cleanups. Enhanced interpretation, such as digital storytelling with virtual reality and interactive touchscreen exhibits, can improve the visitor experience further, and address some of the broader sustainability challenges facing the island. These tools promote sustainable tourism by educating visitors about sustainability, the unique ecosystems in Florida, the increasing pressures and impacts of climate change, and multiple histories representing significant events in the United States. By using international frameworks to guide sustainable tourism, such as the UN SDGs, and drawing lessons from Egmont Key, this chapter offers pathways to promote sustainable coastal and island tourism worldwide.

APPLYING DIGITAL HERITAGE: CHAPTERS 6 AND 7

Chapter 6, "Egmont Key as a Living Learning Laboratory: Participatory Action Research Meets Digital Heritage," by Harrison and Hansen, traces the evolution of the Egmont Key Project, a multiyear initiative integrating Participatory Action Research (PAR) and applied digital heritage methodologies to document and interpret at-risk cultural heritage. In our roles as academics, we partnered with land managers and community organizations to research endangered coastal heritage and develop innovative preservation strategies, including lidar scanning, interactive exhibits (virtual reality, augmented reality, and digital touchscreens), and professional development workshops. The project's four primary objectives were to collaborate on understanding Egmont Key's significance and invisible histories, digitally preserve its extant built heritage, train students and professionals in digital heritage management and sustainable tourism, and enhance public awareness through immersive digital experiences. Findings highlight that action-oriented digital heritage research, combined with community collaboration, is a powerful tool for uncovering hidden histories, protecting vulnerable sites and engaging diverse audiences in sustainability efforts. Our research results demonstrate that participatory heritage research is an effective way to showcase diverse histories, recapture cultural stories, and engage the public in a meaningful and culturally sensitive manner.

In Chapter 7, "Shifting Sands and Rising Seas: Innovations in Lidar and GIS," Harrison, Fernandez, and Fawbush address the question of exactly where and when the continued effects of sea-level rise and coastal erosion will be felt at Egmont Key, to enable thoughtful planning and land management. The National Oceanic and Atmospheric Administration's (NOAA) sea-level-rise projections indicate that if no actions are taken to limit greenhouse gas emissions, Egmont Key will be completely underwater in the coming decades. This sense of urgency drove the research team to pioneer a new fine-grained method for simulating the effects of these scenarios, enabling land managers to visualize the expected destructive impacts of sea-level rise. Battery McIntosh, a Spanish-American War fortification on Egmont Key's fragile western shoreline, serves as a test case for this new methodology. This chapter underscores the invaluable role of lidar and GIS in monitoring coastal dynamics and supporting sustainable decision-making. These results have been communicated to multiple audiences through public-facing presentations and geomatics training workshops, in an effort to heighten awareness of coastal vulnerabilities. Applying lidar and GIS is critical for climate resiliency planning because it helps protect endangered coastal heritage in Florida and worldwide.

REFLECTIONS ON EGMONT KEY: CHAPTER 8

To close the book, in Chapter 8, "Reflections on the Disappearing Island," Harrison and Hansen reflect on the ways Egmont Key has proven to be an unparalleled living learning laboratory in which to explore issues of heritage at risk, climate change, invisible histories, sustainable tourism, complex land management, and application of digital technologies. Over several years, this project has impacted scores of students and community members through workshops, courses, and presentations. Egmont Key has become a crucial training ground for the next generation of heritage and sustainability professionals who have taken the lessons learned from our collaborative work and applied it to new contexts. In this way, the Egmont Key research reverberates beyond the tiny disappearing island's shores.

The work done at Egmont Key was only possible because of strong collaborations forged with multiple partners, from nonprofit entities and government agencies to tour operators and conservation organizations. These relationships will manifest positive change for the resiliency of the region and beyond in the future. Egmont Key has been an incredible touchstone that has something for everyone—from the humanities to the sciences there is an angle, a story to tell, and an issue to be researched. We even featured it in an international project with a US embassy grant with Serbia. Egmont Key's unique capacity to speak to so many issues draws in community collaborators and academic disciplines from across the spectrum. While so many forces have contributed to the disappearance of the island, these relationships will endure and draw inspiration from Egmont Key.

Egmont Key will continue to be a site of learning and collaboration as we incorporate the project into a more comprehensive regional approach to safeguarding Florida's cultural and natural heritage. The work will involve interpreting Egmont Key from other locations and theoretical vantage points that will only deepen our understandings of the role of Egmont Key and share it with new audiences. As we move into other adjacent locations connected to the island through the webs of heritage, tourism, and sustainability, we will be applying our perspectives and methodologies to those places that are also at risk.

Egmont Key is everywhere now. The island—though still difficult to visit physically—is now digitized and can be toured virtually anytime. By virtualizing Egmont Key's iconic heritage sites, we have created an enduring, tangible record of the past that cannot easily be erased. These diverse digital records, which include 3D scans, digital exhibits, GIS visualizations, and virtual reality tours also capture and memorialize intangible histories that were once overlooked. As a result, the island will continue to have a digital afterlife, even if it disappears.

References Cited

El Archi, Y., B. Benbba, M. Kabil, and L.D. Dávid. 2023. Digital Technologies for Sustainable Tourism Destinations: State of the Art and Research Agenda. *Administrative Sciences* 13(8), 184. https://doi.org/10.3390/admsci13080184.

Bechard, A. 2019. Red Tide at Morning, Tourists Take Warning? County-Level Economic Effects of HABSo on Tourism Dependent Sectors. *Harmful Algae* 85: 101689. https://doi.org/10.1016/j.hal.2019.101689.

Buragohain, D., Y. Meng, C. Deng, Q. Li, and S. Chaudhary. 2024. Digitalizing Cultural Heritage Through Metaverse Applications: Challenges, Opportunities, and Strategies. *Heritage Science* 12, 295. https://doi.org/10.1186/s40494-024-01403-1.

Burkey, B. 2022. From Bricks to Clicks: How Digital Heritage Initiatives Create a New Ecosystem for Cultural Heritage and Collective Remembering. *Journal of Communication Inquiry* 46(2): 185–205. https://doi.org/10.1177/01968599211041112.

Díaz-Andreu, M. 2017. Heritage Values and the Public. *Journal of Community Archaeology & Heritage* 4(1): 2–6. https://doi.org/10.1080/20518196.2016.1228213.

Giglitto, D., C. Claisse, L. Ciolfi, and E. Lockley. 2019. Bridging Cultural Heritage and Communities Through Digital Technologies: Understanding Perspectives and Challenges. In *C&T '19: Proceedings of the 9th International Conference on Communities & Technologies*—Transforming Communities, pp. 81–91. Association for Computing Memory, New York. https://doi.org/10.1145/3328320.3328386.

Hansen B., S. Annis, S. Vorce, J. Coates, and A. Farr. 2022. Virtualization Technologies for Sustainable Tourism: Adapting the Matterport 360 Platform to Showcase the UN Sustainable Development Goals in Tampa Bay, Florida. In *The Green Institute: Working Papers*, May 12, 2022, pp. 1–10. https://greeninstitute.ng/visualization-technologies-for-sustainable-tourism-tampa-bay-florida.

Harrison, Laura. 2019. A Roadmap to Applied Digital Heritage. *Studies in Digital Heritage* 3(1): 40–45. https://doi.org/10.14434/sdh.v3i1.27552.

Kidd, J. 2018. Public Heritage and the Promise of the Digital. In *The Oxford Handbook of Public Heritage Theory and Practice*, edited by Angela M. Labrador and Neil Asher Silberman, pp. 197–208. Oxford University Press, Oxford. https://doi.org/10.1093/oxfordhb/9780190676315.013.9.

Legrand, W., J. S. Chen, and G. C. Laeis. 2022. *Sustainability In the Hospitality Industry: Principles of Sustainable Operations*. Taylor & Francis.

Lercari, N., J. Shulze, W. Wendrich, B. Porter, M. Burton, and T. E. Levy. 2016. 3-D Digital Preservation of At-Risk Global Cultural Heritage. In EUROGRAPHICS: Workshop on Graphics and Cultural Heritage, pp. 123–126. The Eurographics Association. UC Merced. http://dx.doi.org/10.2312/gch.20161395.

Munday, J., A. Watts, E. Clark, and T. Crutchett. 2024. Heritage Sites in the 21st Century: Virtual Tours and Digital Artefacts, an Online Example. *International Journal of Heritage Studies* 30(5): 586–596. https://doi.org/10.1080/13527258.2024.2320328.

Shiri, A., D. Howard, and S. Farnel. 2022. Indigenous Digital Storytelling: Digital Interfaces Supporting Cultural Heritage Preservation and Access. *International Information and Library Review* 54(2): 93–114. https://doi.org/10.1080/10572317.2021.1946748

Spenceley, A. (editor). 2021. *Handbook for Sustainable Tourism Practitioners: The Essential Toolbox*. Edward Elgar, Cheltenham, UK.

Stephan, R., A. R. Doery, and C. Simmons. 2025. Virtual Reality Tours as an Immersive Approach to Archaeology in Higher Education. *Journal of Computer Applications in Archaeology* 8(1):1–9. https://doi.org/10.5334/jcaa.185.

Stylianidis, Efstratios, and Fabio, Remondino (editors). 2016. *3D Recording, Documentation and Management of Cultural Heritage*. Whittles, Dunbeath, UK. Accessed March 29, 2025. ProQuest Ebook Central.

United Nations. N.d. Take Action for the Sustainable Development Goals. https://www.un.org/sustainabledevelopment/sustainable-development-goals/, accessed January 7, 2026.

Wood, M. E. 2017. *Sustainable Tourism on a Finite Planet: Environmental, Business and Policy Solutions*. Taylor & Francis.

Xiao, W., J. Mills, G. Guidi, P. Rodríguez-Gonzálvez, S. G. Barsanti, and D. González-Aguilera. 2018. Geoinformatics for the Conservation and Promotion of Cultural Heritage in Support of the UN Sustainable Development Goals. *ISPRS Journal of Photogrammetry and Remote Sensing* 142:389–406. https://doi.org/10.1016/j.isprsjprs.2018.01.001.

2

History Happened Here

A Tiny Island's Remarkable Role in US History

LAURA K. HARRISON, BROOKE HANSEN, DAVE SCHEIDECKER, APRIL MIN, AND RICHARD SANCHEZ

Egmont Key is a fascinating island that reads like a history of the United States from ancient times to events shaping the twenty-first century. The earliest inhabitants were Indigenous people who would have fished, hunted, and camped along its shores. The Spanish and British followed and mapped its strategic location, claiming it for colonial empires. The island served as an epicenter of maritime commerce for over 150 years with Tampa Bay Pilots guiding ships into the ports of Tampa. There are some notable historical figures associated with Egmont Key, including Robert E. Lee, Paul Revere, and Clara Barton. During the mid-nineteenth century members of the Seminole Tribe were incarcerated there, representing one of the last events of Indian Removal in the United States. It is also interesting to note the role Egmont Key played in the Civil War, as a Union outpost and refuge for enslaved people. The outbreak of the Spanish-American War in 1898 brought further changes to the island that became heavily militarized with the construction of Fort Dade and an innovative system of seacoast defenses. During the twentieth century, Egmont Key saw rumrunners hiding their goods, military explosions from target practice, and toward the end of the century, throngs of tourists. In the twenty-first century, a series of cataclysmic hurricanes left a wake of destruction, leaving the island facing an uncertain future. By integrating these histories, Egmont Key's significant involvement in major US history events is revealed. While some of these histories are known, others have been rendered invisible, and with each passing day they recede further into obscurity. This chapter aims to ensure these stories do not disappear, even if the sands of Egmont Key wash away.

The First Inhabitants

The Indigenous people of what is now Florida were composed of diverse tribes and cultures who lived here for thousands of years before Europeans arrived. Their legacy has been preserved in shell mounds, remnants of sites, and the living cultures of some of their descendants, including the Seminole Tribe of Florida. The archaeological record of Egmont Key offers little insight into the first human presence on the island, likely due to the tidal effects and constantly shifting landscapes obscuring any traces of past cultural activity. There is robust archaeological evidence from other locations throughout the region demonstrating that the first humans arrived in Florida at least 12,000 to 14,550 years ago (Faught and Pevny 2019; Halligan et al. 2016; Milanich 2018) and possibly far earlier (Dunbar 2016). Excavations at Little Salt Springs dating to 12,000 BCE (Clausen et al. 1979) and the Page-Ladson site at 14,550 BCE (Halligan et al. 2016) point to the presence of a nomadic hunter-gatherer culture in the southeastern United States, including Florida, which archaeologists refer to as the Paleoindians. These cultures were drawn to the area by megafauna, such as mammoth, and they are the ancestors of all Indigenous groups that reside in what is now called Florida. As people came down through the Panhandle and along the coast, they began to establish small settlements, using shell mounds to keep them stable and above the water line. The Tampa Bay region was settled about 9,000 years ago, at a time when Egmont Key was part of the Florida Peninsula (Milanich 2018).

Around 7500 BCE, Egmont Key became an island as the Ice Age ended (Anderson 1996; James et al. 2006). As the climate warmed and sea levels rose, communities were forced to move inland with the shifting coastline. During the time that the Seminole Tribe refers to as "the ancestral period," Tampa Bay was inhabited by groups known as the Safety Harbor culture, Weedon Island culture, and the Tocobaga, among others. These groups, which are part of the broader Mississippian culture, used wooden dugout canoes to navigate rivers, the coast, the Gulf of Mexico, and the Caribbean (Mol 2014). In 2021, one such canoe emerged from the shore of Egmont Key, after a tropical storm. It has been dated to around 1300 CE (Scott 2020).

The Mississippians were a broad culture group that extended west to Louisiana, north to Wisconsin, and east to Georgia. Their people are considered ancestors of the Muskogean-speaking groups who operated large-scale trade networks. Shark teeth from Florida have been found as far away as Wisconsin and Minnesota and crafted copper goods from the Great Lakes have been found in Florida (Ashley 2002; Hally 2008). The Mississippian culture is known for constructing large earthworks such as Moundville in Alabama, Ocmulgee Mounds in Georgia, and Cahokia in Illinois. In Florida, the Letchworth-Love site near Tallahassee (built between 200 and 900 CE), is an example of Mississippian monumental earthworks, standing 51 ft tall and 300 ft wide at the base.

Although small mounds survive in the Tampa Bay region, there are no surviving monumental earthworks. As the urbanization of Florida's coastline expanded throughout the twentieth century, mounds were routinely destroyed in the construction of new buildings and roads. They now lie under the many golf courses and condos that are part of the tourism matrix of the area. While mounds were common along the coast, there were no permanent Indigenous inhabitants of Egmont Key, perhaps due to a lack of consistent freshwater. The island would likely have been used as a stopover point for fishing and relaxing, much as people do today. It is possible that the gopher tortoise population on Egmont Key was established purposefully by Seminole ancestors to ensure a source of food when visiting (Roa 2025). There are no surviving artifacts or structures from these early inhabitations; most tools were organic and biodegradable and would not survive the humid and stormy environment. In addition, the construction of Fort Dade broke ground in 1898—a time before heritage preservation laws—leading to the destruction and loss of archaeological data that may have been present at the time.

Despite the lack of archaeological evidence in some areas of the state, present-day Seminoles recognize Florida and all its territory as their homeland. They have multiple programs in place, including those of the Tribal Historic Preservation Office (THPO), to ensure that their history and connection to this place, including Egmont Key, is not forgotten. Following the initial period of Indigenous presence, the coming of Europeans launched a tumultuous period that spanned several hundred years. The events at this tiny island are a microcosm of larger historical forces that shaped the early colonial era.

A Contested Land: Incursions into Florida

EUROPEANS ARRIVE

The Spanish began encroachment into what is now Florida in 1513 led by Juan Ponce de León (Hoffman 2002). In the early sixteenth century, a number of Spanish expeditions made their way to the Gulf Coast of Florida, including Diego Miruelo (1516), Francisco Hernandez de Cordoba (1517), Panfilo de Narvaez (1528), and Hernando de Soto in 1539 (Stafford 1980; Thompson and Thompson 2012), the latter of whom is immortalized by his namesake at Fort De Soto Park in Pinellas County and the De Soto National Memorial in Manatee County. In addition to garnering wealth for the Crown, there were two other prominent Spanish objectives on the peninsula: to see if there was a passage connecting the Gulf to the Atlantic Ocean, and to locate stands of tall trees that would be suitable for ship masts (Scott-Ireton and Mitchell-Cook 2018). Mission building was another major goal, and around forty were constructed between the late 1500s into the 1600s (Milanich 1995).

The seventeenth century saw intermittent Spanish incursions into the west Gulf Coast, probably due to the prior tumultuous encounters with local Indigenous peoples. By the eighteenth century, the influx of foreign interests increased significantly. At the behest of the Spanish Crown, Don Francisco Celi arrived in what is now Tampa Bay in 1757 and became the first European to map Tampa Bay and survey Egmont Key, which was then known as Isla de San Blas y Barreda (Stafford 1980). Celi's survey measured the circumference of the island and then determined its area. The sketch below shows the progression of his measurements, starting on the island's southeast end and continuing in a counterclockwise direction (2.1).

Celi's engagement with Egmont Key concluded on May 6, 1757, when he erected a wooden cross on the south end of the island and celebrated a mass (Thompson and Thompson 2012). He then turned his attention to determining the depth of the north channel but was unable to complete the work because of bad weather. He also failed to find the 90-ft depression off the island's north end, today known as the Egmont Deep (Ware 1968). After his survey, Celi considered the south channel between Egmont and Passage Key the main channel, although today the north channel is more widely used by cargo ships and other vessels approaching and departing from the Port of Tampa (2.2).

While Celi was surveying Tampa Bay and its environs, he encountered the local Indigenous population and wrote about the experience in his journal:

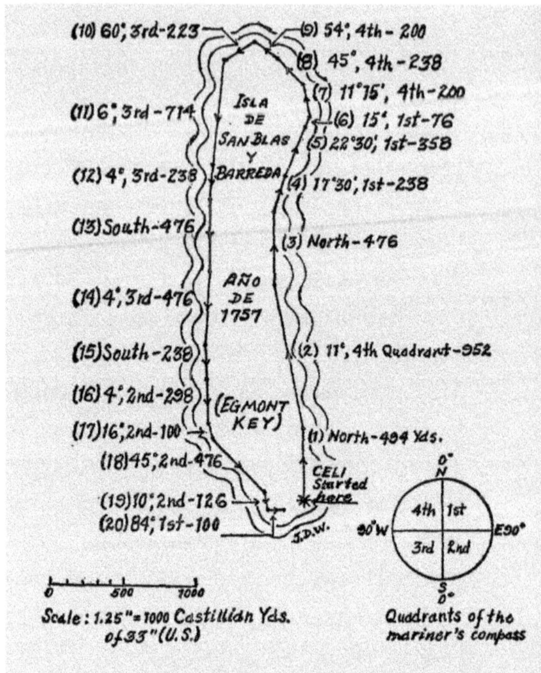

Figure 2.1. Map of Celi's survey of Egmont Key. Reproduced from Ware 1971: 13.

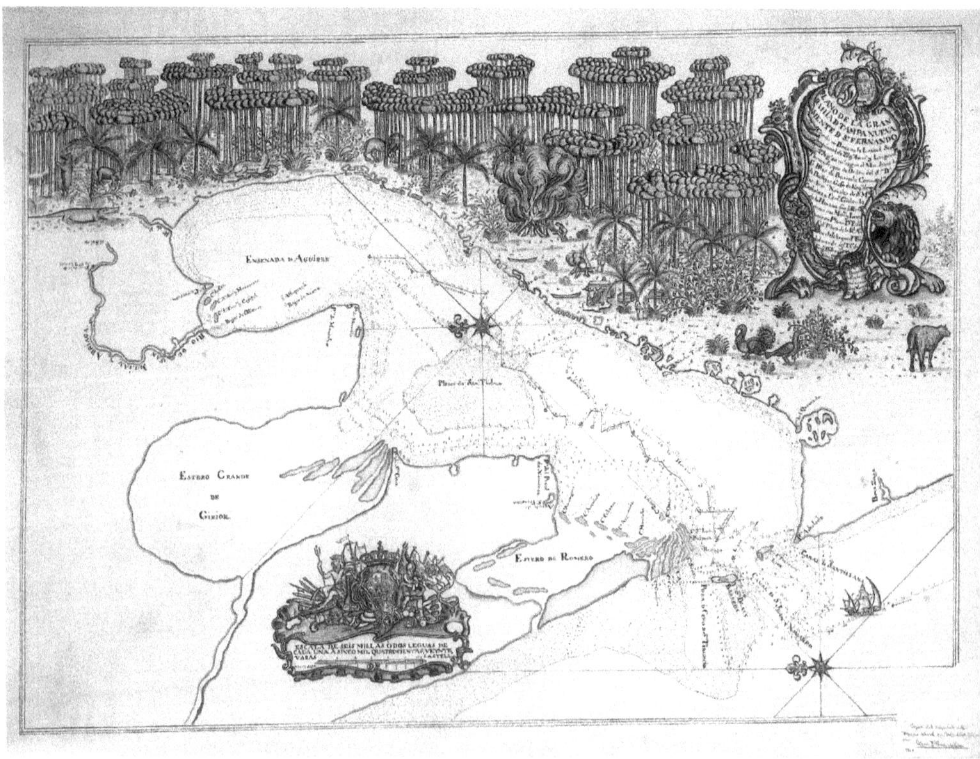

Figure 2.2. Celi's map of Tampa Bay.

> At 8:30 a craft was seen from our stern proceeding toward us; whereupon we anchored in three fathoms to await it. At 11:00 the craft came alongside; it was a canoe with four Indians, natives of this country, who came armed with their muskets. Our captain tried to entertain them, giving them a cask of honey, tobacco, corn, and chickens. At 11:45 they returned to land, and from what we could understand, they left to give part of their gifts to their chief, who remained ashore with four men.
>
> Midday of the 22nd to the 23rd, Saturday noon. The weather continues clear and the WNW wind favorable. At 2:00 P.M. a canoe came alongside with four Indians who came aboard. My captain welcomed them, giving each one tobacco, rum, and a seat in his chairs, showing them great affection. He later gave them a cask of honey, a ration of corn and bread, and handfuls of tobacco, all of which appeared to please the Indians. At 3:00 we set sail, heading NNE with a NW wind. The longboat was ordered to proceed ahead at a distance of one mile, which was traversed in a depth of three and one-half fathoms. The xebec steered NE 50 E a distance of one-half mile in depths of four and four and one-half fathoms. At 3:45 we anchored in three and one-half fathoms in sand bottom, for the longboat had given the signal of shoal water. At 4:30 another canoe came alongside with four other Indians who received the same welcome. All eight Indians slept aboard our vessel that night. (Ware 1971: 178)

It is interesting to note that Celi's interactions with the local Indigenous people seem to have been friendly. Earlier encounters by multiple Spanish expeditions looking for wealth and resources were characterized by hostilities. It would only be 100 years after Celi's purportedly friendly encounter with the local Indigenous people that the Seminole were forcibly removed from their lands by US militias and imprisoned on Egmont Key.

After Celi left the Tampa Bay area in 1757, Egmont Key remained under Spanish control but saw little use until the British arrived in 1763 to conduct a survey. British Naval Pilot George Gauld (sometimes referred to as Gould) surveyed the island and named it Egmont Key, in honor of the Second Earl of Egmont, Sir John Perceval (Thompson and Thompson 2012). The island remained under British occupation, along with the rest of Florida, from 1763 to 1783 (Stafford 1980). The name Egmont Key has endured for centuries, although at various times throughout history the island has also had several other names. At one time, it was called Castor Key—a name associated with the legend of pirate or privateer from the eighteenth century. There are several unreferenced descriptions on the internet to a village called "Castortown," located on Egmont Key's east side about midway down the length. It was supposed to have had about twenty houses, a store, and a dock. No remains of this village can be found today. Was there really a pirate named Castor who inspired this naming?

Pirates and Rumrunners

References to a pirate called Castor or Henry Castor (Kite-Powell 2014), who maybe donned the island with his namesake, persist—yet facts remain elusive. What can be documented is a Florida map made in 1769 by Dutch engineer and deputy surveyor Bernard Romans. Egmont Key was labeled Castor Key on the map that was drawn ca. 1774 (Mohlman 1997), perhaps not in reference to a pirate but to star constellations. While mapping Florida, Romans wrecked his ship in the Manatee River. He trekked across Florida to St. Augustine, keeping notes on his encounters with Native Americans and wildlife. A few years after completing the journey, he published the 1775 book *A Concise Survey of East and West Florida*, with the map (Romans 1999 [1775]; 2.3). An interesting detail is that Paul Revere—the famed silversmith and Patriot of the American Revolution—engraved Romans's 1775 map (Harley 1930).

In Romans's book, he described Tampa Bay and mentioned Captain David Cutler Braddock, a privateer for the Crown who was the first Englishman to explore Egmont Key and surrounding waters. The British expedition that mapped the area included two ships, the *Pollux* and *Castor*, one of which was commanded by Braddock (Romans 1999). The stars called Pollux and Castor are the brightest and second brightest ones in the constellation of Gemini and are well known by mariners for navigational purposes, so it is not surprising to find two ships named for them. Pollux and Castor are also known in Greek and Roman mythology as half-twin brothers who sailed with Jason and the Argonauts. Romans goes into great detail about the geography of Castor Key, and the neighboring island, which he dubbed Pollux Key, today's Mullet Key. There is still a question of why he named the islands after these ships instead of keeping the name already established by Gauld in 1763.

Egmont Key's enigmatic status seems to lend itself to mythmaking and lore. The story of a pirate named Castor who perhaps sailed the local seas is appealing in a place where pirate mythology is central to the region's identity and

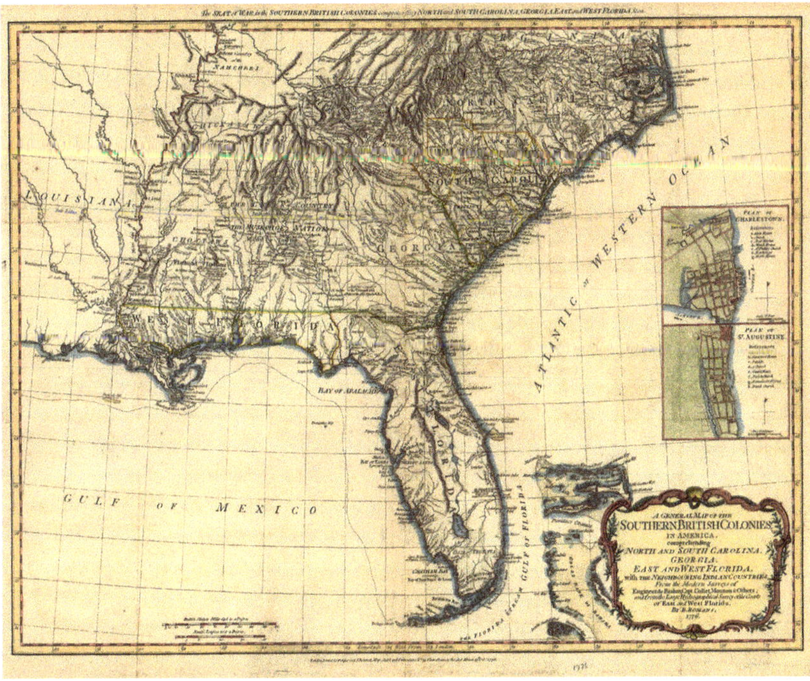

Figure 2.3. Bernard Romans's map of Florida from 1776 (see Romans et al. 1776). State Archives of Florida, Florida Memory.

tourism activities. These stories resonate with tales of another semi-mythical pirate named Gaspar (Kaserman and Kaserman 2011), around which yearlong tourism events take place, including the Gasparilla Parade in downtown Tampa where pirates take the city and steal the key from the mayor of Tampa.

The veracity of the existence of pirates in the waters surrounding Florida can certainly not be questioned. The area had its fair share during the "Golden Age" of piracy in the seventeenth century and throughout the eighteenth and early nineteenth centuries as the United States was forming (Kaserman and Kaserman 2011). Plenty of pirates and privateers roamed the region engaging in trade of goods, humans, and military supplies. It becomes difficult to separate fact from fiction in many of these cases and it is not surprising that Egmont Key as well became bound up in the lore. In the aftermath of the Civil War, the waters surrounding Florida, with mangrove swamps, islands, and inlets made an ideal place to engage in illegal activities from drugs to arms. Trafficking of people, institutionalized by the Confederacy and then outlawed, persisted after

St. Petersburg Times

"St. Petersburg's Biggest and Best Newspaper"

Today's Weather—

Times Telephone Numbers

EGMONT KEY IS SWEPT BY FLAMES

Holdings of E. M. Elliott Are Sold to Syndicate

BIG FIRE IS AFTERMATH TO FEDERAL RAID

DEVELOPMENT OF PROPERTY IS PLANNED

JURY ACQUITS SENATOR WHEELER

Eastern States Hit By Warmest Weather In April On Record

14 ENTRAPPED MINERS FOUND ALIVE IN PIT

Cincinnati "Fans" He'd: Pro Agents Find "Real Beer"

SOLON SMILES WHEN VERDICT IS GIVEN OUT

Motor Tourists Are Angered by License Holdup

MUNICIPAL CAR LINE EXTENSION GETS APPROVAL

Figure 2.4. Headline from the *St. Petersburg Times* mentioning a fire at Egmont Key from April 25, 1925. From Tampa Bay Times Archive.

the 1860s and remains an issue into modern times as well with Florida as an epicenter of human trafficking.

By the early twentieth century, Egmont Key held allure as a hideout spot for a new kind of pirate during Prohibition (1920–1933), involved in the production, hiding, and sale of illegal liquor, for which Egmont Key made an ideal site. The Florida rumrunners found the less populated Gulf side of the peninsula desirable for trade in Cuban rum and British scotch produced in the Bahamas (Kaserman and Kaserman 2011). The liquor pirates of Florida were using Egmont Key's mostly deserted military buildings from Fort Dade as a hideout in the 1920s. In a highly publicized event reported by the *St. Petersburg Times* on April 25, 1925, federal agents attempting to catch the rumrunners and smoke them out started a fire that got out of control leading to the headline in the day's paper that read: "EGMONT KEY IS SWEPT BY FLAMES" (*St. Petersburg Times*, April 25, 1925: 1; 2.4). Sixty-five cases of liquor were discovered, and the criminals were caught after the fire got out of control. The base caretaker Sergeant Fagan and a crew of volunteers worked to put the fire out but were unable to save some of the Fort Dade buildings that had caught fire (Thompson and Thompson 2012). After Prohibition ended and the Great Depression ensued, the buildings of Fort Dade continued to degrade due to weather, disrepair, and more fires on the island.

Fortress, Fever, and Freedom

Egmont Key, strategically positioned at the mouth of Tampa Bay, played a crucial role during the Civil War and the Spanish-American War. The island was a refuge in both conflicts for those embroiled in the Civil War and those seeking asylum from disease in the Spanish-American War. In the Civil War, it served as a Union military base and a refuge for Unionists and enslaved people escaping Confederate control. The Union established artillery, a coaling station, and a hospital on the island, and repurposed the abandoned lighthouse for navigation and blockade runner surveillance.

It is interesting that Robert E. Lee, who later became General in Chief of the Armies of the Confederate States, was involved in a coastal survey of Egmont Key in 1849 and served as the Recorder to the Board of Engineers—the forerunner to the Army Corps of Engineers. He took notes during the trip and contributed to the final report that stated there were two principal maritime entrances to Tampa, one on either side of Egmont "Island." The report noted that Egmont Key was the best entry point for safe harbor between Key West and Pensacola and further recommended that it be reserved to defend against enemies (Mohlman 1997). The report suggested that a defensive work should be built on the north end of the island—anticipating the later decision in 1870 to formally reserve both Egmont Key and Mullet Key for future military use. Ultimately, the Confederacy did not hold the island.

Due to Union control, Egmont Key became a refuge for enslaved people fleeing oppression. Many of them were experts in the salt distilling process, a vital skill for food preservation and leather tanning. The Union Navy, recognizing the value of this expertise, provided a safe haven on Egmont Key. Many of these individuals eventually joined local Unionist militia units. Though the exact number of those who found freedom this way is uncertain, estimates suggest it could be as many as 200 (Zombeck 2016; *New York Times* 1862; Thompson and Thompson 2012).

Egmont Key's role continued as a strategic military site in the 1898 Spanish-American War. It housed important installations and served as a key observation point. Teddy Roosevelt, then Colonel Roosevelt, arrived with the Rough Riders in Tampa Bay in 1898 to prepare the US response in the Spanish-American

War, which brought 30,000 troops to the area (Covington 1998). Tampa was chosen as the official site to launch an offensive on Cuba due to its deepwater port and railway connections (Knetsch and Wynne 2011). The Army remained stationed there awaiting orders through the brief war. This was a major event for Tampa Bay and became linked with tourism as the brigade camped on the lawn of the Tampa Bay Hotel, now a National Historic Landmark with striking Moorish and Turkish architecture (National Park Service n.d.). "The Spanish-American War was sometimes called by locals the 'Rocking Chair War' because the members of the military could be seen in rocking chairs on the Tampa Bay Hotel's veranda discussing strategy, politics, and current events, just waiting for the order to invade Cuba" (National Park Service n.d.: para. 10). It is reported (but not verified) that Roosevelt camped at Egmont Key during this time period with his troops at Fort Dade en route to Cuba where he reportedly opted to stay in the tents with his men, as recounted by Lighthouse Keeper Charles Moore (Cole 1986).

With the explosion of the USS *Maine* in 1898 and the outbreak of the Spanish-American War, noted Red Cross founder Clara Barton was called to address the yellow fever epidemic among US troops. Responding in haste, Clara Barton and the Red Cross followed Theodore Roosevelt and his Rough Riders to Guantanamo Bay (Ardalan 2010–2011; Pryor 2011). Barton, then 76 years old, subsequently left Cuba with her nurse Lucy Graves and headed to Florida to assist in the island quarantine camps, which were set up to prevent US soldiers from bringing yellow fever back to the mainland as they returned home from war. The cause of yellow fever was not known for certain and there was no cure available. With outbreaks in several US coastal cities, quarantine camps were crucial in attempting to mitigate and control the deadly disease.

The Marine Hospital Service established a permanent quarantine camp on Mullet Key, and by 1898 they had placed a new, temporary camp on nearby Egmont Key in response to the urgent need for more locations because of the large number of troops and other personnel returning from Cuba (see 2.5). According to nurse Lucy Graves's diary, Clara Barton spent the duration of her three days on Egmont Key (September 2–5, 1898) recovering from an eye injury she sustained from a fall. On September 3, 1898, Graves writes (Graves 1898: 55–59):

> Early this morning, we arrived at the quarantine station, the doctors came aboard, and we were ordered to Egmont Key for detention and

> disinfection. We are glad to hear we will be there only five days, and so do not complain, though we all know how anxious Miss Barton is to get north. . . . The three ladies are assigned to a very nice house, and the men are made as comfortable as possible in tents. Everything is, however, beautifully clean, and the physicians have given their table to us, eating later themselves. Miss Barton is glad to find in the chief surgeon here, Dr. Geddings, the son-in-law of her old friend, Mrs. Moses of South Carolina. The only drawback to a very pleasant stay here is the mosquitoes—their name is legion, and they are simply ferocious.

Clara Barton recovered from her eye injury and made her way from Egmont Key to Tampa in 1898, where she established a headquarters of the American Red Cross. The quarantine camp on Egmont Key remained in use for several months, and the personal accounts of soldiers who passed through mention a couple of rows of leftover Civil War tents pitched within a swampy area on the east side of the island (see 2.6).

The quarantine camp was surrounded by barbed wire and was widely maligned for its deplorable and rotten food, unbearable mosquitoes, overcrowding, and interpersonal tensions. Notably, a minister and his wife were billeted with a prostitute, who was busy plying her trade while quarantined there. The minister wrote an angry three-page letter to the military complaining about the situation and the indifference of the local soldiers to do anything about it. The minister alleged that the soldiers were partaking of the prostitute's services as well. Despite the detainees' grievances, the quarantine camp was closed not to end their misery but rather to make way for the construction of a new military complex, Fort Dade, which was needed to defend Tampa from the feared Spanish fleet. In 1898, the military requested that the quarantine camp be shut down, and the people relocated to Mullet Key to prevent them from infecting the construction personnel.

Fort Dade was part of a broader coastal defense network designed to protect Tampa Bay from potential naval threats. The fort was named after Major Francis L. Dade, who was killed in 1835 at the outbreak of the "Second Seminole War" (Mohlman 1997). The fort included a series of gun batteries, barracks, and support buildings. The spatial organization of Fort Dade was both functional and self-sufficient, with facilities like a power plant, bakery, and water tower ensuring the garrison could operate independently. This cohesive layout underscores the military's foresight in creating a defensible and sustainable outpost.

Figure 2.5. Sketch of yellow fever quarantine camp made by Alfred G. Mayer. The letter *t* is tents, *p* is privy, and w is water barrel. North is to the right in the drawing. Courtesy of Bruce McCall.

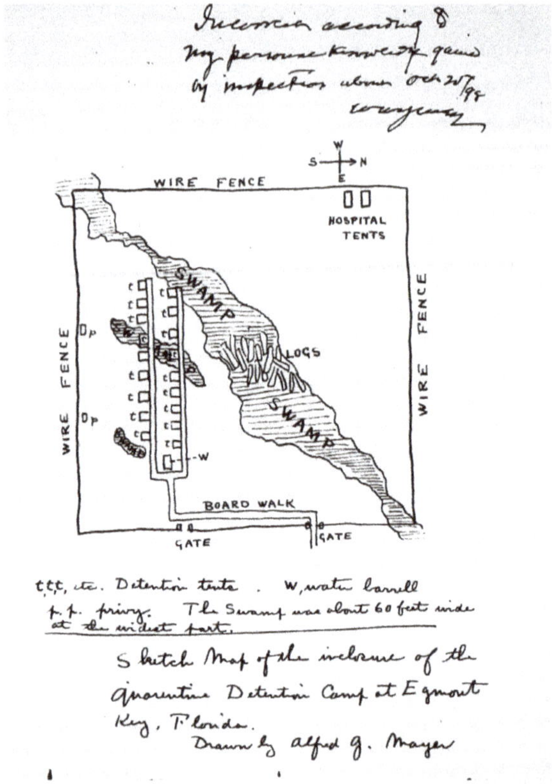

Figure 2.6. Quarantine camp on Egmont Key. Note the lighthouse visible in the upper left of the photo. Courtesy of HathiTrust.

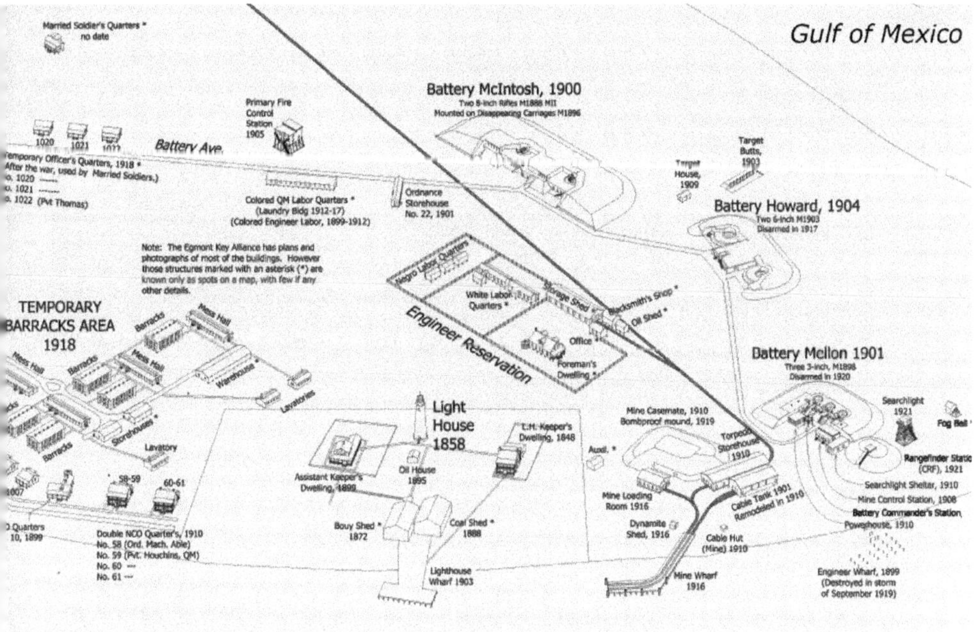

Figure 2.7. Map of Fort Dade. Courtesy of Bruce McCall.

Though it never saw combat, Fort Dade remained active until 1923, serving as a strategic military outpost, when the advent of military aircraft rendered such maritime defenses and batteries obsolete. The Fort's ruins, including the historic brick roads, artillery batteries, and the remains of its once-thriving military community, offer a tangible link to the late nineteenth and early twentieth centuries.

Fort Dade on Egmont Key was characterized by a well-planned architectural layout typical of late nineteenth-century military installations (2.7). The Fort was organized into a linear grid system with brick-paved roads connecting the key structures, including officer quarters, barracks, a bakery, a hospital, mortuary, and a theater. The buildings were designed in a simple, utilitarian style, with wood-frame construction, raised foundations, and wide verandas to facilitate ventilation in the humid subtropical climate. Artillery batteries were scattered along the islands' western shoreline (2.8).

Egmont Key's batteries, the remnants of which can still be seen today, stretch from north to south and include Battery Charles Mellon, Battery Howard, Battery McIntosh, Battery Burchsted, and Battery Page (the latter two are

Figure 2.8. Fort Dade panorama from 1912. Courtesy of the Manatee County Public Library Historical Digital Collections.

now underwater due to sea-level rise and the island's shifting sands). Each of these batteries was constructed of concrete with disappearing guns, concealed behind a sand dune along the shoreline so as to be invisible to invading ships. An electric system triggered a series of underwater mines that traversed the channel and connected Egmont Key with its sister fort, Fort De Soto. This Fourth System of seacoast defenses is a departure from the Third System style, which emphasized brick architecture and monumentality (Berhow 2015; Paloczi-Horvath 1996), conveying an outright image of military might. Only a handful of Fourth System Forts survive in the United States.

While the military history and unique seacoast defense system that typified Egmont is interesting, history is also about the people who lived there. In the years that Fort Dade was an active military installation, many service members were introduced not only to Egmont Key, but also to a vibrant and welcoming community on the St. Petersburg mainland. Soldiers like Julius B. Tiedchen not only served their country here but also found a home. Born on November 7, 1899, in Brooklyn, New York, Tiedchen enlisted in the United States Army in July 1916 (2.9). He was first stationed at Fort Dade as a bugler in June 1918 (Muster Rolls, June 30, 1918, 1st Company, Coast Defenses Tampa), but apparently found a better calling in the kitchen, and was soon transferred to the mess hall, where he became a cook and, later, a baker (Roster of the First Company, December 31, 1918; Morning Reports, 1912–1939).

On March 14, 1920, Julius married Frances Sara Jett, a resident of nearby St. Petersburg whose father ran a local bakery (Florida, US, County Marriage Records, 1823–1982). After receiving his discharge from the Army, Julius went

They're Off to Join Uncle Sam's Navy

—Times Staff Photo by Sandy Gandy

Fifteen local men gathered at the ACL station last night and entrained for Jacksonville to complete final examinations for enlistment in the U. S. Navy. Fourteen are pictured above. Kneeling in the front row, left to right are: Harry M. Killinger, 21, 3027 Fifty-first avenue south; Mack J. Golden, 28, 4955 Forty-first street north; Robert R. Earl, 39, 3733½ Sixteenth avenue south; John T. Cruikshank, 31, 4051 Ninth avenue south; William R. Beegle, 34, 3400 Seventeenth street north, and John W. Tidwell, 32, 1208 Second avenue north. In the row standing (left to right) are: Ernest W. Hunter, 39, 1756 Preston street south; Thomas H. Counihan, 38, 2220 Seventeenth street south; Robert C. Higgins, 31, 3500 Second avenue north; Julius D. Kemp, 43, 2711 Thirteenth avenue south; Avery A. May, 32, 1020 Eleventh street north; Julius B. Tiedchen, 42, 3150 Sixteenth street north; Maurice Gay, 29, Tarpon Springs, and Robert W. Cole, 25, 3027½ Sixteenth street north. A Clearwater boy, Coyt L. Williams, 33, also was scheduled to leave.

Figure 2.9. Julius Tiedchen, the baker of Egmont Key, is pictured in the back row, sixth from the left. From Tampa Bay Times Archive, March 26, 1942.

to work in his father-in-law's bakery on Central Ave. (United States Census, 1930). Julius worked as a baker in St. Petersburg until 1942, when—at the age of 43—he enlisted in the United States Navy Reserves, answering his nation's call once again. After arriving in Midway, he served in the South Pacific theater for about two years. Sadly, upon his return to the United States, as he awaited orders to return home to his family in St. Peterburg, Julius was killed in a car accident on April 30, 1944, at Camp Parks in Alameda County, California. He was laid to rest in St. Petersburg, returning to the place he called home since his arrival on Egmont Key so many years before.

During World War I and World War II, Egmont Key continued to serve important military functions. In World War I, when Tiedchen was stationed at Egmont Key in the waning days of the war, the island was used as a training site and a naval base, with its strategic location at the entrance to Tampa Bay making it valuable for coastal defense and patrol operations. By World War II, Egmont Key's role expanded as it became a base for antiaircraft artillery and a lookout post to monitor potential threats in the Gulf of Mexico. The island's facilities were utilized for military training and to enhance the defense readiness of the region. Throughout both conflicts, Egmont Key's strategic position ensured its continued importance in the defense and security of the US coastline.

Egmont Key's military history is certainly a large part of the island's historical significance, and it is unfortunate that more first-person accounts of what life was like were not recorded. There is some vivid discourse from Roberta Moore Cole, daughter of Lighthouse Keeper Charlie Moore, who was raised on the island in the early twentieth century, about the military activities, including target practice (Cole 1986: 12):

> I will take a moment to mention target practice because it was regularly and carefully scheduled and the only time guns were fired on Egmont. It was one event that had everyone's complete attention and cooperation. Word went out as to the arrival, and when the wooden target frames were towed in place, spread with canvas, then in the Gulf, the military units would be in place, and the word would go out over the telephones—'All is in readiness.' They will go in a half of an hour and last for 20 minutes.

From the many military activities that punctuated and defined Egmont Key from the nineteenth to the early twentieth centuries, there is a little-known dark history of imprisoning people on the island in the mid-1800s, the echoes of which are still felt today.

Seminole Resistance and the Island Prison

Conflict, war, and surveillance have shaped Egmont Key's history for centuries. One of the least known episodes dates to the nineteenth century and involves the Seminole Tribe of Florida. Most historians list the start of the "First" Seminole War in 1817; however, according to the Seminole Tribe, there was only one Seminole War, which started in 1812 and went on until 1858. It began with a group of militias from Georgia, calling themselves Patriots, who invaded Florida to take it from the Spanish. It ended at Egmont Key.

The Seminole War was a war of colonization. At the beginning of the nineteenth century, the Seminoles were working with the Spanish, maintaining a thriving network of farms, towns, and pasturelands for their cattle. The success of these lands caught the eye of farmers and plantation owners in the southeastern United States. Many keepers of enslaved people saw these lands as a threat, because they offered a refuge for those who escaped. In fact, seventeenth-century Spanish Florida offered freedom to any enslaved person who arrived there and pledged loyalty to Spain, making Florida one of the first destinations for enslaved Africans fleeing captivity (Hudson 2006).

The Patriot War of East Florida erupted in 1812, when the Patriots, with tacit support from Washington, invaded Florida, capturing Fernandina on Amelia Island before attacking the Spanish at St. Augustine (Cusick 2007; Stagg 2007). The Seminoles refused to side with the Patriots, and in retaliation, the Patriots attacked Alachua, which was the largest Seminole town in central Florida. By 1814, the Patriots were driven from Florida, but this was soon followed by Andrew Jackson's incursion into Florida in 1817. Jackson's army attacked and burned down three Seminole towns, before taking Pensacola from the Spanish. The US Army continued to attack the Seminole and forcibly claim their land in a bloody series of battles. Amid all the fighting between the US military and the Seminoles, the Spanish ceded Florida to the United States in 1819 with the Adams-Onis Treaty (Bates 2015).

After the Spanish left Florida, the Seminole fought on until 1823. After six years of war, they met with the US military at Moultrie Creek to sign a treaty establishing the first reservation in Florida (Brown 1999). The controversial agreement called for most Seminole to move to the 4-million-acre reservation in central Florida. The entire Orlando metropolitan area and its environs fall within the reservation boundaries. While large, the reservation was designed to isolate the Seminole—cutting them off from coastal lands and thus interrupting their ability to connect with Spanish and British allies in the Caribbean. From the beginning, both sides regularly broke the treaty. US settlers continually pressed into Seminole lands, and many Seminoles refused to relocate in the first place.

The Indian Removal Act of 1830 broke the Treaty of Moultrie Creek and created the framework for breaking all other treaties with Indigenous people in the United States. It displaced all the tribes north of Florida, creating the Trail of Tears as Indigenous people were forced into "Indian Territory" in what would become Oklahoma. Things were different in Florida, where the Seminoles were able to mount a more effective defense than many other tribes. They used guerilla hit-and-run tactics and made extensive use of the hostile environment of the Everglades, which the US Army was neither prepared nor trained for.

The period from 1832 to 1843, known as the "Second Seminole War," became the longest and most costly of all of America's "Indian Wars." The Seminoles won almost every single battle, but every casualty was a blow because there were no reinforcements. While the Americans were losing far more people, their fighting capability never diminished, as they could cycle more soldiers into the conflict. The US Army also broke the rules of war by attacking under a flag of truce and using bloodhounds to track Seminole movements. After decades of fighting and living on the run, several Seminole leaders ultimately agreed to "removal" in 1842. In the same year, the Armed Occupation Act was signed, which incentivized armed homesteaders to claim land a certain distance away from a military base, in an effort to fortify US lands and pressure the Seminole to leave. By 1843, less than 1,000 Seminoles remained in Florida.

In 1849, an Army captain named John Casey was appointed Indian Agent, tasked with working with Billy Bowlegs, a leader of the Seminole Tribe, in order to persuade the Seminole to leave Florida (Wallace 1962). In the 1850s, the US government started a campaign of surveying Seminole lands and harassing Tribal members in an effort to invite conflict or compel them to leave (Knetsch et al. 2018). Casey and Bowlegs made efforts to find a peace, and Bowlegs traveled to Washington in 1854 to make his case to President Franklin Pierce and Congress; however, the US government remained committed to Indian Removal. Bowlegs returned to Florida, and by 1855 the "Third Seminole War" had broken out.

The "Third Seminole War" was a very different phase of the war; the US Army was now committed to targeting Seminole camps—mostly going after women and children. These noncombatants were first taken to a prison camp at Fort Myers; however, the Army grew frustrated as they continually escaped. By 1856, the Army turned to a new solution: an island prison camp. Newspaper records in the *Florida Peninsular* (1857) and others mention plans to purchase lumber for a blockhouse fort (*New Orleans Crescent*, 1857), a wooden building surrounded by an open area and enclosed by sharpened wooden palisade, at Egmont Key.

The first prisoners actually arrived on Egmont Key in 1852 (*Daily Republic*, 1852) followed by a larger wave from 1856 to 1858. The US Army tried to portray their fraught efforts at Indian Removal in a positive light by saying how the Seminole were thriving in their new accommodations. This spin served an obvious political objective, in framing a deeply unpopular southern war in positive terms meant to counteract the Seminole War's unpopularity in the north. Antagonism between the North and South was growing stronger, and opinions on the war were starkly divided along geographical lines, foreshadowing the coming Civil War. Few records survive of the Egmont Key prison camp; however, two short letters were written by M. L. Lothrop in 1857 to Major General Page, the commander of Fort Brooke. Lothrop's letters, written to document the death of two Seminoles, are authored in a very matter-of-fact and dehumanizing way (National Archives, 1979). The exact number of Seminoles who lived and died at Egmont Key is unknown; the US Army didn't treat them as full people and as such did not keep detailed records.

The one well-documented historical event from this period at Egmont Key was the final voyage transporting the Seminoles from the prison camp to New Orleans, where they were then marched north to Oklahoma. On May 6, 1858, all Seminole prisoners boarded the steamer *Grey Cloud*, which set off to make an initial stop at St. Marks. The ship's manifest was published in the *New York Herald* (*New York Herald*, 1858; see 2.10).

At St. Marks, Polly Parker (Emateloye), orchestrated an escape by persuading the guards to let her disembark the boat to collect medicinal herbs. She left with a half dozen other women and escaped into the woods and made her way through occupied territory to rejoin the Tribe at Lake Okeechobee. The *Grey Cloud* continued its journey; the last voyage of Indian Removal east of the Mississippi, a topic that is discussed further in Chapter 3.

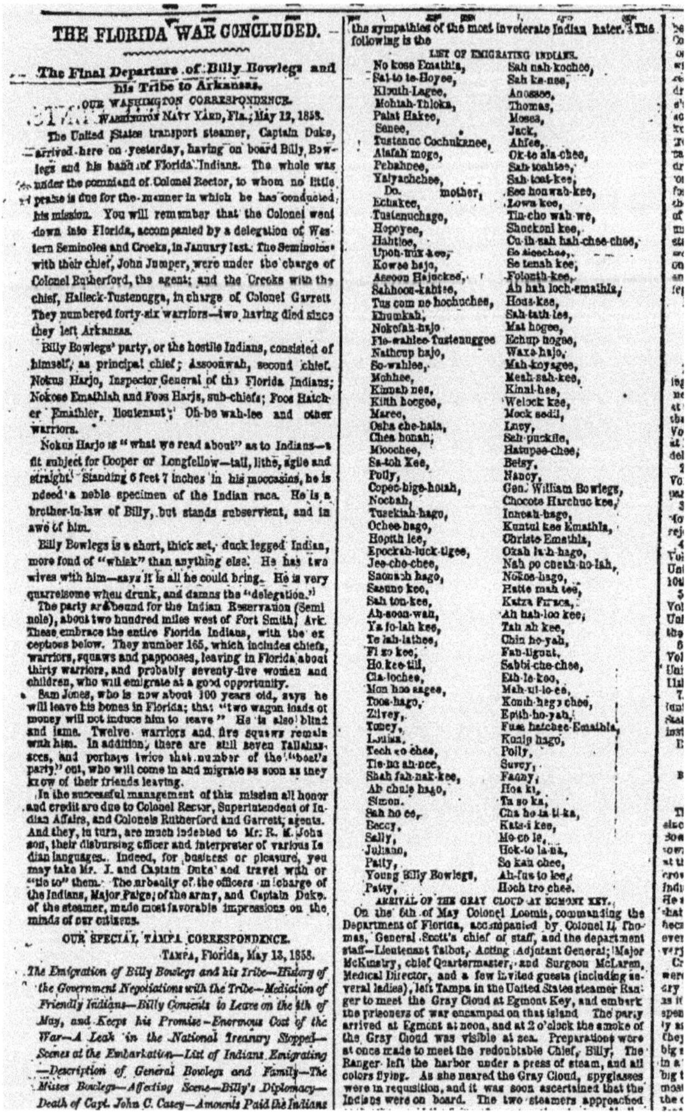

THE FLORIDA WAR CONCLUDED.

The Final Departure of Billy Bowlegs and his Tribe to Arkansas.

OUR WASHINGTON CORRESPONDENCE.

WASHINGTON NAVY YARD, Fla., May 12, 1858.

The United States transport steamer, Captain Duke, arrived here on yesterday, having on board Billy Bowlegs and his band of Florida Indians. The whole was under the command of Colonel Rector, to whom no little praise is due for the manner in which he has conducted his mission. You will remember that the Colonel went down into Florida, accompanied by a delegation of Western Seminoles and Creeks, in January last. The Seminoles with their chief, John Jumper, were under the charge of Colonel Rutherford, the agent; and the Creeks with the chief, Halleck-Tustenugga, in charge of Colonel Garrett. They numbered forty-six warriors—two having died since they left Arkansas.

Billy Bowlegs' party, or the hostile Indians, consisted of himself, as principal chief; Assoonwah, second chief. Nokus Harjo, Inspector General of the Florida Indians; Nokose Emathlah and Foos Harjo, sub-chiefs; Foos Hatcher Emathler, lieutenant; Oh-be wah-lee and other warriors.

Nokus Harjo is "what we read about" as to Indians—a fit subject for Cooper or Longfellow—tall, lithe, agile and straight. Standing 6 feet 7 inches in his moccasins, he is indeed a noble specimen of the Indian race. He is a brother-in-law of Billy, but stands subservient, and in awe of him.

Billy Bowlegs is a short, thick set, duck legged Indian, more fond of "whisk" than anything else. He has two wives with him—says it is all he could bring. He is very quarrelsome when drunk, and damns the "delegation."

The party are bound for the Indian Reservation (Seminole), about two hundred miles west of Fort Smith, Ark. These embrace the entire Florida Indians, with the exceptions below. They number 165, which includes chiefs, warriors, squaws and pappooses, leaving in Florida about thirty warriors, and probably seventy-five women and children, who will emigrate at a good opportunity.

Sam Jones, who is now about 100 years old, says he will leave his bones in Florida; that "two wagon loads of money will not induce him to leave" He is also blind and lame. Twelve warriors and five squaws remain with him. In addition, there are still seven Tallahassees, and perhaps twice that number of the "boat's party" out, who will come in and migrate as soon as they know of their friends leaving.

In the successful management of this mission all honor and credit are due to Colonel Rector, Superintendent of Indian Affairs, and Colonels Rutherford and Garrett, agents. And they, in turn, are much indebted to Mr. R. M. Johnson, their disbursing officer and interpreter of various Indian languages. Indeed, for business or pleasure, you may take Mr. J. and Captain Duke and travel with or "tie to" them. The urbanity of the officers in charge of the Indians, Major Paige, of the army, and Captain Duke, of the steamer, made most favorable impressions on the minds of our citizens.

OUR SPECIAL TAMPA CORRESPONDENCE.

TAMPA, Florida, May 13, 1858.

The Emigration of Billy Bowlegs and his Tribe—History of the Government Negotiations with the Tribe—Mediation of Friendly Indians—Billy Consents to Leave on the 4th of May, and Keeps his Promise—Enormous Cost of the War—A Leak in the National Treasury Stopped—Scenes at the Embarkation—List of Indians Emigrating—Description of General Bowlegs and Family—The Misses Bowlegs—Affecting Scene—Billy's Diplomacy—Death of Capt. John C. Casey—Amounts Paid the Indians

...the sympathies of the most inveterate Indian hater. The following is the

LIST OF EMIGRATING INDIANS.

No kose Emathla,	Sah nah-kochee,
Sal-to te-Hoyee,	Sah ka-nee,
Klouth-Lagee,	Anossee,
Mohlah-Thloka,	Thomas,
Palat Hakee,	Moses,
Senee,	Jack,
Tustenuc Cochukenee,	Ahfee,
Alafah mogo,	Ok-to ala-chee,
Pehahnee,	Sah toahtee,
Yalyachchee,	Sah-toat-kee,
Do. mother,	See honwah-kee,
Echakee,	Lowa kee,
Tustenuchago,	Tin-cho wah-we,
Hopoyee,	Shuckoni kee,
Hahtiee,	Cu-ih-sah hah-chee-chee,
Upon-mix-kee,	So aicechee,
Kowee hajo,	Se tenah kee,
Assoon Hajuckee,	Foloath-kee,
Sahhoon-kahtee,	Ah hah loch-emathla,
Tus com no hochuchee,	Hous-kee,
Khumkah,	Sah-tath-lee,
Nokofah-hajo	Mat hogee,
Fle-wahlee-Tustenuggee	Echup hogee,
Nathcup hajo,	Waxa-hajo,
So-wahlee,	Mah-koyagee,
Mohhee,	Meah-sah-kee,
Kinnah nee,	Kinnl-hee,
Kitth hoegee,	Welock kee,
Maree,	Mock sedil,
Osha che-hala,	Lucy,
Chea honah,	Sah-puckfle,
Moochee,	Hatupee-chee,
Sa-toh Kee,	Betsy,
Polly,	Nancy,
Copee-hige-houah,	Gen. William Bowlegs,
Nocbah,	Chocote Harchuc kee,
Tusekiah-hago,	Inneah-hago,
Ochee-hago,	Kuntul kee Emathla,
Hoptth lee,	Christo Emathla,
Epockah-luck-tigee,	Ozah lah-hago,
Jee-cho-chee,	Nah po cheah-no-lah,
Saonach hago,	Nokos-hago,
Sasuno kee,	Hatte mah tee,
Sah ton-kee,	Katza Furaca,
Ah-soon-wah,	Ah hah-loo kee,
Ya fo-lah kee,	Tah ah kee,
Te lah-lathee,	Chin ho-yah,
Fi so kee,	Fah-ligont,
Ho kee-till,	Sabbi-che-chee,
Cla-lochee,	Eah-le-koo,
Mon hoo sagee,	Mah-ul-lo-ee,
Toos-hago,	Konth-hego chee,
Zilvey,	Epith-ho-yah,
Toney,	Fuse hatchee-Emathla,
Louisa,	Konip hago,
Tech co chee,	Polly,
Tie-no ah-nee,	Suvey,
Shah fah-nak-kee,	Fanny,
Ah chule hago,	Hoa ki,
Simon.	Ta so ka,
Sah ho ee,	Cha ho-la ti-ka,
Beccy,	Kats-i kee,
Sally,	Mo-co le,
Juliano,	Hok-to la-na,
Patty,	So kan chee,
Young Billy Bowlegs,	Ah-fus to lee,
Patty,	Hoch tro chee.

ARRIVAL OF THE GRAY CLOUD AT EGMONT KEY.

On the 6th of May Colonel Loomis, commanding the Department of Florida, accompanied by Colonel L. Thomas, General Scott's chief of staff, and the department staff—Lieutenant Talbot, Acting Adjutant General; Major McKinstry, chief Quartermaster, and Surgeon McLaren, Medical Director, and a few invited guests (including several ladies), left Tampa in the United States steamer Ranger to meet the Gray Cloud at Egmont Key, and embark the prisoners of war encamped on that island. The party arrived at Egmont at noon, and at 2 o'clock the smoke of the Gray Cloud was visible at sea. Preparations were at once made to meet the redoubtable Chief, Billy. The Ranger left the harbor under a press of steam, and all colors flying. As she neared the Gray Cloud, spyglasses were in requisition, and it was soon ascertained that the Indians were on board. The two steamers approached

Figure 2.10. The manifest of the *Grey Cloud*, listing names of Seminoles removed from Egmont Key in 1858. From New York Herald Archive.

Maritime Wayfinding: Beacons, Keepers, and Navigators

Egmont Key has always been a key maritime location for transportation through the dark times of Seminole imprisonment and relocation to other eras where military, defense, commerce, and tourism would come to characterize activities on and around the island. Egmont Key has been a beacon of maritime wayfinding for centuries, because of its location alongside the main channel leading from the Gulf of Mexico to Tampa Bay. The nineteenth century saw the waterways around Egmont Key transform into major throughfares of marine commerce. The shipping industry grew dramatically, and by the 1830s navigational aid was requested for the island (Caignet 2012). In 1836 a barrel painted black and white was placed on 50-ft pole serving as the first beacon. Congress approved a $7,580 appropriation to build a permanent structure and lighthouse keeper's house (Caignet 2012).

The first lighthouse was constructed on Egmont Key in 1848, near the north end of the island. Just months after it was completed, the strongest hurricane to ever hit Tampa Bay made landfall, on September 23–25. This "Great Gale" (Guzzo 2023) leveled nearly all houses in Tampa, leaving a wake of destruction, devastating the region, and destroying Fort Brooke (Brown 1999). Lighthouse Keeper Sherrod Edwards and his family were isolated on the island when the hurricane hit. As the storm surge washed across the island, he and his family tied a small boat to a palmetto tree in the center of the island and rode out the storm, managing to survive. Egmont Key's lighthouse was severely damaged in the storm, and then, as if to add insult to injury, a second storm hit the region later in the season, worsening its condition further. In the years that followed, several repairs were made to the tower, but lighthouse keepers still found it nearly impossible to maintain a steady light due to poor ventilation at the top and the use of low-quality oil. The tower itself was also determined to be 10–12 ft too short to guide vessels into safe harbor (Hurley and Mohlman 2000). The new and current lighthouse, an 87-foot brick tower begun in 1857 following a $16,000 appropriation, was constructed further inland to protect from erosion. It was placed into service in 1858 and still stands today as one of the iconic features of Egmont Key.

During World War II, probably in 1944, the top of the lighthouse was removed by the US Army, as part of a broader effort to install a new lighthouse optic (Hurley 2011). The remnants of the lighthouse top were placed in the woods approximately 100 ft west of the lighthouse, where they remained until

2011, when local volunteers, led by Neil Hurley, obtained a permit from the US Coast Guard to conduct a lighthouse artifact survey. Over the course of four days, the team documented and catalogued 86 iron and bronze lighthouse components, mostly stairs and windowsills. All items were then placed back in the artifact field (Hurley 2011). Since 2011, they have continued to deteriorate in this location, exposed to the elements.

Starting in 1848 and lasting until 1989, there was a succession of 36 lighthouse keepers at Egmont Key (Lighthouse Friends 2025). They bore witness to many historical events that touched the island, from the Seminole incarceration to the Spanish-American War, yellow fever quarantine camp, militarization, and the establishment of the National Wildlife Refuge. Few journals or records remain of their first-person historical accounts. The last lighthouse keeper left in 1989. The life of a lighthouse keeper in the early days of Egmont Key was punctuated with dramatic events such as storms and military activities as well as ample time for appreciating the island's natural beauty. Lighthouse Keeper George V. Rickard held the position for just one year (1860–1861), but was apparently enchanted by the experience, authoring a poem called "The Midnight Hour."

Tis midnight hour the moon shines bright
The dewdrops blaze beneath their rays
The twinkling stars, that trembling light
Like beauty's eyes displays

Sleep no more tho bound by thy heart
Some tender dreams may idly play
For midnight song with magic art
Shall chase that dream away

Tis midnight hour from flower to flower
The wayward gopher floats along
On singers (fingers?) in some shady bower
To hear the night bird song (Rickard 1981)

The end of Rickard's tenure on Egmont Key was decidedly less bucolic. Four days after "The Midnight Hour" was written, Florida seceded from the Union and joined the Confederacy. Rickard became embroiled in the conflict and pretended to sympathize with Union blockaders who appeared in the vicinity of Egmont Key. He soon sensed an opportunity to flee. Under Confederate orders, he dismantled the third-order Fresnel lens from the lighthouse and hid it at Fort Brooke on the mainland (Hurley 2007). The lighthouse remained under Union control throughout the rest of the war (United States Coast Guard n.d.). They used the island as a fuel depot and hospital for the East Gulf Blockade Squadron (Caignet 2012). In Tampa, however, Fort Brooke was under Confederate control and martial law was imposed in 1862 (Caignet 2012).

In the aftermath of the Civil War, the Union spirit perhaps remained on Egmont Key, with the tenure of Senior Lighthouse Keeper Captain Charles Moore (1878–1910), who is quoted as saying, "I am a damn Yankee but I like the town and I like the people and I'm going to stay here—if they'll let me" (Caignet 2012: 44). Charles Moore was the longest-serving lighthouse keeper, well known and respected in the maritime community and throughout the region. His dedicated stewardship of the maritime traditions of Egmont Key passed to his son, Charles "Charlie" Mortimer Moore (1876–1967), who was brought to Egmont Key as an infant and lived in the lighthouse keeper's house with his father for many years. Egmont Key figured prominently into his adult life as well. He moved back and forth between Egmont Key and the mainland with various jobs ranging from medical assistant during the 1898 quarantine to a supervisor with the US Army Engineers building sea walls and fortifications at Egmont Key (Caignet 2012). Eventually he took an office job with the Tampa Bay Pilots Association, the organization responsible for marine commerce, where he served for 25 years.

"Charlie" lived on the island periodically with his family over the years, which had a profound impact on his daughter Roberta Moore Cole, who has recounted many stories of the rhythms of life on Egmont Key (Cole 1981; 1986). In 1986, Libby Warner interviewed Roberta on behalf of the Tampa Bay Pilots Association. In the interview, she says, "You know, Egmont Key is to me a character—a very much-loved character. In my youth she shared some of her secrets with me. I wished she could have told me more. . . . Egmont showed me arrow heads left by Indians. She showed me [a] white sandy rim of beach with spots just ideal for beaching or anchoring a long-ago schooner" (Cole 1986: 1). Roberta also describes Egmont Key's colorful history: "On the knees of my elders, I heard the sagas of the Indians, the Cuban fisherman, the exploration, the conquest, the wars, and in short, the history of the area which extends from the fifteenth century well into the nineteenth century" (Cole 1986: 1)

According to Roberta's recollections, many were attracted to the island:

"There were all kind of people who came—thieves, ruthless murderers, adventurers, loyal soldiers of noble birth, gentlemen, explorers, priests, geographers, map makers. They came from Spain. They came from England, from Holland, and I'm sure, from elsewhere. They came to Egmont and they came into our bay. But none stayed, except the fishermen" (Cole 1986: 3).

With this firsthand reflection, we get a different picture of Egmont Key than the typical histories of Spanish explorers and quarantine camps. Egmont Key was a place where daily life unfolded for many with music, entertaining, and socializing. "The Moore family often enjoyed musical week-ends on Egmont. The music teacher sometimes brought one of her young lady proteges as a guest to inspire her less-talented Egmont people. All of the Lightfoot girls also entertained the family at the piano. And they also entertained their beaus" (Cole 1986: 11). Roberta also spoke of the role of music for the soldiers stationed at Egmont and how much they loved to play honky-tonk music in the auditorium in the center of the island as part of movie nights, with the mockingbirds sometimes singing along.

Roberta Moore Cole bridges the two worlds of the lighthouse keepers and Tampa Bay Pilots; her life was intertwined with both by having a father and a grandfather as such prominent figures in these institutions. This was not unusual, as the men who served in these roles often raised their families on the island and their lives became connected. Despite having such an essential role in coastal commerce, few people know about the Tampa Bay Pilots Association, an organization central to maritime wayfinding and the history of Egmont Key. It remains unknown to most visitors and is often shrouded in mystery. Like the Lighthouse Keepers, the Pilots quietly bore witness to the many historical events of Egmont Key and developed an intimate knowledge of the island and waterways surrounding it.

THE TAMPA BAY PILOTS ASSOCIATION

While the word *pilot* conjures up images of aviation, the profession of maritime "piloting" refers to navigating large ships into ports. Piloting dates back thousands of years and is even referenced in the Old Testament (Caignet 2012; Thompson and Thompson 2012). Pilots perform one of the most critical jobs in maritime wayfinding by contributing their deep knowledge of local waterways to safely navigate ships from distant locales into complex, busy, local ports. In Tampa, highly trained pilots pull a boat alongside an incoming vessel and climb aboard via a rope ladder, referred to as a Jacob's ladder or pilot's ladder. This can be a dangerous endeavor, and many pilots have died or suffered grievous injuries during transfer. In most states, including Florida, piloting is overseen and managed by state governments, each of which has a maritime piloting organization that assigns pilots to incoming and outgoing vessels and coordinates where pilots are stationed and deploy from.

The Tampa Bay Pilots Association was founded in 1886, just 28 years after the last Seminoles were transported off Egmont Key on the *Grey Cloud* and 12 years before the military construction boom of Fort Dade. It is the official navigational group that was established at Egmont Key to ensure the safety and efficiency of steering through the complex waters of Tampa Bay (Caignet 2012). Egmont Key has always been highly strategic and coveted because of its location at the mouth of Tampa Bay—which is why the association chose the island as a base of operations.

Even before the association, Pilots helped safely facilitate maritime commerce into Tampa Bay starting in 1848, and the Pilots were picked up by incoming ships on Egmont Key by the 1850s. Initially, the Pilots stayed at the assistant lighthouse keeper's house to await incoming ships, but by 1911 Pilot John J. Fogarty constructed a small wooden cottage on the east side of the island. By 1916, other Pilots had followed suit, and there were a handful of wooden cottages along with a 40-ft lookout tower, 300-ft pier, a generator, fuel storage tanks, and radio equipment on land that the Pilots had leased from the federal government (Caignet 2012; Thompson and Thompson 2012). In 1928, Hillsborough County purchased the 5.8-acre plot on which the village was located, then leased it back to the Pilots Association. Each Pilot was required to have a home on Egmont Key, even if they also had one back on the mainland. In more recent times, the cottages no longer functioned as primary residences but were used by the Pilots and their families. The village is tucked away down a private road, closed to the public, and many visitors are unaware of its existence or long history. But the village was clearly visible from the water, and many scores of boaters must have wondered who resided in this mysterious cluster of houses on Egmont Key's eastern shore. Adding to the air of mystery, the Pilots, in addition to Florida State Park staff, were the only people authorized to stay overnight on the island, a situation that ended when the housing was destroyed in 2024 (discussed below).

The village serves as a reminder of the history of maritime wayfinding in Tampa Bay that continues to contribute to significant economic impacts through the various ports in the region.

The significance of the Tampa Bay Pilots extends beyond just guiding ships that are essential for the regional economy. Their work is deeply intertwined with the environmental stewardship and safety of the local community. In an interview with John Timmel, a veteran Pilot, he notes, "A lot of people think pilots are there to . . . increase efficiency, which they do, they can bring shifts in and out more quickly, they can dock and undock more quickly, make arrangements do all of that. But our primary purpose is to [be] guardians of Tampa Bay, basically, to look out for the well-being and safety of the environment and, and our citizens here" (John Timmel, personal communication 2024). Timmel's words emphasize that the role of the Pilots is not solely about speeding up maritime traffic but also about protecting the delicate balance of Tampa Bay's ecosystem and ensuring the safety of those who depend on its waters. He emphasizes how piloting is more than just a job but has deep historical roots and an enduring connection to nature. This focus on heritage, history, and stewardship is a theme central to the book *Dedication to Service*, commissioned by the Pilots Association and researched and written by Carrie Caignet (2012).

The involvement of the lighthouse keepers, federal government, and then county in the Tampa Bay Pilots Association underscores a theme that has permeated Egmont Key's history with multiple authorities, municipalities, and entities having a regulatory or administrative role in the activities at the island. For Hillsborough County, the acquisition of acreage to lease to the Pilots meant a foothold in maritime commerce and oversight of the main channel into the Port of Tampa. Interestingly, the whole island is in Hillsborough County, which provides another strategic location as the island comprises the only Gulf-facing coastline in the county. Other key organizations also oversee maritime wayfinding and commerce in Tampa Bay, including the US Coast Guard, which took over the lighthouse operations in 1939 and remains the central authority patrolling America's coasts and coordinating piloting activities.

The end of an era for the Pilots came in 2024. The catastrophic hurricanes in the fall of that year—Helene and Milton—did more than just reshape the landscape of Egmont Key; they erased a vital piece of Tampa Bay's maritime heritage. The back-to-back storms completely leveled the Pilots' Village, bringing an abrupt and devastating end to Pilot operations at Egmont Key where they quietly but crucially guided Tampa's maritime commerce for well over 100 years. The loss of the Tampa Bay Pilots Association's presence on Egmont Key severs a living link to the region's deep-rooted navigational history. Pilot Jack Timmel reflected on the inevitability of this moment, stating, "We hoped it wouldn't be so soon, but we were making preparations for when it happened. We understood that it no longer makes sense to have the entirety of our operations on a small island in a hurricane-prone state" (Guzzo 2025: para. 32). Yet the significance of this loss goes beyond logistical practicality. Few in the region realize the extent to which the Pilots' work has shaped Tampa Bay's economy and daily life. Their departure from Egmont Key and relocation to the mainland is not just a shift in operations—it breaks a long-standing connection to Tampa's maritime past.

Conclusion

Egmont Key's complex history serves as a microcosm of broader national narratives, encompassing themes of colonial expansion, military strategy, forced displacement, maritime commerce, and environmental change. From its early use by Indigenous people to its strategic importance during Spanish, British, and American rule, the island has been a focal point of power struggles, nation building, and human resilience. Its role in the Seminole War, the Civil War, and both World Wars underscores its significance as a site of military occupation and conflict. It was also important for maritime wayfinding and as a base for the Tampa Bay Pilots, establishing itself over the centuries as a place of prominence in Florida's coastal economy. The island has seen both suffering and survival, from the forced imprisonment of Seminole people and isolating quarantine camps to the sometimes-bucolic lives of lighthouse keepers and their families. These histories are at risk of washing away due to the ongoing battle against erosion and sea-level rise.

Despite its historical significance, much of Egmont Key's past remains unknown to the general public. Many of its most compelling narratives—such as the Seminole imprisonment, the role of enslaved people in the Civil War, and the contributions of Lighthouse Keepers and Pilots—are often overshadowed by more widely recognized histories of war and military fortifications. The island's physical landscape has also been shaped and reshaped by both natural forces and human intervention. Hurricanes and rising tides have eroded much of its landmass, threatening the remnants of Fort Dade, the lighthouse, and other historical structures. As the forces of climate change accelerate, Egmont Key now stands at a crossroads, facing an uncertain future that calls for action, collaboration, and reflection (discussed more fully in Chapter 8). Some preservation measures have been undertaken for the extant structures and mitigation of land loss, such as sand emplacement on the vulnerable western shoreline. The question remains what else can and should be done with an island that ultimately will wash away, taking heritage sites and nesting places for birds and turtles with it? What can we do to not let the histories and significance also wash away?

Egmont Key is not just about the past—it is about what we choose to remember and protect moving forward. Understanding the island's layered history allows us to see how global forces—colonialism, war, commerce, and environmental change—play out on a small but significant scale. As conservationists, academic partners, land managers, and local communities strive to steward what remains of Egmont Key, its story continues to evolve, offering lessons on resilience, remembrance, and the interconnectedness of history and place. Whether through digital preservation efforts, public education, or giving voice to invisible histories, the survival of Egmont Key's histories depends on the commitment to keep these stories alive, even as the sands of the disappearing island continue to shift.

References Cited

Anderson, D. G. 1996. Models of Paleoindian and Early Archaic Settlement in the Lower Southeast. In *The Paleoindian and Early Archaic Southeast*, edited by David G. Anderson and Kenneth E. Sassaman, pp. 29–57. University of Alabama Press, Tuscaloosa.

Ardalan, Christine. 2010–2011. Clara Barton's 1898 Battles in Cuba: A Reexamination of Her Nursing Contributions. *Florida Atlantic Comparative Studies Journal* 12: 1–20. https://home.fau.edu/peralta/web/FACS/CLARABARTON.pdf.

Ashley, K. H. 2002. On the Periphery of the Early Mississippian World: Looking Within and Beyond Northeastern Florida. *Southeastern Archaeology* 21(2): 162–177. http://www.jstor.org/stable/40713578.

Bates, C. G. (editor). 2015. *The Early Republic and Antebellum America: An Encyclopedia of Social, Political, Cultural, and Economic History*. Taylor and Francis.

Berhow, M. A. 2015. *American Seacoast Defenses: A Reference Guide*. Coast Defense Study Group Press, McLean, Virginia.

Brown, Canter. 1999. *Tampa Before the Civil War*. University of Tampa Press, Tampa.

Caignet, Carrie. 2012. *Dedication to Service: The History of Piloting on Tampa Bay Through Three Centuries*. Tampa Bay Pilots Association, Tampa.

Clausen, C. J., A. D. Cohen, C. Emiliani, J. A. Holman, and J. J. Stipp. 1979. Little Salt Spring, Florida: A Unique Underwater Site. *Science* 203(4381): 609–614. http://www.jstor.org/stable/1747724.

Cole, R. M. 1981. Interview with Roberta Moore Cole: Memories of Egmont Key. https://

mymanatee.contentdm.oclc.org/digital/collection/p16681coll2/id/1079, accessed March 18, 2025.
Cole, R. M. 1986. "Egmont Key," March 19, 1986. Transcript of a talk given at the Membership Meeting of the Manatee County Historical Society. Manuscript on File, Eaton Room, Manatee County Public Library.
Covington, J. W. 1998. The Rough Riders in Tampa. *Tampa Bay History* 20(1): 3.
Cusick, J. G. 2007. *The Other War of 1812: The Patriot War and the American Invasion of Spanish East Florida*. University of Georgia Press, Athens.
Daily Republic [Washington, DC]. 1852. "Florida Indians." Wed., July 21, 1852.
Dunbar, James S. 2016. *Paleoindian Societies of the Coastal Southeast*. University Press of Florida, Gainesville.
Faught, M. K., and C. D. Pevny. 2019. Pre-Clovis to the Early Archaic: Human Presence, Expansion, and Settlement in Florida over Four Millennia. *PaleoAmerica* 5(1): 73–87. https://doi.org/10.1080/20555563.2019.1597608.
Florida Peninsular [Tampa, Florida]. 1857. "A Trip to Egmont Key." August 1, 1857, p. 2, col. 4.
"Florida, US, County Marriage Records, 1823–1982," entry for Julius Tiedchen and Frances Jett, March 14, 1920, Ancestry.com, online database (index only), https://www.ancestry.com/discoveryui-content/view/1234994:61369, accessed October 6, 2024.
Graves, L. 1898. Clara Barton Papers: Diaries and Journals: Diarists Other Than Barton; Graves, Lucy, June 17–December 30, Spanish-American War Relief, June 17–December 30. Manuscript/mixed material, retrieved from the Library of Congress, https://www.loc.gov/item/mss119730062/.
Guzzo, Paul. 2023. Letter from 1848 Details Tampa's Damage from a Major Hurricane. *Tampa Bay Times*, September 11, 2023. https://www.tampabay.com/life-culture/history/2023/09/11/tampa-hurricane-1848-history-robert-jackson/, accessed June 15, 2025.
Guzzo, Paul. 2025. USF Is Digitally Preserving Egmont Key's Historic Harbor Pilot Village. USF Newsroom, March 17, 2025. https://www.usf.edu/news/2025/usf-is-digitally-preserving-egmont-keys-historic-harbor-pilot-village.aspx, accessed June 15, 2025.
Jessi J. Halligan, Michael R. Waters, Angelina Perrotti, Ivy J. Owens, Joshua M. Feinberg, Mark D. Bourne, Brendan Fenerty, and others. 2016. Pre-Clovis Occupation 14,550 Years Ago at the Page-Ladson Site, Florida, and the Peopling of the Americas. *Science Advances* 2(5): e1600375. https://doi.org/10.1126/sciadv.1600375.
Hally, D. 2008. *King: The Social Archaeology of a Late Mississippian Town in Northwestern Georgia*. University of Alabama Press, Athens.
Harley, A. F. 1930. Bernard Romans's Map of Florida Engraved by Paul Revere, and Other Early Maps in the Library of the Florida Historical Society. *Florida Historical Society Quarterly* 9(1): 47–57. http://www.jstor.org/stable/30149718.
Hoffman, P. E. 2002. *Florida's Frontiers*. Indiana University Press, Bloomington.
Hudson, J. B. 2006. *Encyclopedia of the Underground Railroad*. McFarland, Jefferson, North Carolina.

Hurley, Neil. 2007. *Florida's Lighthouses in the Civil War*. Middle River Press, Florida.

Hurley, Neil. 2011. Egmont Key, Florida: Lighthouse Artifact Survey Results. Unpublished manuscript.

Hurley, N. E., and G. Mohlman. 2000. *Lighthouses of Egmont*. Key. CD-ROM Book. Historic Lighthouse Publications. Chesapeake, Virginia.

James, Stephen R., Jr., Charles C. Pearson, and M. C. Krivor. 2006. *Historic Assessment, Remote Sensing Survey and Diver Evaluations at Egmont Key, Hillsborough, Florida*. Prepared for the US Army Corps of Engineers, Jacksonville District, under subcontract to the US Army Corps of Engineers, Memphis District. Panamerican Consultants, Memphis, Tennessee.

Kaserman, S., and J. Kaserman. 2011. *Florida Pirates: From the Southern Gulf Coast to the Keys and Beyond*. History Press, Charleston, South Carolina.

Kite-Powell, Rodney. 2014. Pirates, Real and Legendary, Left Their Mark on Tampa Bay. *The Tribune*, June 15. https://www.newspapers.com/article/the-tampa-tribune-pirate-history-tampa-b/66479185/, accessed June 15, 2025.

Knetsch, J., and N. Wynne. 2011. *Florida in the Spanish-American War*. History Press, Charleston, South Carolina.

Knetsch, J., J. Missall and M. L. Missall. 2018. *History of the Third Seminole War, 1849–1858*. Casemate, Havertown, PA.

Lighthouse Friends. 2025. Egmont Key Lighthouse. https://www.lighthousefriends.com/light.asp?ID=370, accessed June 15, 2025.

Milanich, J. T. 1995. *Florida Indians and the Invasion from Europe*. University Press of Florida, Gainesville.

Milanich, J. 2018. Original Inhabitants. In *The History of Florida*, edited by Michael Gannon, pp. 12–24. University Press of Florida, Gainesville.

Mohlman, G. 1997. An Island Fortress: Egmont Key's Fort Dade. *Sunland Tribune* 23(7): 1–20. https://digitalcommons.usf.edu/sunlandtribune/vol23/iss1/7.

Mol, A. A. 2014. *The Connected Caribbean: A Socio-Material Network Approach to Patterns of Homogeneity and Diversity in the Pre-colonial Period*. Sidestone Press, Leiden, the Netherlands.

"Morning Reports, 1912–1939." 1919. Morning Report, Camp Merritt, New Jersey, School for Bakers and Cooks, October 1919, Fold3.com, online database with images. https://www.fold3.com/image/708218452/oct-1919-page-11-us-morning-reports-1912-1939, accessed October 6, 2024.

"Muster Rolls, June 30, 1918, 1st Company, Coast Defenses Tampa." 1918. Organizations, Coast Defenses, Record Group 392, Box 405, Entry 370, File 320.2, National Archives and Records Administration—East Point, Georgia.

National Archives. 1979. Letters Sent, Registers of Letters Received by Headquarters, Troops in Florida, and Headquarters, Department of Florida, 1850–1858. National Archives Microfilm Publications. Microfilm Publication M1084, Roll 8, Letters Received by Headquarters, Department of Florida Registered, H-Q, 1857.

National Park Service. N.d. Tampa Bay Hotel. https://www.nps.gov/places/tampa-bay-hotel.htm, accessed June 15, 2025.

New Orleans Crescent [New Orleans, Louisiana]. 1857. "Pensacola Democrat States That the Indians Captured Since the Commencement of the War, Are to Be Placed on Egmont Key, Under the Charge of an Adequate Guard. The Lumber Is Now on the Ground to Erect a House for Their Accommodation." https://chroniclingamerica.loc.gov/lccn/sn82015753/1857-08-01/ed-1/seq-1/.

New York Times. 1862. "West Coast of Florida." November 17, 1862. https://www.nytimes.com/1862/11/17/archives/west-coast-of-florida-the-blockade-of-tampa-bay-description-of-the.html.

New York Herald. 1858. "The Florida War Concluded." May 27, 1858.

Paloczi-Horvath, G. 1996. *From Monitor to Missile Boat: Coast Defense Ships and Coastal Defense Since 1860*. Naval Institute Press, Annapolis.

Powell, M. T. 1993. Mariner and Privateer to the Crown: A Modest Analysis of the Life of Captain David Culter Braddock. Undergraduate paper, printed in *Savannah Biographies*, Vol. 23, housed in the Florence Powell Minis Room of Lane Library, Georgia Southern University. Digitized in 2011 and available at https://digitalcommons.georgiasouthern.edu/sav-bios-lane/23.

Pryor, E. B. 2011. *Clara Barton, Professional Angel*. University of Pennsylvania Press, Philadelphia.

Rickard, G. 1861, Jan. 6. The Midnight Hour. [Poem written at Egmont Key Light Station]. From Tampa Bay History Center Archives.

Roa, Ray. 2025. Egmont Key Is More Fascinating Than We Could Ever Imagine. The Skinny, WMNF. January 17. https://www.wmnf.org/egmont-key-is-more-fascinating-than-we-could-ever-imagine/, accessed July 15, 2025.

Romans, B. 1999 (1775). *A Concise Natural History of East and West Florida*. Edited by K. Braund. University of Alabama Press.

Romans, B., J. G. W. De Brahm, Robert Sayer, and John Bennett. 1776. A general map of the southern British colonies in America, comprehending North and South Carolina, Georgia, East and West Florida, with the neighboring Indian countries, from the modern surveys of Engineer de Brahm, Capt. Collet, Mouzon, & others, and from the large hydrographical survey of the coasts of East and West Florida. London, Printed for R. Sayer and J. Bennett, map, chart, and print sellers. Map/ Retrieved from the Library of Congress, https://www.loc.gov/item/gm71005467/.

"Roster of the First Company, Tampa, Coast Artillery Corps, at Midnight." 1918. December 31. Organizations, Coast Defenses, Record Group 392, Box 405, Entry 370, File 320.2, National Archives and Records Administration—East Point, Georgia.

Scott, D. 2020. Hugely Significant Canoe Found at Egmont Key. *Seminole Tribune*. January 3. https://seminoletribune.org/hugely-significant-canoe-found-at-egmont-key, accessed June 15, 2025.

Scott-Ireton, D., and A. Mitchell-Cook. 2018. The Maritime Heritage of Florida. In *The History of Florida*, edited by Michael Gannon, pp. 394–416. University Press of Florida, Gainesville.

St. Petersburg Times. 1925. [St. Petersburg, Florida]. "Big Fire Is Aftermath to Federal Raid." Vol. 43 (115), p. 1.

Stafford, John W. 1980. Egmont Key: Sentinel of Tampa Bay. *Tampa Bay History* 2(1), article 4. https://digitalcommons.usf.edu/cgi/viewcontent.cgi?article=1037&context=tampabayhistory.

Stagg, J. C. A. 2007. George Mathews and John McKee: Revolutionizing East Florida, Mobile, and Pensacola in 1812. *Florida Historical Quarterly* 85(3): 269–296. http://www.jstor.org/stable/30150062.

Tampa Bay Times (TBT) [Tampa, Florida]. 1942. "They're Off to join Uncle Sam's Navy." March 26, 1942.

Thompson, D. H., and C. Thompson. 2012. *Egmont Key: A History*. History Press, Charleston, South Carolina.

"United States Census, 1930," St. Petersburg, Florida, Julius Tiedchen in the household of William H. Jett, Ancestry.com, database with images. https://www.ancestry.com/discoveryui-content/view/103418462:6224, image 13 of 33, accessed October 6, 2024.

United States Coast Guard. N.d. Egmont Key Light, July 25, 2019. https://www.history.uscg.mil/Browse-by-Topic/Assets/Land/All/Article/1915905/egmont-key-light/, accessed June 15, 2025.

Ware, John D. 1971. Tampa Bay in 1757: Francisco Maria Celi's Journal and Logbook, Part 1. *Florida Historical Quarterly* 50(2), article 6: 158–179. https://stars.library.ucf.edu/fhq/vol50/iss2/6/, accessed June 15, 2025.

Ware, J. D. 1968. A View of Celi's Journal of Surveys and Chart of 1757. *Florida Historical Quarterly* 47(1): 8–24. http://www.jstor.org/stable/30147404.

Wallace, F. W. 1962. The Story of Captain John C. Casey. The Florida Historical Quarterly, 41(2): 127–144. http://www.jstor.org/stable/30339913.

Zombek, Angela. 2016. Paradise Lost: Florida's Egmont Key During the Civil War. August 31. *Journal of the Civil War Era*. https://www.journalofthecivilwarera.org/2016/08/paradise-lost-floridas-egmont-key-civil-war/.

3

Seminole Perspectives on Egmont Key

TINA OSCEOLA AND DAVE SCHEIDECKER

Egmont Key is a solemn place for the Seminole people. This island epitomizes the struggle and suffering that marked the end of the Seminole War. While the United States recorded three "Seminole Wars," Tribal members view it as one sustained war fought in defense of their homeland. The war began when Andrew Jackson led an invasion into Florida in 1817. Intensification occurred in the periods from 1832 to 1843 and also in the "Billy Bowleg's War," as it was called at the time, from 1855 to 1857. Throughout this time period, the Tribe remained under attack continuously from settlers, local militia, and American slave hunters seeking to capture their free African allies. They fought the settlers in both retribution and anger, and every violent action made the opposing side call for revenge in a bloody cycle. Throughout these ordeals, the United States pressured the Seminole to "remove" themselves willingly while breaking treaties and encouraging actions against them. The Armed Occupation Act of 1841 offered land to Americans who brought their own weapons explicitly to show the Seminole they would never be safe in their homeland.

Seminole Lands Under Siege: Nineteenth-Century Conflicts

When the so-called Billy Bowleg's War began in 1855, the military had learned the lessons from their previous efforts. They had equipment for traversing the Florida wetlands and gear better suited for the environment. But one of the main lessons they had learned was the difficulty of hunting down Seminole soldiers in their own territory. The Seminole knew the wetlands better and had previously caught the soldiers in ambush after ambush before disappearing back into the swamps, using guerilla tactics the American soldiers had never been trained for. As noted by Quenton Cypress (Wind Clan),

> In Seminole War times during the Indian Removal Act, the soldiers were taking us to Fort Myers and they would hold us at Fort Myers and wait for another Calvary to come by and pick us up and take us off to Oklahoma. But we knew the land so well, and we knew what to use, what resources to use to help us escape, that they never were able to hold us there, to hold us in a place where they could keep us and not have to worry about us being able to escape. (Ah-Tah-Thi-Ki Museum 2019: 01:35)

Secretary of War Jefferson Davis was determined to remove the Seminoles and pacify Florida, and he knew a different approach was needed to succeed. Rather than targeting Seminole soldiers directly, the Army struck their home camps when the warriors were away in the field, capturing everyone they could. Then they would find one of the captives, usually one of the women, who would be released to relay a message, "Your family is going to be sent west. Give up your arms and surrender if you want to be with them."

This tactic began to pay dividends early on. However, it also left the Army needing to contain a large prisoner population, almost entirely women, children and elders: the noncombatants who were declared prisoners of war. At first, they were held at Fort Myers, the frontline military command at the time. Difficulties holding people in a region the captives knew better than the soldiers, however, compelled those in command to choose a new location.

Establishment of Egmont Key as a Prison Camp

Egmont Key had been scouted for use as a military outpost in 1846, as part of the larger Army survey that took place as American land claims extended. By 1852, some Seminoles were brought to the island and detained. In 1857 the order was given to create a "stockade" on the island for Seminole prisoners. Lumber was purchased from the mainland and taken out to build a standard blockhouse fort—a small, fortified building enclosed within a wooden stockade—a style that had become emblematic of the war. The new stockade was placed under the command of nearby Fort Brooke, and soon more prisoners began to arrive. Among the last of these was Billy Bowlegs, the leader of the Seminole Tribe in Florida.

Within this prison camp, several hundred Seminoles would be held, and

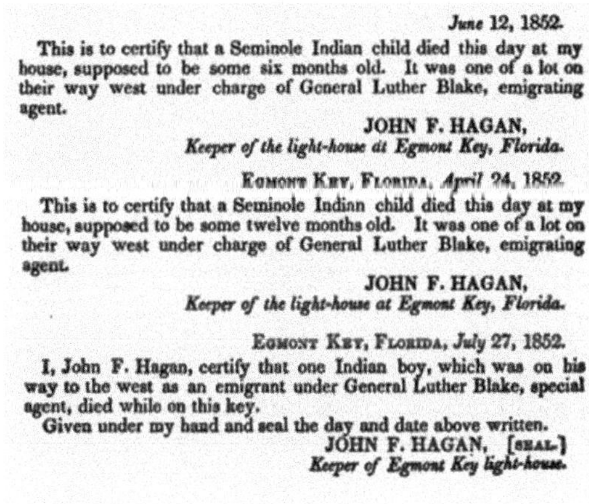

June 12, 1852.

This is to certify that a Seminole Indian child died this day at my house, supposed to be some six months old. It was one of a lot on their way west under charge of General Luther Blake, emigrating agent.

JOHN F. HAGAN,
Keeper of the light-house at Egmont Key, Florida.

Egmont Key, Florida, April 24, 1852.

This is to certify that a Seminole Indian child died this day at my house, supposed to be some twelve months old. It was one of a lot on their way west under charge of General Luther Blake, emigrating agent.

JOHN F. HAGAN,
Keeper of the light-house at Egmont Key, Florida.

Egmont Key, Florida, July 27, 1852.

I, John F. Hagan, certify that one Indian boy, which was on his way to the west as an emigrant under General Luther Blake, special agent, died while on this key.

Given under my hand and seal the day and date above written.

JOHN F. HAGAN, [SEAL.]
Keeper of Egmont Key light-house.

Figure 3.1. Correspondence listing the deaths of three Seminole children in 1852. From Congressional Serial Set 702 1853.

an unknown number would face their deaths. The US government's overall attitude toward the Seminole is reflected in the sparse archival records of the time, which document few deaths during their detainment and treat those they do record in a cold and dehumanizing manner. The rare documents that do mention Indigenous deaths on the island are notably dismissive. There is a reference to the death of an elder only recorded as "Chief Tommy" and an unnamed 11-year-old girl. A commandant's report from the time dismissed the Indigenous girl's death by writing simply, "A female child has died of influenza. It was eleven years of age" (3.1, Congressional Serial Set 702).

Oral histories from the Seminole Tribe recall a mass grave somewhere on Egmont Key from the time of the prison camp. As noted by Tribal member Rita Youngman (Bird Clan), "I was looking for a mass grave . . . in the middle there where the Seminoles were, they found some doorlatches where maybe they had them locked up, chains, stone bullets . . . but they took them all and they cataloged it" (Roa 2025: 17:15).

Yet, as discussed in Chapter 2, no physical remains of the prison camp structure survive. A forest fire in 2016 incinerated much of the island's underbrush, and the Seminole Tribal Historic Preservation Office (THPO) seized on this opportunity to conduct an archaeological survey of the island aimed at locating the remains of the grave or other artifacts connected with the prison camp. The ground-penetrating radar (GPR) survey and excavation test pits did not find evidence of the prison camp, suggesting that the mass grave had already washed into the sea—a likelihood given the island's shifting shoreline.

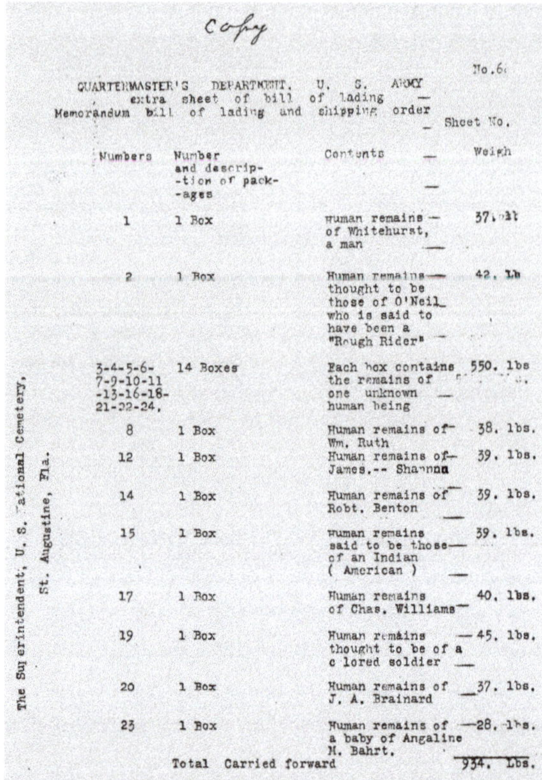

Copy

No.6

QUARTERMASTER'S DEPARTMENT, U. S. ARMY
extra sheet of bill of lading
Memorandum bill of lading and shipping order

Sheet No.

Numbers	Number and descrip- -tion of pack- -ages	Contents	Weigh
1	1 Box	Human remains of Whitehurst, a man	37. lbs
2	1 Box	Human remains thought to be those of O'Neil who is said to have been a "Rough Rider"	42. Lb
3-4-5-6- 7-9-10-11 -13-16-18- 21-22-24,	14 Boxes	Each box contains the remains of one unknown human being	550. lbs
8	1 Box	Human remains of Wm. Ruth	38. lbs.
12	1 Box	Human remains of James.-- Shannon	39. lbs.
14	1 Box	Human remains of Robt. Benton	39. lbs.
15	1 Box	Human remains said to be those of an Indian (American)	39. lbs.
17	1 Box	Human remains of Chas. Williams	40. lbs.
19	1 Box	Human remains thought to be of a colored soldier	45. lbs.
20	1 Box	Human remains of J. A. Brainard	37. lbs.
23	1 Box	Human remains of a baby of Angaline M. Bahrt.	28. lbs.
	Total Carried forward		934. Lbs.

The Superintendent, U. S. National Cemetery, St. Augustine, Fla.

Figure 3.2. Documentation of the removal of Seminole human remains from Egmont Key. Courtesy of the National Archives.

Figure 3.3. Sign installed at the Egmont Lighthouse Cemetery listing deaths of Seminole people. By permission of Laura Harrison.

There are few physical reminders of Seminole death on the island. The handful of Indigenous people buried in the Lighthouse Cemetery were disinterred in 1912, when the US government decided to remove them and bury the remains to the National Cemetery in St. Augustine, Florida. Throughout the disinterment, the dehumanization of Indigenous people continued: A list of human remains that were removed records non-Indigenous people by name (and weight) but documents the remains of unnamed Indigenous people by weight only (3.2). While this list references only a few Seminoles perishing at Egmont Key, it is likely that many more died in the difficult conditions on the island. In one instance, recorded as an oral history, conditions were so harsh and the fate of deportation so dire, that a Seminole man named Tiger Tail swallowed glass to end his life while at Egmont Key. The only public-facing interpretation at Egmont Key referencing Seminole deaths, or the later prison camp and associated casualties, is one small sign, approximately 8 1/2 × 11 in, mounted on a pole at the entrance to the Lighthouse Cemetery (3.3).

Indian Removal and the *Grey Cloud*

In 1858, the final deportation orders were carried out with the steamer *Grey Cloud* chartered for the voyage. The captives at Egmont Key were mostly noncombatants, whose capture had been used to compel Billy Bowlegs and his men to turn themselves in. The imprisoned Seminoles were reunited with the warriors who were also destined for the voyage. The guards allowed the prisoners to greet the men who had fought for them. Cheers erupted on both sides as many saw friends or family members for the first time since they were taken. As the two groups embraced, neither the island prisoners nor Bowleg's men had known what had happened to the other. Cries of joy rang out as family members were reunited. Alongside them were wails of mourning from those whose learned their family members had died. The Seminole were given one final night to be reunited with their people on the island that had been their prison.

The following day on May 6, approximately 165 Seminoles boarded the vessel, although accounts differ on the exact number and all of those onboard may not have been named in reports (see 3.4). On May 6, 1858, Army officer Elias Rector reported the following to Colonel Loomis at Fort Brooke:

> Sir: I left Fort Myers on the 4th instant with the steamer Grey Cloud, which was turned over to me for the purpose of transporting the Semi-

> nole and Creek delegations and the hostile Florida Seminoles (who have consented to emigrate) to New Orleans, on their way to their country west of Arkansas. I have on board the steamer with me one hundred and twenty-three hostile or Florida Seminoles, of which number thirty-eight are warriors (men and youths capable of bearing arms) and eighty-five women and children, who have consented to emigrate voluntarily; and forty-one hostiles who have been captured; making in all, with the woman "Polly," one hundred and sixty-five Indians who leave Florida for their new homes west. . . . 'Bowlegs' says that if the boat party can be found they will undoubtedly desire to emigrate. . . . I have been particularly requested by 'Bowlegs' and several of the Seminole men with me that hostilities may not be resumed until the Tallahassees and Boatmen can have an opportunity to emigrate. . . . The steamer Grey Cloud, as requested by Assistant Quartermaster McKinstry, will be returned from New Orleans immediately after the delivery of the Indians at the place. (Seminole Tribe of Florida 2019: 19).

The *Grey Cloud* departed from Egmont Key bearing the last of the Seminoles forced to leave Florida after nearly half a century of war. Also on the voyage was the casket of US Army Captain John C. Casey, a longtime friend of Billy Bowlegs and the former head of Indian Affairs in Florida. Together they had petitioned for the Seminole to be able to remain in Florida. Now, at the end of the Seminole War, both left together for the last time. This was one of the very last events in the period of Indian Removal instituted by Andrew Jackson. While the *Grey Cloud* voyage effectively closed the US government's campaign of "removal" in Florida, it was not the end of Seminole presence in the region—rather, it marked the survival of those who evaded capture.

Emateloye Estenletkvte: "Polly Parker got away"

There were no known escapes from the Egmont Key prisoner camp, but there was one from the *Grey Cloud* after it left. It was orchestrated by Emateloye, known to the Americans as Polly, a woman whose life had been defined by the war, and who had survived it by her wits. Emateloye was born into the Bird Clan among the Red Stick Creek people who had taken refuge in Florida following the Creek Civil War, their homes stolen by Andrew Jackson and the United States. Chipco, a respected leader during the rebellion, led many of his

The following is the list of Emigrating Indians

No Kose emath'a,
Set-to te-Hoyee,
Klouth-Lagee,
Muhtah Thloka,
Palat Hakee,
Senee,
Tusteanuc Cochukanee,
Alafah moge,
Pedahnee,
Yalyachchee,
Do. Mother,
Echakee,
Tustenuchago,
Hopoyee,
Hahtlee,
Upoh-huk-kee,
Koweehajo,
Assoon Hajuckee,
Sahhoon-kahtee,
Tus com ne hochuchee,
Ehumkah,
Nokefah-hajo,
Fle-wahlee-Tustenuggee
Nathcup hajo,
So-wahlee,
Mohhee,
Kinnah nee,
Kirh hoogee,
Sah nah-kochee,
Sah-ke-nee,
Anoggee,
Thomas,
Moses,
Jack,
Ahfee,
Ok-te ala-chee,
Sah-loahlee,
Sah-koat-kee,
Sac tensh kee,
Folonth-kee,
Ah hah Koch-emathla,
Lowakee,
Tin-cho wah we,
Shuckoni kee,
Cu-ih-sah hah chee-chee,
So ticschee,
Se tensh kee,
Folocth-kee,
Ah hah loch-emathla,
Houg-kee,
Echup-nogee,
Waxa-hajo,
Mah-koyagee,
Meah-sah-kee,
Kinni-hee,
Welock kee,
Marec,
Osha che-hala,
Chee honah,
Mioochee,
Sa-toh Kee,
Pully,
Copec-bige-holah,
Noobah,
Tusekiah-hago,
Ochee-hago,
Hopith lee,
Epockah-luck-tigee,
Jee-che-chee,
Saonash hago,
Sauno kee,
Sah ton kee,
Ah-soon-wah,
Ya fo-lah kee,
Te iah-lathee,
Fi so kee,
Ho kee till,
Cla-lochee,
Mon hoo sage,
Toon-hago,
Zilrey,
Toney,
Louisa,
Tech go chee,
Tie no ah-nee,
Shah fah hak-kee,
Ah chule hago,
Simon,
Sah ho ee,
Beccy,
Sally,
Julian,
Paity,
Young Billy Bowlegs,
Ptty,
Mock sedil,
Lucy,
She-puckile,
Betsy,
Nancy,
Gen William Bowlegs,
Chocota Harchuckee,
Inneah-hago,
Kuntul kee emathla,
Christe-Emathla,
Okah lah-hago,
Nap po chen no-la,
Nokos-hago,
Hatte mah tee,
Kqatza Fraca,
Ah hah loo kee,
Tah ah kee,
Chin ho-yah,
Fah-ligout,
Sabbi-che-chee,
Eth-le-koo,
Mah-ul-lo-ee,
Kouth-hego chee,
Epish-ho-yah,
Fux hachee- Emathla,
Konip hago,
Polly,
Surey,
Fanny,
Hoa ki,
Ta so ka,
Cha hola ti-ka,
Kats-I kee,
Hocd le,
Hok-to la-na,
So kan chee,
Ah-fus to kee,
Hoch tre chee

Figure 3.4. Names of Seminoles taken on the *Grey Cloud.* From Seminole Tribe of Florida's 2019 High School Curricula Guide.

Figure 3.5. Seminole Indians Lucy Tiger, daughter of Old Aunt Polly Parker, and Naha Tiger, youngest son of Captain Tom Tiger, in White Springs, Florida. State Archives of Florida, Florida Memory.

followers to Florida. This included Emateloye's parents, as well as a young boy named Osceola of mixed Indigenous and non-Indigenous ancestry.

When the Army raided the Seminole camp at Fish-Eating Creek in 1857, Polly was one of the many women who was taken captive. She was held at Egmont Key for the better part of a year. Much of what we know about the Seminole experience there comes from her recollections, told to her daughter, Lucy Tiger (3.5). Lucy later shared them with Florida Historian Albert DeVayne in 1953. Polly had spoken of being held behind walls, under constant watch by armed military guards, only allowed outside the walls of the fort under escort to gather food or medicine. Around a hundred Seminole were held there at any given time, all of them noncombatants. Ships occasionally arrived to bring new prisoners, or to take others away, beginning their "removal" to Oklahoma. They survived on food provided by the Army.

On May 6, 1858, Emateloye was forced on to the *Grey Cloud* for deportation. Although Polly boarded the vessel when it left Egmont Key, she was not on it when it docked in New Orleans. Nor were several other women. During the voyage Polly orchestrated the escape that made her one of the heroes of the Seminole War and a major figure for the Tribe today. The *Grey Cloud*'s route between Egmont Key and New Orleans was a long one. The ship had to keep close to shore, stopping several times to replenish their supply of coal. By the time the ship stopped for the first refueling at St. Marks, a small station just south of Tallahassee, an outbreak of yellow fever was spreading through the ship. Both crew and prisoners were coming down with the disease. Polly found her opportunity there. She shared her plan with the elders and leaders on board, including Billy Bowlegs. She saw a chance to save some of the women. Everyone agreed.

Polly spoke to the soldiers on the ship and explained that there was medicine the Seminole knew that could help treat the fever. She persuaded them to allow several of the women to leave the ship, under guard, to gather the plants needed. They looked for the right spot and began gathering, with Polly keeping an eye on the guards. The soldiers had been cooped up on a ship that was quickly becoming a hospital, and were laxer in their watch, seemingly unconcerned about a group of women. Polly waited for the right moment and gave a signal, and the women broke for the tree line. The women worked to elude their pursuers, running and hiding through the Florida terrain. Roughly half of them escaped in the end, Polly among them.

Their escape was not over, however. They would end up traveling around 350 miles, by foot, through lands already occupied and settled by Americans. Not only were they fugitives now, but their very existence in Florida as Seminole was illegal, and some were already coming down with the sickness themselves. The journey was an ordeal for the women, but eventually they arrived home, finding the remnants of the Tribe who had followed Abiaka (Sam Jones) into safety in the wetlands of what is now South Florida.

Polly's escape made her one of the only women left in Florida from the Bird Clan, and she is credited today with the clan's survival in the state. She would go on to marry another Tribal member, Henry Parker (named for his American friend Henry Parker) and is often remembered now as Polly Parker. She would live a long life after her escape, raising a family and becoming matriarch of her clan. She would pose for a photograph in 1913 that would make her image famous as a Florida postcard (3.6). The picture introduced her as Aunt Polly Parker, The Oldest Seminole Indian in the State, Florida.

It was the legacy of Polly Parker, Billy Bowlegs, and the *Grey Cloud* that brought the Seminole back to Egmont Key 155 years later in 2013 on a voyage that retraced the steps of the Seminole people on the Trail of Tears removal. Chairman James E. Billie invited Tribal members on this moving voyage that stopped at Egmont Key and St. Marks. Chairman Billie had commemorative

Figure 3.6. Painting of Polly Parker (Emateloye). Parker was captured by the US Army near Lake Okeechobee during the Seminole War and forced aboard the *Grey Cloud* steamship to New Orleans. She escaped when the vessel stopped at St. Marks, and made her way south to rejoin her people in the lands of southern Florida. Parker survived and started a family that continues today in the Seminole Tribe of Florida. The painting was composed by Robert Butler in 1913. State Archives of Florida, Florida Memory.

gold "challenge coins" created for the trip with the seal of the Tribal Council on one side (medicine colors with a chickee) and an engraving of Polly Parker on the other side crouching in some palmettos with the *Grey Cloud* in the background anchored at St. Marks. Lorene Gopher, a direct descendant of Polly Parker, was asked to give the coin a title, which was Emateloye Estenletkvte: "Polly Parker got away" (Gallagher 2013).

Seminole Historian Willie Johns (Wild Cat Clan) was on that voyage to honor this legacy, returning to the island this time as an honored guest. Johns reflected, "I don't know how she did it, but I am glad she did. Because, if she hadn't escaped, we would not be in Florida now. . . . Polly Parker's escape was a brave and defining moment in both Seminole and American history" (Gallagher 2013: para. 10). The Seminole group brought a framed copy of the Polly Parker image to be hung in the Island's small museum with the help of Medicine Man Bobby Henry (Otter Clan), who performed proper services for those who lost their lives on the island.

Norman "Skeeter" Bowers (Snake Clan) was also on the Polly Parker voyage and offered these reflections: "I kept trying to imagine how it was for the Seminoles being taken up the Gulf like that . . . I mean, the fog was so thick we couldn't see much further than the boat. How depressed those Seminoles

Figure 3.7. Willie Johns with the photo of Polly Parker at Egmont Key. By permission of the *Seminole Tribune*.

must have been, forced to leave their homeland for a place they didn't know, in conditions like this. Then I remembered, they were probably all locked up deep in the hull of the boat. They couldn't see anything at all. That was worse. How painful that must have been" (Gallagher 2013: paras. 6–7).

In this epic journey Johns, along with Henry, other elders, and the Tribal Historic Preservation Office (THPO) that helped to organize the trip, met with representatives of the Florida and federal governments during their stops. The relationships built with this return continued and the Tribe began the work to tell the story of Egmont Key with many efforts led by the THPO: "It's just amazing that the incredible history of Polly Parker's escape has stayed in the background so long," said Paul Backhouse (Gallagher 2013: para. 35), former director of the THPO and Ah-Tah-Thi-Ki Museum (and since 2023 senior director of the Environmental Protection Office).

These stories are emerging from the background and important statements about the Seminole experience at Egmont Key have now been published, including *Egmont Key: A Seminole Story* (see Tribal Historic Preservation Office n.d.) and the curriculum guide created by the Ah-Tah-Thi-Ki Museum: *Egmont Key: A Seminole Story, High School Curricula Guide* (Seminole Tribe of Florida 2019). Since 2013 other collaborators have also worked with the Seminole Tribe of Florida to ensure that this critical history is not erased or forgotten. These efforts have been coordinated with the THPO, which has been instrumental in protecting and preserving the Tribe's history and cultural patrimony. The cultural resources and oral histories related to Egmont Key and the ancestry of the Seminole people are carefully maintained and safeguarded, often in secure vaults under lock and key with controlled access.

The Seminole Tribal Historic Preservation Office and Egmont Key

The Seminole Tribe of Florida's THPO is one of the largest and most well-funded among Native nations, something that has allowed the THPO to expand the work it can do for the Tribal community. The THPO was founded on July 15, 2002, under the direction of Billy Cypress, through Tribal Council Resolution C-185-02 (Tribal Historic Preservation Office n.d.), in accordance with the National Historic Preservation Act (NHPA). This act established the ability for federally recognized Indigenous tribes to form tribal historic preservation offices that would have authority over cultural, historic, and archaeological resources within the Tribe's lands. The mission of the THPO is to identify, document, and protect sites of cultural, historical, and archaeological significance to the Seminole Tribe, both within their ancestral lands and beyond. The THPO is committed to protecting these resources with Tribal priorities first in mind, and to educate those wishing to use these resources on the Seminole perspective rather than the often poorly misinformed, colonial narrative. This aligns with broader objectives of preserving Seminole traditions, educating the public, and ensuring compliance with cultural preservation laws.

The Seminole Tribe of Florida THPO has grown consistently in recent years. In 2012 the THPO authored the book *We Come for Good*, that articulated new ideas of what a THPO can do to help the community with proper Tribal guidance (Backhouse et al. 2017). One of the highest priorities of the THPO is to promote and defend Tribal sovereignty and heritage. The Seminole history at Egmont Key has become an important area of focus for the THPO: "The offshore island of Egmont Key has become the front line for the Tribe in a community effort to remember a difficult past that is today threatened with being washed away. Community engagement, archaeology, and climate change collide on Egmont, an island that is central to the past, present, and future of the Tribe" (Backhouse 2018: 25). The THPO's involvement has been instrumental in making sure that the experiences at Egmont Key and Polly Parker's heroic journey and impact on the Tribe are not forgotten.

While memories of Egmont Key had faded for many, some Tribal members still remembered the stories. According to Norman "Skeeter" Bowers (Snake Clan), "It's been handed down in my family. We have always known about it . . . but, I guess so much time has passed most everyone else forgot about it" (Gallagher 2013: para. 16). Paul Backhouse recollects how the discussions over erosion at Egmont Key, initiated by the Army Corps of Engineers in 2012, prompted the re-emergence of memories about the Seminole experiences (Hamilton et al. 2022). The THPO was instrumental for the reconnection with Egmont as they planned the 2013 commemorative trip following the path of Polly Parker (Backhouse et al. 2017).

In June 2016, a chance event brought the focus back to Egmont Key. A single lightning strike started a wildfire on the densely wooded island that would last for three days and burn down 87 acres. Once the fire was contained, this area was clear for the first time in decades. The THPO was able to conduct an archaeological survey, looking for signs of the prison camp the Seminole had been held in. No trace could be found. The archaeological record had been irrevocably disturbed by the creation of Fort Dade during a time when there were no historical protection laws. With no archaeological pathway, the THPO turned to historical sources to tell the story.

In 2020, another event brought the THPO back to Egmont Key after Hurricane Dorian, one of the most powerful hurricanes ever recorded, hit the Gulf Coast. An interesting artifact emerged and washed up on the western shore of Egmont Key that was described as "hugely significant" by Damon Scott, writer for the *Seminole Tribune* (Scott 2020). It was piece of wood about 16 ft long with a dugout part in the center. It was part of a canoe. Land managers on the island called the THPO for a consultation. Members of the THPO and Seminole carver Pedro Zepeda went to investigate. Based on Zepeda's observations, the canoe was very old—an intuition confirmed by radiocarbon dates indicating the wood used to make the canoe was from approximately 1350 CE. The canoe is would have had a mast for a sail, indicating it was outfitted for longer, ocean voyages. As noted by Bernard J. Howard of the THPO, "you don't use a sail in [Everglades] canoes . . . a canoe with sails is specifically for ocean going, back and forth around the islands in the Gulf [of Mexico] or trading with Cuba. There are oral histories of Indigenous People trading with Cuba" (Scott 2020; para. 27).

Figure 3.8. Wooden canoe from 1350 CE found at Egmont Key in 2020 after Hurricane Dorian. By permission of Laura Harrison.

Contemporary Reflections on Egmont Key: Trauma, Remembrance, and Legacy

For many years, the story of Egmont Key and its connection to the Seminole Tribe was forgotten. It was only in 2013 that many members of the Tribe became reacquainted with this history, through the work of the THPO, who began organizing commemorative voyages and trips to the island. The first major event was the 2013 "Polly Parker Got Away" voyage retracing the path of Removal through Egmont Key. Parker's courageous journey helped the Seminole Tribe maintain a foothold in their homeland during a period of intense conflict with the US government, and embodies the Tribe's motto, "The Unconquered Seminole Tribe of Florida." Bringing the Tribe's connection to Egmont Key's history back into the spotlight has been painful yet poignant experience for many.

TRAUMA

Egmont Key is a stark reminder of the trauma endured during the Seminole War and Indian Removal. The Tribe often describes Egmont Key as a "dark place," or as their own "Alcatraz," because of the island's association with imprisonment, suffering, and loss. The removal itself—an act of ethnic cleansing carried out by the US government—happened amid many other atrocities that were part of a broader governmental strategy to dehumanize and dispossess the Seminole in order to seize their ancestral lands. As Rita Youngman (Bird Clan) notes,

> They didn't even have a roof over the top of them. They talked a lot about the soldiers raping the girls, and the children, and even the men. These things happen in war—this is a hurtful thing that she was talking about, the painful things that need to be brought to light. This is what happened to our people. And when you try to fight back, then they take your kid and cut it up right in front of you. These are the things that are told to me, hurtful things—and they still do it today in war . . . it's war and they want the people to be submissive and they want to remove the people out of the land. (Roa 2025: 15:10)

As discussed earlier in this chapter, Indigenous deaths on Egmont Key were not handled with the same care and reverence as the deaths of whites or soldiers in the US Army; they were often recorded simply by the weight of their collective bones, exemplifying the objectification of Indigenous people that was prevalent at the time. In some cases, oral histories are all that survive.

Although many Seminoles likely died at Egmont Key, there are only two named Indigenous people who died on the island: Chief Tommy (who died in 1852), and Tiger Tail (who died sometime between 1856 and 1858). Quenton Cypress (Wind Clan) recounts the tragic story of Tiger Tail—who was forcibly taken to Egmont Key and ended his life there in protest of further removal to Oklahoma:

> And one of the stories I'm told is that there was a leader by the name of Tiger Tail. And he felt so strongly that he did not want to leave the island that he would rather kill himself before he was ever taken off and taken to Oklahoma. So he actually crushed up glass and with his daughter standing next to his side telling him not to do it, he drank water with broken glass and killed himself. (Ah-Tah-Thi-Ki Museum 2019: 02:20)

For Aaron Tommie, who is a descendant of Polly Parker, the story of Egmont Key is a window to a long legacy of intergenerational and intersectional trauma wrought by the US government through decades of wars and policies founded on colonialist ideologies. The histories of Indigenous people are often left unwritten and reclaiming them is a crucial part of the Tribe's continued efforts to maintain and assert Tribal sovereignty. Visiting and reflecting on Egmont Key is a catalyst for preserving these histories for future generations and honoring the sacrifices of our Indigenous ancestors. As Tribal member Aaron Tommie says:

> The aftermath of slavery has created a people who are descendants of lost cultures and identities. The genocide and displacement of Native Americans have caused Natives' rights to continue to be dismissed and disrespected. Society has marginalized us, and systemic racism continues to breed broken families, low senses of dignity, and cultural misrepresentations in our communities. These issues will continue to plague us if we stop developing resources that encourage solidarity and empowerment amongst our people. . . . The Atlantic slave trade and the Trail of Tears have shown that there is nothing we cannot overcome. Despite centuries of hardships, our presence is still here, and this is just the beginning for us as people Black and Native. (Tommie 2018a: para. 10)

On a 2016 voyage to Egmont Key organized by the Tribe, Tommie connected with other Tribal members and elders and learned he was a descendant of Polly Parker. In recounting the trip, he reflects on how the histories of Indigenous removal and displacement reverberate across centuries:

> At some point in time, we're going to have to face our past. And I believe that's what some of the elders were trying to mention to me in that it's really important that we know the true history so that we can teach the future generations and have them be educated about it so that our history is not going to be washed away, as many aspects of history are within US history. And then lastly for me, just as a Seminole with African descent, it hit doubly hard, because just like my Seminole ancestors were enchained and imprisoned so were my African ancestors. We were forced from our homelands to go to a foreign place, so it really resonated with me strongly (Tommie et al. 2021: 5).

Many Tribal members today feel compelled to confront the darkest events of Indian Removal as a way to counteract the whitewashing of history. Mainstream journalistic accounts of Indigenous displacement from ancestral lands often omit descriptions of the protracted violence and cruelty wrought by government actors, erroneously describing scenes in which Tribal members willingly accept their own displacement. Quenton Cypress (Wind Clan), emphasizes the urgency of amplifying Indigenous voices and perspectives as a way to reclaim Tribal history:

> The US still isn't telling that story. They're trying to hide and push it away and push it underneath the rug. We're here to try and voice and tell that story and share it and make sure that the general population and everybody else knows our story, knows why we're the 'Unconquered Seminole Tribe of Florida,' and know that there's that fight that we had in us and that we still have in us to this very day. (Morrow 2019: para. 11)

The THPO's organized trips to Egmont Key have become powerful acts of remembrance and education for the Tribe. Among these journeys was the marathon organized by Chairman James E. Billie in 2013, which retraced the journey that hundreds of captured Seminoles were forced to endure in the nineteenth century, during Indian Removal. Billie's inspiration for organizing the journey was to honor the legacy of Polly Parker, whose destiny was to "create the Seminole Tribe as we know it today" (Billie 2013). He says,

> Back in earlier days when I was flying my airplane and going to Tallahassee, there was a VOR (VHF Omnidirectional Radio) range transmitter at Egmont Key, just off the Gulf Coast in St. Petersburg. It gave out a radio

> signal so you can track where you are when you are flying through the air. I always thought of the many Seminoles, including Billy Bowlegs, who were put in the stockade there on Egmont and then shipped north on the Grey Cloud. Egmont Key is a very important part of our Seminole history. (Billie 2013: para. 9)

REMEMBRANCE

The 2013 journey to Egmont was followed with a number of additional trips organized by the THPO. Quenton Cypress (Wind Clan) became a driving force in ensuring the Seminole community could access and experience Egmont Key. Cypress stated,

> I made it a mission . . . to try to make sure I got as many Tribal members out there as possible. You know, because if it wasn't for me working with the Tribal Historic Preservation Office, I myself wouldn't have known about Egmont Key and it was through them I was able to learn that. And as a community engagement coordinator, it's my obligation . . . to get everything I learned out to the community, and this was a big part of my history that has been forgotten. You know it's been slipped under a rug somewhere and someone thought they forgot about it, but we were able to dig this up and unearth it. (Tommie et al. 2021: 7)

The trips to Egmont Key had a profound impact on many attendees. As Rita Youngman (Bird Clan) describes, "There is a sadness and a sense of pride because we survived. The voices are here. The ancestors wanted to be found, remembered, and not lost" (Bidney 2020; para. 19). Similarly, Brighton Councilman Larry Howard (Bird Clan), a descendant of Polly Parker, noted the personal significance of his visit: "I wanted to stand on these grounds and visualize what happened here. It speaks volumes to me" (Bidney 2020: para. 18).

The trips were also a time for the younger generation to learn about their Seminole heritage and the Tribe's enduring connection to Egmont Key. Joseph Toneges (18) said, "It's crazy how they sacrificed themselves to get out of here. . . . It's pretty cool to be out here to experience it" (Bidney 2020: para. 13). Rylee King (14) said "It's pretty creepy . . . I learned about it in Miss Jade's class. I thought it was just some island, but my people stayed and died here. There is a lot of history here" (Bidney 2020; para. 13). Edna Bowers, a descendant of Parker from Brighton, was glad to see so many young people in attendance. "I want them to be interested in their history . . . we have informed them about it and wanted them to see it for themselves" (Bidney 2020: para. 10). Many Tribal elders believe that sharing the story of Egmont Key and Polly Parker with the younger generation helps ensure that it will not be lost amid the distractions of modern life. They see these stories not only as a connection to the past but as a guide for the future, a sentiment captured by Aaron Tommie:

> Many of the elders mentioned that they hope that more tribal members continue and that these trips continue to take place and that more tribal members continue to go. Especially the younger ones because it's easy, just in history. Just in general, it's easy for us as people to be distracted by you know, TV, Fortnite, whatever. But at some point in time, you know there's gonna be a point in time where we're going to have to face our past. And I believe that that's what some of the elders were trying to mention to me in that it's really important that we that we know that we know the true history so that we can teach the future generations and have them be educated about it so that it's not going to be our history is not going to be washed away as many aspects of history are within US history. (Tommie et al. 2021: 8)

LEGACY

The erosion of Egmont Key presents challenges for its preservation, but the Seminole Tribe and partners at the University of South Florida are committed to ensuring its history is not forgotten. Quenton Cypress (Wind Clan) aims to ensure that even when Egmont Key disappears entirely (a fate most climate experts deem not "if" but "when?"), its somber lessons will live on in the memories of those who visited. He says:

> This is a way I can preserve our history. . . . Everything I learn with the [Ah-Tah-Thi-Ki Seminole] Museum and Tribal Historic Preservation Office, I'm going to take to my community and teach them—and not just teach them, but take them there so they can see and experience it in person. The island is eroding away. It's not going to be there much longer, so we want to take as many trips out there as we can. Pretty soon, it's only going to be in the books we write and stories we speak. (Smith 2021: para. 16)

This sentiment is echoed by Rita Youngman (Bird Clan), who says,

> I talked to a couple of elders and yes, you can keep pouring money into [beach renourishment] . . . but there's already 2/3 of [the island] gone,

> so you're talking about saving 1/3. At some point, nature is going to win. It just does. The earth is alive. So especially here in Florida, hurricanes are going to happen, fires are going to happen, this is just the way of the world. . . . The creator has a plan, and to go against it is going to be fruitless. If the ocean wants to reclaim this island, it wants to reclaim Florida, it's going to happen and there's not really anything we can do—I don't care how much money you spend on it. It's just the way the earth is, it's alive. (Roa 2025: 20:26)

Quenton Cypress (Wind Clan) also discusses preservation and beach renourishment:

> The officials of the island wanted to see if they should save the island or just let Mother Nature take it. So they came to the Tribe about it. To ask us whether we should keep it or not. [They asked,] Is it important enough for you guys to want to keep? And we told them yes, we have significant history there. History that will help us understand and remind ourselves where we came from and what we had to do to even be here today. (Ah-Tah-Thi-Ki Museum 2019: 03:28)

Carmello Shenandoah reflects on the value of technological preservation:

> Because of the great advancements in technology, it is now possible to make a virtual duplicate of the place. The real location is still being claimed by nature. . . . The work done at the USF 3D lab educates many people about the island's history, heritage, and climate change impacts. (Osceola and Shenandoah 2022; para. 3)

Quenton Cypress (Wind Clan) also discusses the theme of resilience:

> People ask me, how did you feel when you're on the island? Did you feel sad? Or did you feel that? And as you can see with the big fat smile on my face and other faces, we were happy. You know, sure. It's because we're on a boat ride going to an island for work. But, you know I felt that I was happy and I feel that I'm happy right now because we did that, we endured that we fought, you know. For us to be here today as the Seminole people. . . . We're still fighting and Indian country is still fighting. (Tommie et al. 2021: 6)

On educating the public, Quenton Cypress (Wind Clan) notes,

> I feel deeply that more people, more of our tribal members need to hear about this and the outsiders too . . . it amazes me to see the amount of people that have no idea that Native Americans still exist. I mean, we had a group of people come up to us—me and our weapons team, who are all Seminole and from the Big Cypress Reservation—and tell us you guys are Seminole? Or you guys don't look Seminole—you guys look like Mexicans. You know that is insane. That they came up to pure tribal members and said you don't look Indian. You look like Mexicans, you know. So this is why we want this history out there to everyone. Not, you know, not just to us, to remind, us. But to everybody and to remind our tribal members that people don't know we exist still. Because of things like this, this is why people think Native Americans don't exist and we need to get that out there even more so now you know we need to make sure everybody knows we're still here. (Tommie et al. 2021: 8)

On public outreach, Quenton (Wind Clan) notes,

> Any museum you go to you see artifacts with Native Americans, that kind of gives the wrong image that we're not here no more because it's an artifact. But we're still here, and our artifacts may not be arrowheads anymore. You know, there might be necklaces and not even just beads. You know, there's all kinds of innovative things tribal members are doing nowadays. And you know, with the history of this island. We can finally get that message out there. (Tommie et al. 2021: 10)

Tribal member Aaron Tommie, a descendant of Polly Parker, reflects on their transformative impact, emphasizing the importance of facing history to teach future generations:

> The water was a little atrocious, but the weather itself was overall pretty nice and I felt like that was pretty ironic compared to like the history that that existed within that that the Seminoles experience that might we as Seminoles and my ancestors experienced. But I really, really enjoyed the trip. It was definitely life changing and then after I left the trip, I started reflecting and I started thinking about [how] the opportunities that a lot of my fellow tribal members are able to experience now are because of what our ancestors went through. And I think it's something that we have . . . to continue to honor and to think about because of their sacrifices or their experiences (Tommie et al. 2021: 9)

As Mahala Billie Osceola recounts,

> "She [Parker] was told to just go. Don't worry about the people she was collecting medicine for—the sick on the boat—because they said she needed to warn the Seminole people they were going to die eventually. So she saved herself to warn as many as she could." Osceola, a descendant of Parker, reflects on the importance of this legacy: "Polly Parker's legacy continues to live on through her family, which continues to grow bigger throughout the years. . . . I made [a family tree] for me and other family members who wanted it to show how we are all related." (Osceola and Shenandoah 2022: paras. 2–15)

Conclusion

Egmont Key stands as both a site of historical trauma and a testament to the resilience of the Seminole people. For the Seminole Tribe of Florida, the island encapsulates the struggles of the Indian Removal era and serves as a reminder of the Tribe's ability to persevere against overwhelming odds. The stories of captivity, loss, and survival are emblematic of broader Indigenous experiences during this dark chapter of US history. Polly Parker's escape highlights the determination of the Seminole people to fight forced removal and maintain connection to their ancestral lands.

Today, Egmont Key continues to hold strong cultural and historical value for the Seminole Tribe. Efforts by the Seminole Tribal Historic Preservation Office to preserve and interpret the island's history have been instrumental in reclaiming and sharing these narratives. Commemorative voyages, archaeological surveys, and community engagement initiatives have ensured that the legacy of Egmont Key remains part of the Tribe's collective memory.

The loss of Egmont Key's physical landscape would not diminish its symbolic significance, as the stories and lessons of the island are carried forward by the Seminole people. In this way, Egmont Key serves as a reminder of the resilience of the Seminole Tribe of Florida—The Unconquered.

References Cited

Ah-Tah-Thi-Ki Museum. 2019. Egmont Key—Told by Quenton Cypress. YouTube, November 14. https://www.youtube.com/watch?v=SSfIJR2bEVw, accessed April 2, 2025.

Backhouse, P. N., B. R. Weisman, and M. B. Rosebrough (editors). 2017. *We Come for Good:*

Archaeology and Tribal Historic Preservation at the Seminole Tribe of Florida. University Press of Florida, Gainesville.

Backhouse, Paul. 2018. Made from the Sands of Florida: Egmont Key, Section 106, Climate Change, and the Seminole Tribe of Florida. *SAA Archaeological Record* 18(1): 25–31.

Bidney, B. 2020. Egmont Key Trip Evokes "Sadness and Sense of Pride" for Seminoles. *Seminole Tribune,* March 30. https://seminoletribune.org/egmont-key-trip-evokes-sadness-and-sense-of-pride-for-seminoles/, accessed April 2, 2025.

Billie, J. E. 2013. Emateloye's Escape Gave Birth to Today's Tribe. *Seminole Tribune,* August 1. https://seminoletribune.org/emateloyes-escape-gave-birth-to-todays-tribe/, accessed April 2, 2025.

Congressional Serial Set No. 702. 1853. 33rd Congress. US GPO, Washington, DC. Library of Congress. https://www.loc.gov/resource/llserialsetpdf.00702_00_00/?st=pdf, accessed April 2, 2025.

Gallagher, P. 2013 Emateloye Estenletkvte: Polly Parker Got Away. *Seminole Tribune,* December 17. https://seminoletribune.org/emateloye-estenletkvte-polly-parker-got-away/, accessed April 2, 2025.

Hamilton, A., H. Brown, B. Burton, J. W. Walker, and C. Guevara. 2022. Island Impermanent, Part 1: Erosion and Erasure on Egmont Key. Pulitzer Center. *The Marjorie.* https://pulitzercenter.org/stories/island-impermanent-part-1-erosion-and-erasure-egmont-key.

Morrow, E. 2019. "We're Still Here": Seminole Tribe Shares Dark History of Egmont Key. *10 Tampa Bay,* November 25. https://www.wtsp.com/article/news/local/pinellascounty/seminole-tribe-egmont-key/67-a6ee7a61-ceb9-45e6-a2cd-f699a7e72fd1, accessed March 31, 2025.

Osceola, M. B., and C. Shenandoah. 2022. On Egmont: Words from Tribal Members. *The Marjorie,* October 3. https://themarjorie.org/2022/10/03/on-egmont-words-from-tribal-members/, accessed April 2, 2025.

Roa, R. 2025. Egmont Key Is More Fascinating Than We Could Ever Imagine. The Skinny, WMNF. January 17. https://www.wmnf.org/egmont-key-is-more-fascinating-than-we-could-ever-imagine/, accessed April 2, 2025.

Scott, D. 2020. "Hugely Significant" Canoe Found at Egmont Key. *Seminole Tribune,* January 3. https://seminoletribune.org/hugely-significant-canoe-found-at-egmont-key/, accessed April 2, 2025.

Seminole Tribe of Florida. 2019. *Egmont Key: A Seminole Story, High School Curricula Guide.* https://www.ahtahthiki.com/downloads/Egmont-Key-Curricula-12.5.2019.pdf

Smith, J. 2021. Seminole Tribe, USF Sustainable Tourism and USF Access 3D Lab Preserve History at Egmont Key. *83 Degrees Media.* https://www.83degreesmedia.com/features/seminole-tribe-and-USF-work-to-preserve-egmont-key-in-Florida072021.aspx, accessed July 15, 2025.

Tommie, A. 2018a. "My ancestors have invested in me, so I want to be an investment to my Tribe": Aaron Tommie Discovers His Seminole Heritage. *Native Max Magazine,* July 15.

https://nativemaxmagazine.com/my-ancestors-have-invested-in-me-so-i-want-to-be-an-investment-to-my-tribe-aaron-tommie-discovers-his-seminole-heritage/, accessed April 2, 2025.

Tommie, A. 2018b. Tribe Recounts History at Egmont Key. *Seminole Tribune*, April 30. https://seminoletribune.org/tribe-recounts-history-at-egmont-key/, accessed August 1, 2025.

Tommie, A. Q. Cypress, and D. Scheidecker. 2021. Egmont Key: The Seminole Story. Transcript of online public presentation, delivered on March 25, Florida Humanities Council, Tampa.

Tribal Historic Preservation Office. N.d. Our Mission Statement. https://stofthpo.com/about-the-seminole-tribal-historic-preservation-office/, accessed January 7, 2026.

4

Key Lessons for Managing Heritage at Risk

BROOKE HANSEN AND LAURA K. HARRISON

Managing Egmont Key's Heritage

The question of how to approach heritage management on Egmont Key is not a simple one. Egmont Key holds a multitude of cultural and natural resources that have been overseen by many different agencies and organizations. These irreplaceable assets are of great concern given the uncertain future where erosion and sea-level rise continue to bear down on the island. The unique marine and terrestrial ecosystems and species have drawn the attention of many, from early Indigenous inhabitants who used the area for fishing and food foraging to modern-day visitors. Due to its geographical isolation from the mainland, some species have evolved separately from their mainland counterparts, such as the gopher tortoise population. The island is also notable as one of the most active bird-nesting sites along Florida's central Gulf Coast, providing critical coastal habitat in a region otherwise characterized by extensive development.

Egmont Key's location as a sentinel of Tampa Bay also led to its development as a military base, center of maritime navigation, and popular tourist attraction. After military decommissioning in 1923 and a brief reoccupation during World War II, the island became an undersupervised playground for boaters. Tales of parties, piles of beer cans, and refuse dumping are well known from locals during the mid-twentieth century and led to local politicians taking action to protect and preserve the island in the 1970s. Congressman Sam Gibbons, a frequent visitor to Egmont Key with his family, knew how important the island was and spearheaded a plan for oversight that "would be so complicated that no one would ever be able to undo it" (Hare 2022: 12). This plan built upon the island's 1974 designation as a National Wildlife Refuge and involved the US Fish and Wildlife Service (USFWS), the Florida Department of Environmental Protection, Florida Park Service, the US Coast Guard, Hillsborough County, and several other entities, which would all have a stake in the island and its protection.

To amplify these efforts to protect Egmont Key, Rep. Gibbons organized a massive cleanup dubbed "Egmont '88" (Sanchez 2025). It involved dozens of agencies and groups with hundreds of miliary and civilian volunteers. They removed over 70 tons of trash in what became a watershed moment in Egmont's history (a moment that was repeated on a smaller scale in the aftermath of the devastating 2024 hurricanes that left the island in shambles). Rep. Gibbons continued his efforts to secure the island and its heritage with sand replenishment from the Army Corps of Engineers. The island became a Florida State Park in 1989. Despite these efforts, and the multiple agencies involved in its protection, Egmont Key's location as the outermost island in Tampa Bay has placed it in the crosshairs of climate change impact and increasing numbers of tourists. In 2017, Egmont Key was listed as one of the most endangered sites in the state by the Florida Trust for Historic Preservation (see Florida Trust for Historic Preservation 2025).

This chapter explores insights and lessons about managing heritage at risk at Egmont Key. We address the problem of endangered cultural and natural heritage in the context of a myriad of threats, most being fueled from anthropogenic (or human-induced) causes, such as climate change, hurricanes, erosion, overtourism, and vandalism of heritage structures. Managing Egmont Key's heritage is profoundly complex, with many federal, state, private, and nonprofit entities involved. According to Roberta Moore Cole (1986: 10), who lived on the island with her lighthouse keeper family, "there were so many agencies, when people ask me who was the boss of Egmont, what government agency? . . . It would take a couple of minutes to answer." The intentional entanglement of multiple interests was designed to safeguard the island from development pressures, but it has also had some unintended consequences. Each year, these problems become more urgent as the waters of the Gulf of Mexico erode the fragile shoreline an inundate the island during strong storms, endangering habitats and heritage sites.

Academics and university partners can enhance heritage management plans by conducting collaborative research with land managers and stakeholders on interpretation, preservation, and virtualization. This approach is especially valuable at endangered heritage and tourism sites, which often lack the resources to pursue this research independently and are plagued by immediate problems of site management rather than long-term comprehensive planning. Incorporating partnerships into heritage conservation and public engagement aligns with international frameworks, including the UN Sustainable Development Goals (SDGs) that champion the protection of cultural and natural heritage (promoted by SDG 11.4). These approaches are especially salient in the wake of natural disasters, including Hurricane Helene and Hurricane Milton that made landfall at Egmont Key in 2024.

Heritage at Risk as a Global Problem

When tangible elements of history—such as buildings and landscapes—disappear, not only is that heritage lost, but the memories connected to these places of cultural significance become disconnected too. Intangible cultural heritage is fragile and often more difficult to protect than physical sites. If both tangible and intangible cultural heritage are not preserved and accounted for, they may disappear or be erased. The case of the Seminole experiences at Egmont Key is an exemplar of the vulnerable nature of cultural heritage. No physical remains were left of the camp where they were imprisoned on Egmont Key. The intangible heritage and stories were carried forward by Seminole people and documented in a handful of archival materials. This episode of history was largely forgotten for over a century and only began to re-emerge recently through the efforts of the Seminole Tribe of Florida (STOF). While the STOF has invested in a robust Tribal Historic Preservation Office (THPO) to help protect and preserve their cultural heritage for future generations, many endangered sites do not have such protections in place. As a result, heritage at risk is a major challenge facing societies around the world from urbanization, industrialization, armed conflict, climactic pressures, and willful destruction, all forces that are intensifying in the twenty-first century.

Cultural heritage, including structures and archaeological sites, and intangible elements like stories, memories, and languages, face increasing threats from anthropogenic sources. Climate change poses one of the most severe risks, causing extreme weather events that degrade and destroy sites (Hall et al. 2016). Increased flooding and sea-level rise threaten coastal sites (Zarley et al. 2016), while changes in precipitation can lead to mud slides or droughts. Climate-driven threats extend to intangible heritage as well (Higgins 2022), as communities are often displaced or forced to endure trauma, losing connections to ancestral lands and practices.

Development and infrastructure expansion are also significant threats to cultural heritage around the world. The need for new housing, roads, dams, and industrial development often leads to the demolition or alteration of historic buildings and archaeological sites. Rapid urbanization can result in poorly regulated construction that encroaches on or even destroys heritage sites. Even strong regulations are often not enough to protect against such development. For example, coastal areas in Florida and elsewhere are highly sought after for housing and tourism, and the pressures of development are often greater than interest in preservation and conservation.

Cultural heritage sites are often highly vulnerable to natural disasters. Earthquakes, hurricanes, and wildfires can devastate entire regions by destroying architectural heritage, damaging infrastructure that protects sites (e.g., guardhouses, fencing, facilities, shelters), and causing heritage tourism destinations to close due to damage. For instance, in regions where wildfires are becoming more frequent and intense, historic wooden structures are at high risk, as are cultural landscapes that have shaped regional identities for generations. Egmont Key has faced numerous fires caused by lightning and people (intentional and unintentional) over its history, erasing all wooden structures between its shores and underscoring the immediacy of this issue.

Disasters instigated by humans, particularly warfare and armed conflict, pose significant threats to cultural heritage, with sites facing both accidental and deliberate destruction (Neglia et al. 2024). Despite global outcry, iconic sites like the Bamiyan Buddhas in Afghanistan and the ancient city of Palmyra in Syria have been intentionally destroyed for political or ideological reasons. The erasure of cultural heritage is a well-known tactic used to exert control over cultural identity. As a result, heritage sites have become casualties of armed conflicts throughout history; their destruction representing the collateral damage of warfare that prioritizes strategic gains and ideological control over preservation. The Seminole War of the 1800s caused not only physical casualties among the people but cultural ones, too, as communities and homelands were disrupted and destroyed and defining historical events were almost erased. The Spanish-American War of 1898 transformed Egmont Key into a small military city that was built atop centuries of cultural heritage, including the site where Seminoles were held. This development also threatened its natural environment and the species that call the island home.

Another pressure endangering cultural heritage is mass tourism and over-tourism which can degrade sites and cultural practices; a problem that is compounded by inadequate, inaccurate, or out-of-date interpretation and visitor services. Popular destinations may suffer from overcrowding, which accelerates wear and tear on physical structures, contributes to pollution, and can lead to unsustainable economic dependence on tourism. This situation has typified much of Egmont Key's recent history, as tourists and locals have sought to recreate on the island's beautiful shores, a situation that was exacerbated when outdoor tourism was at its height during the COVID-19 pandemic in Florida. Most visitors to the island during this busy time were completely unaware of the island's dark and complex histories. As anthropogenic threats to heritage preservation grow, they underscore the urgent need for integrated documentation and preservation strategies that address both environmental and human impacts, ensuring that cultural heritage can endure for future generations.

Frameworks for Preserving Heritage at Risk

INTERNATIONAL ORGANIZATIONS AND INITIATIVES: SETTING THE GLOBAL STAGE FOR HERITAGE PROTECTION AND PROMOTION

Global organizations play a critical role in preserving at-risk cultural heritage through collaborative, cross-border strategies that address threats from armed conflict, climate change, human impact, and development—all issues that have affected Egmont Key. Prominent entities like the United Nations Educational, Scientific, and Cultural Organization (UNESCO), the International Centre for the Study of the Preservation and Restoration of Cultural Property (ICCROM), and the International Council on Monuments and Sites (ICOMOS) lead initiatives to identify vulnerable sites, implement protective measures, and facilitate emergency response frameworks. International and intergovernmental frameworks advocate for embedding cultural preservation within broader disaster preparedness and sustainability goals, as seen in the Sendai Framework for Disaster Risk Reduction and the UN SDGs (UN n.d.). Most of these efforts were initially framed around the protection and preservation of tangible heritage (buildings, sites, and monuments), with initiatives such as the 1954 Hague Convention. The preservation of intangible heritage (language, traditions, cultural practices) was introduced later in 2003, with the UNESCO Convention for the Safeguarding of Intangible Cultural Heritage (UNESCO 2003).

Another major effort of UNESCO is the World Heritage Centre, which oversees the World Heritage Sites program. Sites are designated for having outstanding cultural, historical, or scientific value for all of humanity. They function as popular tourism sites globally, especially through the passport initiatives that encourage travelers to visit sites and get stamped. We recognized that Egmont Key held the attributes of qualifying for such a designation, and in 2019 we convened a research group to evaluate the feasibility of application. While the exercise proved informative in showing the applicability of these international criteria to Egmont Key's heritage, ultimately the bureaucratic requirements of applying and the fact that Egmont Key is disappearing into the sea (with heritage assets already submerged) led to a conclusion that a National Marine Sanctuary may be a more appropriate designation. Made possible by the National Marine Sanctuaries Act of 1972 and overseen by the National Oceanic and Atmospheric Administration (NOAA), these sanctuaries are meant to protect their "natural and cultural features while allowing people to use and enjoy the ocean a sustainable way. Sanctuary waters provide a secure habitat for species close to extinction and protect historically significant shipwrecks and artifacts" (NOAA n.d.: 7). To date, no such UNESCO international or national marine protection designations have been sought for Egmont Key.

Another organization highly invested in protecting heritage at risk internationally is ICOMOS (see ICOMOS 2025). They have made significant strides by developing influential policies and best practices, many of which can be applied to Egmont Key. Notably, ICOMOS's "Heritage at Risk" program has raised global awareness of threatened sites and facilitated rapid responses to crises through documentation and intervention recommendations. The ICOMOS "Guidelines on Disaster Risk Management for Cultural Heritage and the Principles for the Analysis, Conservation, and Structural Restoration of Architectural Heritage" have become cornerstones in heritage preservation, articulating a framework for protecting monuments and sites from natural disasters and other threats. ICOMOS's advocacy for integrating heritage preservation within the UN SDGs has reinforced the importance of safeguarding cultural sites as part of broader sustainability efforts. Additionally, ICOMOS has promoted the use of digital documentation and participatory approaches, used extensively by the contributing authors of this book, to empower local communities in heritage management.

ICCROM is another global organization that works to protect heritage at risk (see ICCROM 2025). ICCROM's "First Aid to Cultural Heritage in Times

Figure 4.1. One of the key frameworks for heritage management work at Egmont Key is the UN Sustainable Development Goal's Target 11.4: Protect the World's Cultural and Natural Heritage. By permission of the United Nations.

of Crisis" program has become a global model, training professionals and communities to respond swiftly and effectively to threats from conflict and natural disasters. ICCROM's "Disaster Risk Management framework and the Integrated Emergency Response" guidelines enable proactive planning, encouraging heritage managers to assess vulnerabilities and develop tailored emergency protocols. By prioritizing capacity-building and localized training, ICCROM works toward ensuring that heritage professionals worldwide have the tools and knowledge to protect at-risk cultural assets in a wide range of challenging environments.

The UN SDGs have successfully integrated heritage preservation into global development agendas, notably through SDG 11, which emphasizes making cities inclusive, safe, resilient, and sustainable. Specifically, Target 11.4 highlights the need to strengthen efforts to protect and safeguard the world's cultural and natural heritage, which has prompted countries to incorporate heritage protection within urban planning, disaster risk management, and sustainable tourism (UN n.d.; 4.1). This approach has led to policies that balance conservation with economic and social development, promoting heritage as a source of community resilience, identity, and sustainable livelihoods.

The SDGs have spurred funding and technical support for heritage initiatives in vulnerable regions, especially those facing threats from climate change, development, and natural disasters. Initiatives like the UNESCO Urban Heritage Programme and UNESCO's partnership with the UN Office for Disaster Risk Reduction (UNDRR) are direct results of the SDG framework, offering best practices in risk assessment and sustainable site management. By aligning heritage preservation with sustainable development, the SDGs have helped mainstream heritage protection, creating a global recognition of its importance to both cultural identity and sustainable futures. SDG 11.4, and SDG 13 Climate Action, are the two most frequently used SDGs in the USF team's work at Egmont Key (discussed in detail in Chapter 6) and have been included in many of the presentations of the project.

The integration of heritage preservation into the SDGs has raised awareness of heritage as a sustainability issue, but it risks oversimplifying heritage as a component of economic development rather than recognizing its intrinsic cultural value. By prioritizing heritage tourism and economic benefits, preservation efforts may inadvertently encourage exploitation of cultural assets, shifting focus away from genuine preservation and long-term resilience, all of which are needed at Egmont Key.

While global heritage frameworks and organizations such as the UN SDGs, UNESCO, ICCROM, and ICOMOS play essential roles in protecting at-risk cultural assets, these initiatives often face significant limitations. The reliance on top-down approaches, particularly in UNESCO's World Heritage Convention, can be at odds with local, community-led approaches. Their large, global scale sometimes fails to account for the specific social, political, and cultural nuances of each heritage site (Di Giovine 2018). Although the frameworks emphasize community engagement, in practice, local voices are sometimes sidelined in favor of external expertise or universal standards, which may not always align with community needs or priorities. Global preservation bodies have, in recent years, also faced critiques stemming from an overreliance on top-down approaches, limited local input, and resource disparities that make implementation difficult, especially in lower-income regions. Balancing economic development with the intrinsic cultural value of heritage remains a core challenge in ensuring that preservation efforts meet both global standards and local needs effectively.

Another important consideration relates to digital heritage approaches, promoted by these international organizations and discussed frequently throughout this book. While digital tools and databases are celebrated for their role in documenting heritage, their implementation is often hindered by resource disparities. Many countries and communities, especially those most vulnerable to climate change or conflict, lack the technological infrastructure or financial support to maintain and utilize these tools effectively. This disparity creates an imbalance where heritage in wealthier regions may receive more attention and resources, leaving many sites in lower-income regions insufficiently protected.

While keeping these challenges in mind, it can be stated that in recent years, digital tools and databases have started to transform the work of cultural heritage preservation. Site documentation is faster and often more accurate with digital tools like terrestrial lidar scanning. Remote sensing can locate hidden sites, and satellite imagery can identify looting from outer space—a "space archaeology" pioneered by Sarah Parcak (Parcak 2019). Digital databases such as Open Context use peer review, standard vocabularies, and open linked data architecture to increase the discoverability of archaeological finds. This approach also promotes data reuse and sharing. In addition, digitalization and virtualization are transforming dissemination and public outreach, with WebVR, virtual and augmented reality, and digital exhibits increasing public engagement with heritage. We have incorporated digital documentation, digital tools, and storytelling into our work at Egmont Key to promote heritage interpretation in keeping with the goals of international frameworks, while acknowledging the ongoing issues of accessibility, inclusiveness, and affordability.

NATIONAL ORGANIZATIONS AND INITIATIVES: PROTECTING HERITAGE

National organizations and initiatives embed preservation into several policy frameworks that address domestic heritage needs. In the United States, programs like the Advisory Council on Historic Preservation (ACHP), and the Native American Graves Protection and Repatriation Act (NAGPRA) emphasize ethical stewardship, cross-sector partnerships, and public awareness. Other federal initiatives include the National Register of Historic Places and the National Historic Landmark designations (with Egmont Key holding the former). While these have established needed protections for cultural heritage in the United States, they are often plagued by bureaucratic issues, particularly with ACHP's Section 106 reviews. NAGPRA also faces challenges in compliance and verifying cultural affiliations, which can hinder the repatriation process. Many of these mandates are applicable to and in fact required at Egmont Key.

ACHP's Section 106 of the National Historic Preservation Act (NHPA) and the National Environmental Policy Act (NEPA) have significantly advanced the protection of heritage at risk in the United States by embedding historic preservation into federal decision-making processes. Section 106 requires federal agencies to consider the impacts of their projects on historic properties, enabling communities and stakeholders to engage in consultations that can lead to project modifications to avoid, minimize, or mitigate harm to cultural resources. The integration of NEPA, which mandates environmental assessments for federally funded projects, complements Section 106 by broadening the evaluation scope to include both natural and cultural resources, facilitating more comprehensive planning and protection strategies. ACHP's efforts to streamline Section 106 reviews through tools like Programmatic Agreements and Memoranda of Agreement have improved the efficiency of preservation reviews, establishing best practices for collaboration between agencies and local communities. These frameworks have not only saved historic sites from potential adverse effects but have also set a national precedent for stakeholder-driven heritage protection that aligns cultural preservation with responsible development.

NAGPRA is perhaps the most iconic cultural heritage legislation in the United States and has led directly to the protection and return of Native American patrimony by mandating the repatriation of ancestral remains and sacred objects from museums and federal agencies to their affiliated tribes. Since its enactment in 1990, NAGPRA has facilitated the return of thousands of human remains, funerary items, and sacred artifacts, restoring them to the custody of Native communities and honoring their cultural and spiritual rights. This legislation has also set a high standard for ethical stewardship, encouraging institutions to establish best practices in handling and documenting Native American collections with respect, transparency, and collaboration. With an occupation site at Egmont Key, a history of detainment and deaths of Seminole people, and the archival documentation of Native American graves and their disinterment on the island, NAGPRA is a fundamental piece of legislation for the subject matter of this book.

Recent updates to informed consent guidelines, influenced by NAGPRA and the United Nations Declaration on the Rights of Indigenous Peoples (UNDRIP), emphasize Indigenous sovereignty and equitable collaboration in the management of Native American collections and cultural heritage sites. These frameworks mandate meaningful consultation with tribal representatives, ensuring that research practices respect Indigenous cultural protocols, particularly regarding sacred or sensitive materials. Additionally, streamlined repatriation processes require institutions to proactively identify and return funerary items, sacred objects, and other culturally significant materials. This paradigm shift prioritizes ethical stewardship and reinforces the rights of Indigenous communities to control and protect their cultural heritage, advancing a more inclusive and respectful approach to heritage management.

National heritage initiatives in the United States play an essential role in the protection of at-risk cultural assets, though they are not without critical challenges. ACHP's Section 106 review process, while foundational for integrating preservation considerations into federal projects, often faces criticism for procedural inefficiencies that can delay necessary preservation actions. In 2025, Section 106 was weakened due to an executive order under President Trump declaring a national energy emergency that directs federal agencies to circumvent the traditional Section 106 process, potentially leading to fast-tracking projects, reduced consultation with tribes and the public, and less protection for historic sites (ACHP 2025). NAGPRA has made significant advances in repatriating culturally sensitive items to Native American communities. However, insufficient funding and intricate cultural-affiliation requirements are cited as barriers to timely compliance. Overall, these initiatives reflect a committed approach to heritage preservation but could achieve greater effectiveness through enhanced procedural efficiency, resource allocation, and responsiveness to the specific needs of heritage communities across diverse contexts.

Safeguarding Heritage at Risk in Florida: From Government Agencies to Nonprofit Organizations

Managing Egmont Key's heritage has proven to be a deeply complex and challenging task, with federal, state, private, community, and nonprofit stakeholders having different perspectives and agendas that do not all align. The intricate network of land managers did not arise by accident—it was put in place intentionally starting in the 1970s to safeguard the island from development pressures (Hare 2022; Sanchez 2025). Congressman Sam Gibbons was instrumental in this regard, and many others have followed in his footsteps to engage in collaborations to protect the island. Yet the complexity of these overlapping interests has, at times, led to inefficiencies and unintended consequences. The entangled web of organizational oversight has impeded the development of new and much needed approaches to heritage management and sustainable tourism. Top-down decisions at Egmont Key are enacted by federal agencies, primarily the US Fish and Wildlife Service (USFWS), the Army Corps of Engineers, and the US Coast Guard, along with state agencies such as the Florida Park Service that often manage the day-to-day oversight. Some of these agencies have developed laudable conservation and management plans. These, however, have not been fully executed for several reasons, including lack of funding, the hierarchy of authority, staff and management turnover, and serious infrastructural hurricane damage caused in 2024 that took out all the docks and many of the buildings.

Egmont Key is unique in that a multitude of government agencies are responsible for the island, although they are not fully able to carry out its protection, interpretation, and promotion. Nonprofits and community organizations such as the Friends of the Tampa Bay National Wildlife Refuges and the Egmont Key Alliance have stepped in to fill that void, in addition to projects conducted through local educational institutions such as Eckerd College and the University of South Florida. The state-funded Florida Public Archaeology Network, which is active in the West Central Florida region where Egmont Key sits, has pioneered an innovative citizen science heritage monitoring program that could complement existing activities and benefit the island's vulnerable resources, but it has not been implemented as of yet.

While partnerships between governmental and community-led organizations are a keystone of effective heritage management, they can also be plagued by a multitude of challenges. At Egmont Key, nonprofit organizations have made substantive accomplishments, although being volunteer-driven and underfunded has been a constant challenge. Interpersonal frictions have also hampered efforts at collaboration. The following paragraphs will provide an overview of the key organizations involved in stewarding Egmont Key's at-risk heritage along with a discussion of notable successes and challenges.

GOVERNMENT EFFORTS AT EGMONT KEY

To help save Egmont Key from ongoing erosion, in 2006 the Army Corps of Engineers (Jacksonville District), in collaboration with USFWS, conducted a study to assess the feasibility of stabilizing the west shore of the island and its historic fortifications. The loss of land from 539 acres in 1877 to 280 acres in 2006 was a deciding factor in initiating the Egmont Key Shore Protection Plan (James et al. 2006). The project was prompted by the severe state of endangerment of Egmont Key's cultural resources that have long been recognized by its placement on the Florida State Cultural Resources Inventory (site No. 8-HI-117) and the National Register of Historic Places in 1978.

The Army Corps of Engineers commissioned Panamerican Consultants,

Inc., to carry out an extensive study that was done in compliance with Section 106, the Archaeological and Historic Preservation Act, NEPA, and a variety of Florida statues (James et al. 2006). Methods included remote sensing, ground-penetrating radar, terrestrial surveys, and a comprehensive literature and record review for a full inventory of the land-based and submerged heritage assets. The features that are already underwater (and frequently explored by snorkelers and divers brought to the island almost daily by tour boats) include a fog bell, ammunition bunkers, Battery Burchsted, Battery John Page, and other Fort Dade remains (James et al. 2006).

Panamerican Consultants, Inc., concluded that the cultural resources on the island are under continuous threat from pronounced shoreline erosion and may be addressed with breakwaters, submerged reefs, groins, and beach renourishment. Of these solutions, replenishing the sand on the western shore has been the primary action taken that has significantly stabilized land loss on the island (discussed in greater detail in Chapter 7). Other key recommendations from the report state that the island's protective boundaries should be expanded to include the offshore cultural resources and that its status be elevated as a National Historic Landmark. The 2006 report is an excellent summary and overview of Egmont Key's cultural resources that embodies the concept of heritage at risk.

During the same time as the Army Corps of Engineers study, in 2006, USFWS hired Panamerican Consultants, Inc., to create a topographic base map of the historic transportation network of Fort Dade (Ambrosino and Driscoll 2007), likely because they were already on the island conducting extensive surveys. According to the report, "The work completed during this project will enable the US Fish and Wildlife Service and the Florida Park Service to preserve, protect, and interpret a significant cultural resource on Egmont Key, and will also aid the US Fish and Wildlife Service in the proposed rehabilitation and subsequent maintenance of the brick road" (Ambrosino and Driscoll 2007: ii). Over the course of two weeks, archaeologists used a total station to collect approximately 3,700 measurements of the transportation network, while also excavating five test units to examine construction techniques, recovering 454 artifacts that date from 1821 to 2006 (Ambrosino and Driscoll 2007: ii). Once excavated, the artifacts were taken to the Florida Division of Historical Resources in Tallahassee. As of 2025, the collection has received little scholarly attention and has not been incorporated into exhibits or public-facing interpretation.

While the Panamerican Consultants' reports are very informative and contain many proactive recommendations, the responsibility to carry those forward ultimately falls under the purview of multiple organizations, including the State of Florida's Department of Environmental Protection (DEP) and the Florida Park Service. The DEP oversees cultural and natural resource management programs in the state, coordinating with programs like the Florida Master Site File (FMSF). The DEP contributes to heritage protection through the Unit Management Plans for state parks, which mandate comprehensive site management plans that address conservation needs for both natural and cultural resources. The Florida State Park System maintains Unit Management Plans organized by district for almost every park in the state (https://floridadep.gov/parks/parks-office-park-planning-2). As of 2025, within District 4 (Suncoast Region), all parks listed on the website have a clickable link to a management plan. Egmont Key is listed, but its management plan is conspicuously absent. Other nearby parks within the same district, such as Honeymoon Island State Park and Caladesi Island, have comprehensive Unit Management Plans that articulate a vision for management of cultural resources, beaches, visitors, and land use.

The likely reason that Florida State Parks (FPS) never authored a Unit Management Plan for Egmont Key is that another government agency—USFWS—authored a Comprehensive Conservation Plan for the island in 2010. Additionally, the hierarchy and entanglement of government agencies on the island is such that USFWS has greater autonomy in decision-making than FPS, which is primarily responsible for managing daily activities and recreation on the island. But these activities only proceed under the oversight of federal agencies—the US Coast Guard and USFWS—that have enacted a "cooperative management agreement" with the Florida DEP (USFWS 2010). This agreement could be terminated, at which point the island would no longer be part of the state park system; a possibility that has presented itself on various occasions over the years. As Thompson and Thompson note (2012: 137),

> Another challenge facing Egmont Key is its future status as part of Florida's State Park system. Should Egmont Key not remain under the watchful eye of the park system with full time rangers, it is feared wildlife would suffer, and the island's unspoiled beauty would deteriorate. . . . Vandalism and just plain ignorance of the island's ecology and nesting birds could

destroy what previous and present generations have worked so hard to preserve.

USFWS COMPREHENSIVE CONSERVATION PLAN: TAMPA BAY REFUGES

The "Comprehensive Conservation Plan: Tampa Bay Refuges" (USFWS 2010) outlines strategies for the preservation and management of both cultural and natural heritage across the Tampa Bay area's National Wildlife Refuges. The Tampa Bay Refuges include Egmont Key, Passage Key, and the Pinellas National Wildlife Refuge, which are respectively located in three different counties (Hillsborough, Manatee, and Pinellas), complicating efforts by necessitating intercounty cooperation. The plan emphasizes protecting sensitive ecosystems, such as coastal habitats, wetlands, and estuaries, while also recognizing the importance of safeguarding cultural resources, including historical sites and archaeological artifacts. Key objectives include maintaining biodiversity, restoring habitats, and addressing climate change impacts, all while ensuring the conservation of historical and cultural landscapes within the refuge areas.

BIODIVERSITY AT EGMONT KEY: "WHERE BIRDS CAN BE BIRDS"

A focal point of the Comprehensive Conservation Plan is the description of wildlife including reptiles (snakes and turtles), amphibians, and birds. More than 110 species of birds have been documented at Egmont Key, including numerous local and migratory birds from royal terns and black skimmers to great blue herons and ospreys. According to USFWS (n.d.:1):

> 35,000 pairs of colonial beach-nesting birds. Royal and sandwich terns, brown pelicans, and laughing gulls make up the majority of the colony. Known as colonial nesters, these birds find safety in numbers. Egmont Key holds the highest nesting colony of laughing gulls in the entire state of Florida. Over 7,000 pairs of royal terns have nested on Egmont Key, which makes it one of the highest nesting royal tern colonies in the state.

The island's sandy beaches and low vegetation create an ideal environment for these birds to nest and raise their young. Sand replenishment on the quickly eroding western side of the island has kept these nesting grounds intact, but whether this practice is sustainable in the long run is unknown. A bigger threat may be human activity that has disrupted nesting areas both in the refuge area, which is off-limits to people, and other areas of the island where nesting occurs alongside beachgoers and boaters. Serious wildlife disruptions were seen in the past during periods of military occupation, and they persist with increased tourism. Sadly, "In past years, instances of human disturbances have caused total failure of all nesting colonies" (USFWS 2010: 57). Despite signs posted at the southern end of the island for people to keep out of the refuge, frequent incursions occur and cannot be fully monitored by the limited staff on the island.

Figure 4.2. Gopher tortoise at Egmont Key. By permission of Laura Harrison.

Perhaps a more unusual case occurred in 2024, when a man landed his helicopter at the southern tip of the island, citing a need to check his engine. Video footage "shows the helicopter's whirring rotors stirring up sand and flocks of shorebirds retreating from their beach nests on the restricted wildlife refuge on May 12. Shortly after landing, a woman exited the helicopter and started taking photos, according to a Florida wildlife incident report" (Chesnes 2024: 2). Since the fall of 2024 with hurricanes Helene and Milton, when most structures that were habitable on the island were destroyed, there has been no daily presence of any supervisory staff on the island to oversee bird protection.

Egmont Key is also home to box turtles and gopher tortoises, the latter of which is a keystone species in the region. Gopher tortoises play a vital role in maintaining ecological balance by digging burrows that provide habitat for other animals, such as frogs and snakes. The population at Egmont Key is the largest concentration in the state. Their protected status is well marked on the island with signage. Historically, their presence on the island has contributed to the resilience of the island's ecosystems, which include many native plant species as well, and delighted many visitors (4.2).

A CALL FOR COLLABORATION IN THE COMPREHENSIVE CONSERVATION PLAN: CHALLENGES ABOUND

In addition to sections of the Comprehensive Plan aimed at further protecting wildlife, other specific actions outlined include promoting public education and outreach to raise awareness about the cultural significance of the region and the natural resources. The document advocates for collaborative partnerships with local communities, Tribal nations, and other stakeholders to ensure that cultural heritage is integrated into resource management practices. The plan also supports archaeological surveys and the protection of historically significant sites, acknowledging the need for effective stewardship that balances ecological restoration with the protection of cultural and historical assets. The alignment is clear with international global heritage frameworks and organizations like UNESCO, ICCROM, ICOMOS, and the UN SDGs discussed earlier; however, the vision has yet to be realized due to several factors discussed below. The Comprehensive Plan described pressing issues at Egmont Key such as global warming and overtourism and the areas that were in need of improvement by USFWS (USFWS 2010: 85):

> There is a general lack of awareness regarding the Service's mission, purpose, and management objectives, particularly as it relates to the Tampa Bay Refuges. Minimal outreach is being conducted, and environmental education and interpretation opportunities are lacking at the refuges. Passage Key and Pinellas National Wildlife Refuge (NWRs) are closed for public use; however, there are still opportunities for Tampa Bay Refuges wildlife observation and photography from the water. Egmont Key NWR has very good vantage points for wildlife observation and photography, and the Service could provide good opportunities for environmental education and interpretation. However, lack of facilities at the refuge and staff located off-site and outside the Tampa Bay/St. Petersburg vicinity undermines these opportunities.

The need to take action at Egmont Key regarding visitors was also noted in the report (USFWS 2010: 85):

> Problems are occurring on Egmont Key NWR due to overcrowding and overuse. Unregulated commercial tours bring over 70,000 visitors to Egmont Key NWR annually. Boaters, anglers, swimmers, and sunbathers gather at Egmont Key NWR where there is no available freshwater for public consumption and sanitation facilities are sparse or unavailable.

The main issue with the 2010 Comprehensive Conservation Plan is that much of it was not executed and remains aspirational. Problems raised in 2010 have worsened over time and have not been addressed, such as overtourism on the island and increasing numbers of tour boats and recreational boaters who often bring their dogs (which are prohibited on the island to protect the birds and turtles). As of 2024, it was estimated that the island received over 200,000 visitors per year, who still have no access to bathroom facilities, leaving them to their own devices when nature calls. Built heritage also continues to degrade, and as the structures appear abandoned, overgrown, and decrepit, they invite vandalism and graffiti. This situation worsened during the COVID-19 pandemic when many of Florida's parks saw an uptick in numbers as people sought outdoor activities.

An additional issue is that the USFWS Comprehensive Conservation Plan has not been updated on a regular schedule, despite the mandatory 10-year re-evaluation date of September 25, 2019, for the NEPA compliant and approved uses at Egmont Key listed in Appendix D (USFWS 2010: 183). These uses covered mosquito management, photography, video, filming, or audio recording (commercial, news, and educational), beach use, shelling, picnicking, snorkeling, concessions, and more. A review of other USFWS Comprehensive Conservation Plans shows that Egmont Key is in good company; most others have not been updated either (USFWS n.d.).

While government-authored heritage management and conservation plans are a step toward responsible stewardship, limited funding and personnel can hinder effective implementation, potentially leaving some vulnerable sites without adequate protection measures. Even if the necessary pieces were in place for moving forward with an implementable plan for Egmont Key, all the different agencies involved would need to be at the table (USFWS, US Coast Guard, Florida State Parks, etc.) and all of the applicable laws, regulations, and policies that govern any changes would need to be considered. The Comprehensive Plan lists over 28 policies, including the Antiquities Act of 1906, the Migratory Bird Conservation Act of 1929, the National Wildlife Refuge System Administration Act of 1966, the Emergency Wetlands Resources Act of 1986, and NAGPRA. Here's is a more comprehensive list of policies, acts, and laws relevant for Egmont Key (from earliest to most recent):

The Property Clause of the U.S. Constitution, Article IV, Section 3, Clause 2 (1787)

The Commerce Clause of the U.S. Constitution, Article I, Section 8 (1787)

Antiquities Act of 1906 (34 Stat. 225)
Migratory Bird Treaty Act of 1918 (15 U.S.C. 703–711; 40 Stat. 755)
Migratory Bird Conservation Act of 1929 (16 U.S.C. 715r; 45 Stat. 1222)
Migratory Bird Hunting Stamp Act of 1934 (16 U.S.C. 718–718h; 48 Stat. 451)
Refuge Revenue Sharing Act of 1935, as amended in 1978 (16 U.S.C. 715s; 92 Stat. 1319)
Criminal Code Provisions of 1940 (18 U.S.C. 41)
Bald and Golden Eagle Protection Act of 1940 (16 U.S.C. 668–668d; 54 Stat. 250)
Refuge Trespass Act of June 25, 1948 (18 U.S.C. 41; 62 Stat. 686)
Fish and Wildlife Act of 1956 (16 U.S.C. 742a–742j; 70 Stat. 1119)
Refuge Recreation Act of 1962 (16 U.S.C. 460k–460k-4; 76 Stat. 653)
Wilderness Act of 1964 (16 U.S.C. 1131–1136; 78 Stat. 890)
Land and Water Conservation Fund Act of 1965
National Historic Preservation Act of 1966, as amended (16 U.S.C. 470 et seq.; 80 Stat. 915)
National Wildlife Refuge System Administration Act of 1966 (16 U.S.C. 668dd, 668ee; 80 Stat. 927)
National Environmental Policy Act of 1969 (NEPA) (42 U.S.C. 4321 et seq.; 83 Stat. 852)
Use of Off-Road Vehicles on Public Lands (Executive Order 11644, as amended by Executive Order 10989) (1972)
Endangered Species Act of 1973 (16 U.S.C. 1531 et seq.; 87 Stat. 884)
Archaeological Resources Protection Act of 1979
Memorandum of Understanding Between U.S. Fish and Wildlife Service (Chassahowitzka Refuges Complex, Tampa Bay Refuges, Homosassa, Florida) and US Coast Guard, St. Petersburg Group, St. Petersburg, Florida, dated February 7, 1984
Management Agreement for Certain Sovereignty Submerged Lands Surrounding Passage Key National Wildlife Refuge in Manatee County, Agreement No. 750-0013, dated February 7, 1986
Emergency Wetlands Resources Act of 1986 (S.B. 740)
Abandoned Shipwreck Act of 1987
Cooperative Agreement between the U.S. Department of the Interior and the Florida Department of Natural Resources (now Florida Department of Environmental Protection), November 24, 1989

- Native American Graves Protection and Repatriation Act (NAGPRA), Public Law 101–601, 25 U.S.C. §§ 3001–3013. 1990
- Board of Trustees of the Internal Improvement Trust Fund Amendment to Sovereignty Submerged Land Management Agreement No. 750-0013, dated April 7, 1992
- Executive Order 12996: Management and General Public Use of the National Wildlife Refuge System, March 25, 1996
- National Wildlife Refuge System Improvement Act of 1997 (Public Law 105–57, USC 668dd)
- Water Resources Development Act of 2000, Section 420

Despite the good intentions of those involved in its management, Egmont Key's valuable cultural, natural, and historical resources have suffered from the lack of a cohesive, comprehensive strategy with the resources to enact it, which has ultimately hindered long-term protection and preservation. This has invited proposals for the development of recreational facilities within Florida State Parks. In 2024, the State of Florida launched the Great Outdoors Initiative, which aimed to convert portions of nine state parks into recreational facilities, including pickleball courts, golf courses, and hotels. At Honeymoon Island State Park, which is within the same managerial purview as Egmont Key, an amendment to the Unit Management Plan in 2024 described plans to construct four new pickleball courts on lands that had previously been conserved for environmental protection. This triggered a widespread bipartisan public outcry across the state, and eventually Governor Ron DeSantis withdrew the proposal. This controversy is part of a broader conversation about the appropriate uses of public lands that contain valuable and vulnerable natural and cultural heritage. Should attention focus on developing sustainable tourism options such as ecotours that are mindful of preservation, or should commercial development be the primary focus of public lands? Of note, Egmont Key was not included in the Great Outdoors Initiative, most likely because of its inaccessible location and entanglement of many state and federal agencies.

NONPROFIT ORGANIZATIONS AND STEWARDSHIP EGMONT KEY

Against the challenges of government-led plans to conserve and safeguard Egmont Key are several nonprofit organizations that have stepped in to develop and implement models for monitoring and safeguarding at-risk heritage.

Figure 4.3. Chapter authors and colleagues at the Tidally United conference in 2019. *From left*: Dave Scheidecker, Seminole Tribal Historic Preservation Office; Brooke Hansen, USF; Laura Harrison, USF; April Min; and Lacee Cofer. By permission of Brooke Hansen.

As of 2025, some of these models are in the development phase, some have been ongoing for years, and others have recently disbanded after decades of community-led work.

The Florida Public Archaeology Network (FPAN), funded by the Florida state legislature, is a world-renowned heritage preservation organization that pioneers heritage management and public engagement. Among their many activities, FPAN implements citizen-led documentation of at-risk sites throughout the state, including through its Heritage Monitoring Scouts (HMS) program (Miller and Murray 2018). They also organize the Tidally United conference to raise awareness and explore future-ready solutions to protect heritage sites from climate-related threats. The co-editors of this book have done several presentations about Egmont Key at Tidally United, including at the 2019 conference with representatives from the Seminole Tribal Historic Preservation Office (4.3). As the island is now known as one of the 11 most threatened historic properties in the state (Florida Trust for Historic Preservation 2025), it is an informative case study for the Tidally United discussions on how to protect heritage against the rising tides.

FPAN's marquee citizen science program, the Heritage Monitoring Scouts, trains volunteers to monitor sites threatened by climate change, erosion, and development with photographs and a site condition form (Miller and Murray 2018). According to FPAN there are 35,000 known at-risk cultural resources spread across 8,000 miles of Florida's coastline. HMS focuses on 5–6,000 of the most vulnerable sites (FPAN n.d.). Observations are uploaded into a continuously updated database that allows the state to track at-risk sites while also empowering local communities to participate in preservation efforts. FPAN's reliance on volunteer engagement and resource availability can sometimes influence the consistency and effectiveness of its programs. Despite these challenges, FPAN stands out as a leading model for integrating public participation into heritage protection strategies, aligning with international efforts to preserve cultural heritage under threat. As Rachel Kangas (personal communication 2024) director of FPAN's West and Central Regions, states,

> the fact that we're able to train people how to ethically and legally visit these [archaeological] sites and help us collect data is really where the strength is in that whole program . . . it's really changed the way that we look at site prioritization and responses to storms and responses to development and other things that are happening at sites. [Volunteers] learn everything they need to know to legally and ethically visit a cultural site, and we work really closely with the state Division of Historical Resources to make sure that even once [HMS scouts are] trained, that sensitive site information isn't shared unless we have specific land manager permission.

While FPAN is active in the West Central region of Florida, an HMS monitoring station has not been installed at Egmont Key. We did offer HMS training in one of our professional development workshops at Egmont Key in 2020. One outcome of the training was gaining provisional approval by land managers to install an HMS station on the island, but staff turnover and the hardships of working collaboratively during the COVID-19 pandemic put the project on hold. This is emblematic of the many efforts to steward Egmont Key that prove to be difficult for a myriad of internal and external reasons. Installing the HMS monitoring station would significantly improve heritage documentation and monitoring at Egmont Key, especially important because of the numerous threats facing the island from erosion, overtourism, strong storms, and other forces. It would also empower FPAN to serve as a liaison between land managers and the community—a role that they have successfully fulfilled at many other heritage sites around the state. As Rachel Kangas notes (personal communication 2024):

> [FPAN] brings those two voices together and helps advocate for land managers to have conversations with the community and advocate with the community and help [communicate] about what the land managers are doing. That sometimes is also the same for Tribal interests too.

Other nonprofit organizations have played an essential role at Egmont Key and have worked closely with the land managers at the federal and state levels, including the Friends of the Tampa Bay National Wildlife Refuges and the Egmont Key Alliance (EKA). The Friends group works in collaboration with USFWS, and they host cleanups, conduct bird- and turtle-nesting counts, coordinate bird stewards, and organize occasional volunteer docent staffing to the Egmont Key Guardhouse. Education and outreach are the main activities of the Friends group. In 2022, they released an award-winning short film titled *Where Birds Can Be Birds—The Remarkable Refuges of Tampa Bay* (Friends of the Tampa Bay National Wildlife Refuges 2022).

Another community-led initiative working to preserve and protect Egmont Key is the Egmont Key Alliance (EKA), a 501c3 nonprofit founded in 1991. Like FPAN, the EKA served as a liaison between the land managers and the community and was the official citizen support organization (CSO) of the Egmont Key Florida State Park until 2023. Over the years, the EKA was primarily focused on monthly cleanup days and monitoring the health of bird and sea turtle populations with a landmark public outreach event called Discover the Island with vendors and interpretive tours of the island. As of 2023, the Egmont Key Alliance transitioned away from its CSO role and was subsumed as a committee under the nonprofit Take MAR that continues to sponsor cleanups on the island (Take MAR 2024). In 2025, Take MAR led the efforts for a rebooting and reorganization of the EKA as an independent entity again to continue its role in stewarding Egmont Key in the wake of the 2024 hurricanes that destroyed many parts of the island (EKA 2025).

The EKA has been a significant player in carrying out hands-on work to preserve, protect, and restore Egmont Key's natural and cultural heritage (Sanchez 2025; Thompson and Thompson 2012). They were one of the driving forces behind initiating sand replenishment at Egmont Key, which was implemented by the Army Corps of Engineers. This has been a relatively effective means

Figure 4.4. The Egmont Key Guardhouse, which was restored as part of an initiative led by community nonprofit the Egmont Key Alliance, with additional assistance provided by USFWS. As of 2025, this is the only historic building to have been restored at Egmont Key, although the interpretive exhibits inside are only open occasionally, when volunteers are available. By permission of Laura Harrison.

of stabilizing the island's vulnerable western shoreline (discussed further in Chapter 7).

The EKA also carried out the full restoration of the Fort Dade Guardhouse starting in 1999 (4.4). At the time, the US Coast Guard had been using the vacant building to store large metal palettes. Later in the twentieth century, vandals set fire to the structure, leaving nothing but concrete walls and the metal debris. The EKA raised nearly $500,000 to restore the structure and arranged for a barge with a crane to remove the steel pallets that were left inside. The EKA organized the project that was endorsed by the park manager at the time, Bob Baker, and the USFWS refuge manager. The restoration included replacing the roof and refinishing the exterior walls. The USFWS refuge manager allocated another $150,000 to install interpretive exhibits about the island's history and ecology; however, in the following years the renovated space was closed most days, and only open to the public intermittently on weekends when volunteers were available. A 3D virtual tour of the space was created in 2020 during one of our professional development workshops to enhance accessibility to the information on the interpretive panels inside (discussed in greater detail in Chapter 6).

Richard Sanchez, the last president of the Egmont Key Alliance CSO before it was transitioned to a subcommittee of Take MAR and then an independent organization again, reflected on differences between how heritage has been handled at Egmont Key as compared with neighboring sites like Fort DeSoto. He notes,

> There is so much more that could have been done—if you look at Fort DeSoto and Fort Dade [on Egmont Key], they were built by the same people for the same purpose. But look at the difference between the two. One has been preserved, and one hasn't. It shouldn't be that way. Why is one more important than the other one? There's no reason that it should be except that there's no will among the agencies to do anything . . . and the island is just far enough away—it's the farthest west and farthest south part of Hillsborough County (Richard Sanchez, personal communication 2025).

In considering the legacy of the nonprofits that are currently engaged at Egmont Key (Friends of USFWS, Take MAR, the Egmont Key Alliance), and those that might develop a foothold and engage more in the future (FPAN), it is clear that community-led initiatives have and can play an integral role in protecting and preserving Egmont Key's at-risk heritage.

Cultural Heritage at Egmont Key: Stories of Destruction and Resilience

Egmont Key is a prime example of how a lack of consistent strategic planning for stewardship, preservation, and interpretation creates an existential threat for a heritage site. Despite admirable community-engaged initiatives such as the Florida Public Archaeology Network and the Egmont Key Alliance, land managers have been unable to author a Unit Management Plan for the island or fully enact elements of the Comprehensive Conservation Plan that include sustainable tourism. One reason these goals are left unrealized is a lack of financial support from the state and federal government—a situation seen commonly around the world, especially in the aftermath of the COVID-19 pandemic, which placed a heavy financial burden on most governments. As a result, much of the island's tangible cultural heritage has been destroyed by repeated environmental and anthropogenic forces like strong storms, erosion, vandalism, and overtourism. Hurricanes Helene and Milton in 2024 not only did severe damage to physical heritage sites on the island, but they also actually destroyed more recent infrastructure (housing and docks) and prevented land managers from maintaining a presence on the island post-hurricanes.

The built heritage at Egmont Key that has been under threat for decades mostly pertains to maritime and military histories. For instance, after Fort Dade was formally abandoned in 1923, only one primary caretaker, Sgt. Fagan, was left in charge of the island (Thompson and Thompson 2012). Throughout the 1920s and 1930s, the island effectively became a ghost town, with many buildings burned down or demolished (Stafford 1980). One notable fire occurred in 1925 when federal agents attempted to flush out rumrunners and the island was set on fire (Thompson and Thompson 2012). Sgt. Fagan worked to stop the fire after the bootleggers fled and were captured.

Former Park Ranger Bob Baker recounted how bootlegging was stamped out at Egmont Key (Manatee County Public Library 1996):

> Customs ran some bootleggers to ground, and I am sure nobody around here got in trouble for having a few toddies during the prohibition period, but they ran, I believe it was 11 bootleggers jumped off the boat. They got 33 cases of whiskey and they couldn't figure out how to get these guys out of the buildings, so one guy said, "Well, let's light the grass on fire and smoke them out." They did, and the Tampa Trib[une] reported the blaze was visible at Ybor City. Thirty-five buildings were lost in that fire, and eventually the Army came back and destroyed the rest.

The rumrunners are but another chapter in the story of Egmont Key as a coveted island, a disappearing island, and a forgotten island. After the 1921 hurricane, the 1923 decommissioning of Fort Dade, and the obsolescence of the seacoast defense system, Egmont Key became a bygone place in Tampa Bay—an abandoned outpost. This state of neglect crystallized and eventually became a beacon for unlawful activities that has permeated Egmont Key's history for over a century. This was a recurring theme in the 1950s and '60s, when the island became a party destination for beachgoers, before the National Wildlife Refuge was established in 1974 to protect it from unsupervised, unregulated visitors, and impending threats of development. The theme of Egmont Key as a hinterland is also present in the aftermath of Hurricanes Helene and

Figure 4.5. Battery Burchsted in 1995. Courtesy of Bruce McCall.

Figure 4.6. Battery Page in 1977. Courtesy of Bruce McCall.

Milton; the island has been left without consistent oversight of law enforcement and land managers, impeding efforts to safeguard heritage.

As of 2025, the military forts and lighthouse at Egmont Key are in varying states of decay. Battery Burchsted and Battery Page are underwater and have become popular snorkeling destinations for tourists visiting the island (4.5, 4.6). Battery McIntosh now sits just 20 m from the western coastline, and despite a lack of conservation work the structure is still fully standing, albeit with significant corrosion evident on its iron elements (4.7). The roof of Battery Howard has collapsed in on itself, leaving the structure as a pile of rubble (4.8). And finally, Battery Charles Mellon is the best-preserved structure of the group, with some damage to the concrete and water intrusion visible in certain areas, but no major structural issues, though its condition is likely to deteriorate without routine maintenance and preventive measures to stop

Figure 4.7. Remains of Battery McIntosh. Note the weathering of the paint and large cracks visible in the concrete. By permission of Laura Harrison.

Figure 4.8. The intact portion of Battery Howard. Behind the trees on the left of the photo is a collapsed section of the structure that is closed to visitors. This structure is situated on Egmont Key's highly dynamic western shoreline and is at risk of washing into the sea. By permission of Laura Harrison.

Figure 4.9. Battery Charles Mellon, which sits on what is now the northwestern tip of Egmont. Key. It was constructed in 1901 at the north end of the island. By permission of Laura Harrison.

Figure 4.10. The Egmont Key Lighthouse, constructed in 1858. While the top was removed in the 1940s, the overall structure is in fairly good shape. It is set back far enough from the coast that it has avoided the most extreme erosion that has impacted the military fortifications. By permission of Laura Harrison.

the intrusion of water into the concrete through visible cracks (4.9). The 1858 lighthouse is far enough inland that it is somewhat protected from the most severe of the erosion, but its exterior paint has weathered over the years (4.10). The interior, which is closed to visitors, is in fairly good shape.

The Fort Dade power plant/mess hall on Egmont Key's western shoreline was already deteriorating by the 1990s, and a concern that it was "too dangerous to anyone who went near it" (Ballingrud 1999: para. 4) led the Florida state park manager, Bob Baker, to organize a detonation of the remains. Despite Baker's acknowledgment that "the building undeniably had historical value," he worked with Sgt. Jim Diamond of the Tampa Police Department's bomb squad to jam 300 lb. of dynamite and TNT "into hundreds of holes bored in the side of [the historic building]" (Ballingrud 1999: para. 9). Because the structure was so strong—with seaward walls up to 2 ft thick reinforced with steel cable—it took two blasts to finally reduce it to rubble. Curiously, no one

Figure 4.11. Ruins of the 1901 power plant/mess hall that was degraded by erosion for over a century and ultimately destroyed by dynamite in 1999. By permission of Laura Harrison.

thought to photograph or otherwise document the historic structure before lighting the explosives, a sentiment perhaps motivated by a general lack of public engagement with Egmont Key's cultural heritage at the time. As Baker noted, "there were no protests, only some concern expressed for the wildlife" (Ballingrud 1999: para. 10). Today, the crumbling remains of the power plant and mess hall are slowly washing away into the Gulf of Mexico (4.11).

Despite all the human assaults on the built heritage, what remains is no match for mother nature. During the writing of this book, two strong hurricanes in 2024 wreaked havoc on the island and completely destroyed the historic Tampa Bay Pilots Association village. The quaint cottages that were used by active-duty pilots and their families were not built to withstand the powerful storms that intensified as a result of climate change. Some of the buildings were also used as management centers for USFWS personnel. The loss of these, in addition to the structure near the lighthouse that housed the one full-time Florida Park Service ranger, led to a situation where no land managers were consistently present on the island. In late 2024, the island was closed to visitors due to the dangers of the debris, yet there were reports of visitors still going there. It reopened in the spring of 2025, a somewhat apocalyptic site of destruction still littered with trash, dead foliage, and broken bits of structures throughout the island.

Two days after Hurricane Helene, volume editor Harrison traveled to Egmont Key with members of the Timmel family, with three generations of Tampa Bay Pilots in their genealogy, to help clean out their family cottage and 3D scan what remained of the village.

> As the boat pulled up to eastern shore of the island, the remains of the dock came into view. We tied the boat to a piling and waded to shore. I was initially struck that several houses in the village had physically moved; they were no longer arranged in two orderly rows. Debris was littered everywhere, with houses reduced to rubble and intermixed with gopher tortoise skeletons, golf carts broken in half, and waterlogged furniture. In one place, I saw the roof a house sitting on the ground far away from what was left of the main structure. All the houses had been lifted from their foundations. It was almost as if a supernatural force had picked them up and moved them. And I was told that during the storm one of the structures—a guardhouse used for communications—had completely disappeared, washing out to sea. (Laura K. Harrison)

Conclusion

The story of Egmont Key serves as a microcosm of the challenges and opportunities inherent in managing heritage at risk. Over the years, this small island has faced a multitude of threats—natural, anthropogenic, and organizational. From hurricanes that have reshaped its physical landscape to overlapping and often fragmented management structures that complicate its protection, Egmont Key's heritage is a reflection of the broader challenges that international frameworks attempt to address.

Egmont Key's history of degradation—whether through intentional destruction, such as the razing of structures during the bootlegging era, or unintentional losses, like those caused by severe hurricanes—is a stark reminder of the fragility of both tangible and intangible heritage. Yet, alongside this history of destruction, there is resilience. The efforts of community-led organizations, such as the Egmont Key Alliance and the Friends of the Tampa

Bay National Wildlife Refuges, and academic partnerships demonstrate the potential for grassroots and collaborative approaches to fill gaps left by limited government resources. These efforts, from volunteer cleanups to innovative heritage monitoring programs, highlight the critical role of public participation in safeguarding heritage at risk.

Egmont Key remains a cautionary tale of what can happen when resources, coordination, and long-term planning fall short. The island's plight exemplifies the urgent need for integrated management strategies that prioritize both cultural preservation and ecological resilience. The overlapping jurisdictions of federal, state, and nonprofit entities have often created inefficiencies, but they also highlight the importance of collaborative frameworks that align the interests of many stakeholders. International frameworks like the UN Sustainable Development Goals provide guiding principles, but their effectiveness depends on consistent funding, localized action, and political will.

Egmont Key's significance extends beyond its shores. It is a lens through which to examine broader discourses on heritage management, climate resilience, and the intersections of history, culture, and the environment.

References Cited

Ambrosino, James, and Kelly Driscoll. 2007. *Mapping of the Fort Dade Historic Transportation Network, Egmont Key, Hillsborough County Florida*, Vol. 1. Prepared for US Fish and Wildlife Service. Panamerican Consultants, Memphis, Tennessee.

American Council on Historic Preservation (ACHP). 2025. Section 106 Emergency Provisions and the Executive Order Declaring a National Energy Emergency. https://www.achp.gov/taxonomy/term/26, accessed October 4, 2025.

Ballingrud, D. 1999. Egmont Key Explosion: Fort's Hall Goes Down Fighting. *Tampa Bay Times*, May 21. https://www.tampabay.com/archive/1999/05/25/egmont-key-explosion-fort-s-hall-goes-down-fighting/, accessed July 5, 2025.

Chesnes, M. 2024. Man Lands Helicopter Amid Protected Bird Nests on Egmont Key. *Tampa Bay Times*, May 31. https://www.tampabay.com/news/environment/2024/05/31/egmont-key-state-park-helicopter-landing-birds/, accessed June 15, 2025.

Cole, R. M. 1986. "Egmont Key," March 19, 1986. Transcript of a talk given at the Membership Meeting of the Manatee County Historical Society. Manuscript on File, Eaton Room, Manatee County Public Library.

Di Giovine, M. A. 2018. The Heritage-Scape: Origins, Theoretical Interventions, and Critical Reception of a Model for Understanding UNESCO's World Heritage Program. *Via Tourism Review* 13. https://doi.org/10.4000/viatourism/2017

Egmont Key Alliance (EKA). 2025. Restore, Preserve, Protect: We Are the Egmont Key Alliance. https://www.egmontkey.org/, accessed October 1, 2025.
Florida Public Archaeology Network (FPAN). N.d. Documents. https://www.fpan.us/about/documents/, accessed June 15, 2025.
Florida Trust for Historic Preservation. 2025. Florida's 11 to Save. https://floridatrust.org/11-to-%20save/, accessed March 31, 2025.
Friends of the Tampa Bay National Wildlife Refuges. 2022. Where Birds Can Be Birds—The Remarkable Refuges of Tampa Bay. YouTube, June 8. https://www.youtube.com/watch?v=Cp_l_-ld-m8, accessed January 10, 2026.
Hall, C. Michael, Tim Baird, Michael James, and Yael Ram. 2016. Climate Change and Cultural Heritage: Conservation and Heritage Tourism in the Anthropocene. *Journal of Heritage Tourism* 11(1): 10–24. https://doi.org/10.1080/1743873X.2015.1082573.
Hare, K. 2022. Lighthouse Preservationist and Egmont Key Champion Was a "Fierce Defender of History." *Tampa Bay Times*, March 21. https://www.tampabay.com/life-culture/2022/03/21/lighthouse-preservationist-and-egmont-key-champion-was-a-fierce-defender-of-history/, accessed March 31, 2025.
Higgins, N. 2022. Changing Climate; Changing Life—Climate Change and Indigenous Intangible Cultural Heritage. *Laws* 11(3), 47. https://doi.org/10.3390/laws11030047.
International Centre for the Study of the Preservation and Restoration of Cultural Property (ICCROM). 2025. Showcasing Innovation in Disaster Risk Reduction and Preparedness for Cultural Heritage. https://www.iccrom.org/news/call-abstracts-showcasing-innovation-disaster-risk-reduction-and-preparedness-cultural, accessed June 15, 2025.
International Council on Monuments and Sites (ICOMOS). 2025. World Heritage. https://www.ICOMOS.org/world-heritage/, accessed June 15, 2025.
James, S. R., Jr., C. C. Pearson, and M. C. Krivor. 2006. Historic Assessment, Remote Sensing Survey and Diver Evaluations at Egmont Key, Hillsborough, Florida. Prepared for the US Army Corps of Engineers, Jacksonville District. Panamerican Consultants, Memphis, Tennessee.
Manatee County Public Library. 1996. MCHS-A-0053 Baker, Robert; on Egmont Key 5-15-1996; Eaton Room, Egmont Key, General file; McCall, 6; McCarthy, 95; Sarles, 27–28; Stafford, 26–27.
Miller, S. E., and E. J. Murray. 2018. Heritage Monitoring Scouts: Engaging the Public to Monitor Sites at Risk Across Florida. *Conservation and Management of Archaeological Sites* 20(4): 234–260. https://doi.org/10.1080/13505033.2018.1516455.
Neglia, Grazia, Mariarosaria Angrisano, Ippolita Mecca, and Francesco Fabbrocino. 2024. Cultural Heritage at Risk in World Conflicts: Digital Tools' Contribution to Its Preservation. *Heritage* 7(11): 6343–6365. https://doi.org/10.3390/heritage7110297.
NOAA. N.d. National Marine Sanctuary Frequently Asked Questions. https://sanctuaries.noaa.gov/about/faqs/, accessed March 31, 2025.
Parcak, S. 2019. *Archaeology from Space: How the Future Shapes Our Past*. Macmillan+ ORM.

Sanchez, R. 2025. *Egmont Key: Stories from Eyewitnesses to History*. Self-published.

Stafford, John W. 1980. Egmont Key: Sentinel of Tampa Bay. *Tampa Bay History* 2(1), article 4. https://digitalcommons.usf.edu/cgi/viewcontent.cgi?article=1037&context=tampabayhistory.

Take MAR. 2024. We are MAR: More Action for Regeneration. https://www.takemar.org/, accessed June 15, 2025. (Take MAR changed its name to MAR in late 2025.)

Thompson, D. H., and C. Thompson. 2012. *Egmont Key: A History*. History Press, Charleston, South Carolina.

United Nations Educational, Scientific and Cultural Organization (UNESCO). 2003. Tex of the Convention for the Safeguarding of Intangible Cultural Heritage. https://ich.UNESCO.org/en/convention, accessed June 15, 2025.

United Nations. N.d. The 17 Goals. https://sdgs.un.org/goals, accessed June 15, 2025.

US Fish and Wildlife Service (USFWS). 2010. Comprehensive Conservation Plan: Tampa Bay Refuges. May. Southeast Region, Atlanta, GA. https://iris.fws.gov/APPS/ServCat/Reference/Profile/168154, accessed June 15, 2025.

US Fish and Wildlife Service (USFWS). N.d. Comprehensive Conservation Plans. https://www.fws.gov/library/collections/comprehensive-conservation-plans, accessed July 15, 2025.

Zarley, A., S. Witte, and G. Burgess. 2016. Heritage At-Risk: Vulnerability of Cultural Resources along Florida's Coast to Sea Level Rise and Hurricanes. University of Wisconsin-Madison Geography, pp. 1–34. http://digital.library.wisc.edu/1793/74999.

5

Footprints in the Sand

Building a Sustainable Tourism Future for Egmont Key

BROOKE HANSEN AND LAURA K. HARRISON

From Militarism to Tourism: The Intertwined Past and Present of Egmont Key

When viewed with a long lens, the small island at the mouth of Tampa Bay has always been a destination for visitors to partake in a variety of activities. This enigmatic island has been a beacon for many, from the early Indigenous inhabitants who camped and fished there, including the ancestors of the Seminole Tribe of Florida, to the many modern-day tourists who enjoy the island's beauty and mystery. The military interests in Egmont Key became a prime factor in visitation for several hundred years as the Spanish, English, and then Americans jockeyed to claim and name the key. The Tampa Bay Pilots Association took up residence there in the mid-1800s to guide the ever-increasing maritime traffic into Tampa Bay, which today includes all the cruise ships coming into the Port of Tampa. A lighthouse was built in 1848 that began an era of lighthouse keepers, their families, and visitors that has lasted into the twenty-first century. It was the threat of war at the end of the nineteenth century, however, that changed the function, landscape, and purpose of Egmont Key dramatically and brought the military, followed by many other government agencies from the US Coast Guard to the US Department of the Interior.

The island's history of government interventions reflects shifts in its role, from a bustling military town and site of target practice to a protected historical landmark, National Wildlife Refuge overseen by US Fish and Wildlife Service, and popular tourist destination only accessible by boat. Today's visitors, numbering well over 200,000, ramble around the massive concrete ruins of gun batteries and the ghost town of Fort Dade while admiring the historic lighthouse, glistening beaches, turquoise waters, and abundant wildlife. Egmont Key is home to a unique gopher tortoise population and many species of birds and marine animals, making it an attractive nature tourism location.

Military tourism is most certainly a draw for visitors to the island today. It in fact cannot be ignored as the ruins of Fort Dade are everywhere and the one restored building, the Guardhouse, contains a museum with interpretive displays (though the building is rarely opened and was damaged by the hurricanes of the fall of 2024). Fort Dade was established in 1898 as part of the US coastal defense strategy in response to the short-lived Spanish-American War. Despite not ever being directly involved in the war and being decommissioned in 1923, the fort remained under military control throughout the mid-twentieth century and saw intermittent use for target practice and military drills during World War II. In the aftermath of the Great War, the US government recognized the need to protect and preserve Egmont Key's historical and environmental significance, despite a landscape littered with remnants of buildings and military debris.

While the Spanish-American War initiated a new era for Egmont Key, it also coincided with the rise of tourism in Tampa Bay, which went from a steamy outpost with tales of alligators, renegades, and brothels to a desired destination with the help of early icons. Vicente Martinez Ybor founded Ybor City, which, by 1900, became the cigar capital of the world and is still one of the most popular tourist destinations in Tampa today. Henry B. Plant was laying the infrastructure in the form of railroads for commerce and tourism that reached Tampa in 1884. He also built the Tampa Bay Hotel, an iconic symbol of Tampa with its gleaming spires and turrets. Plant's grand plan was to establish Tampa Bay as a premiere tourist destination, a vision that has certainly come to pass with 27 million visitors in 2023.

The Tampa Bay Hotel is the famed site where Lieutenant Colonel Theodore "Teddy" Roosevelt and the Rough Riders took up residence in 1898 to serve as a volunteer cavalry regiment during the Spanish-American War (Knetsch and Wynne 2011). Tampa was the main embarkation point for US troops headed to Cuba. The Spanish-American War was sometimes jokingly referred to as the "Rocking Chair War" because of the scene at the Tampa Bay Hotel, a luxury resort turned into military headquarters, where Roosevelt and the officers spent time lounging on the hotel's grand verandas in rocking chairs, waiting for orders to be shipped to Cuba. There were long delays due to poor planning, miscommunication, and overcrowding. Well-dressed officers relaxed in rocking chairs while enlisted men camped in the sweltering heat nearby, a surreal moment in military history that was captured in photographs depicting a scene when war was imminent, but it looked more like a vacation retreat for some.

Today the Tampa Bay Hotel is part of the campus for the University of Tampa and houses the Henry B. Plant Museum where photos of Roosevelt and the Rough Riders can be viewed. Visitors still inquire if Teddy Roosevelt slept in one of the rooms (Knetsch and Wynne 2011). The Museum also presents the history of military planning during the war and famous figures who visited the area during the 1898 yellow fever outbreak, including Clara Barton, who was briefly quarantined at Egmont Key. It is rumored that Teddy Roosevelt himself camped at Egmont Key en route to Cuba in mid-June 1898, but evidence of this has not been found. It is interesting to note early on the intertwining of militarism and tourism in Tampa that would punctuate much of the existence of Egmont Key as well.

After the military periods of the 1800s and World War II, the transition to tourism was well under way. By the mid-twentieth century, tourism began to boom along the Gulf Coast. The 1960s ushered in ever-increasing numbers of tourists and development to Florida. "As the 1960's drew to a close, it became apparent that the fantastic growth tourist business in Florida in that decade surpassed that of any other resort area in the world. In 1960, the tourist total was approximately 10,800,000; in 1969, this more than doubled" (Wright 1970: 302). By 2024, Florida tourism was bringing in 143 million visitors a year.

Egmont Key, with its idyllic location, became a site of interest during the tourist boom of the 1960s and '70s with some wanting to shield it from impact. To protect the island from the pressures of development and tourism and retain space for wildlife, the Egmont Key National Wildlife Refuge (NWR) was established in 1974 (US Fish and Wildlife Service [USFWS] n.d.). The 328-acre refuge includes 97 acres of sanctuaries that are closed to the public year-round. This move was part of a broader effort at the time to conserve critical coastal and marine environments across the United States. The refuge designation helped to curb further development that would impact the island's natural resources and historical structures. To further these efforts, in 1978, William Thurston, the chief preservation planner of the Florida Division of Archives, History, and Records Management, filed a historic designation for the entire island of

Egmont Key and it was placed on the National Register of Historic Places in 1978. This foreshadowed further involvement by the state in efforts to protect and preserve Egmont Key (discussed at length in Chapter 4).

While these measures prevented tourism development in the form of resorts, restaurants, and marinas, they also made the island a desirable location to visit. Throngs of tourists and locals flocked to Egmont Key's shores throughout the 1970s and 1980s, drawn by its rich heritage, natural beauty, and remoteness. The island's transition to a tourist destination was facilitated by the expanding urbanized Florida coastline, increasing numbers of people with boats, and the overall uniqueness of the tourism experience that blended the ruins of historic structures with long expanses of beach and excellent birdwatching. The National Wildlife Refuge status was intended to provide a framework for sustainable tourism practices, ensuring that visitor activities did not negatively impact the island's ecosystems. However, with little oversight even after attaining National Wildlife Refuge status, people knew they could travel to Egmont Key and partake of many activities unsupervised. Congressman Sam Gibbons, longtime visitor to the island with his family, began lobbying hard in the mid-1980s to protect the island with multiple preservation efforts that included coordination with the US Fish and Wildlife Service (USFWS) and Florida Park Service (Sanchez 2025). He orchestrated a well-known cleanup of the island in 1988 that involved multiple agencies and community groups in an effort that was unprecedented and yielded 70 tons of trash being removed from the island.

In 1989, through the efforts of Sam Gibbons, part of the northern end of Egmont Key became a Florida State Park with the promise of on-site park rangers to monitor the island. This was seen as a major victory in the stewardship of Egmont Key. Ten years later, the state threatened to cut funding and close Egmont Key State Park, harkening back to the old "Wild West" days. In newspaper coverage from the time Barbara Schmidt, a historian of the island, stated, "It would be a tremendous loss to turn that back into a party island. During spring break it takes every volunteer and park rangers to keep that place under control and keep young people from coming out there from destroying everything" (Salinero 2009: para. 15).

During the late 1980s, the US Coast Guard was preparing to leave the island and automate the last manned lighthouse in Florida. At that time, Susan Kessel of the Southwest Florida Water Management District was quoted as saying, "When the Coast Guard leaves, the last symbol of authority on the island will be gone. You can already find beer cans and old flip-flops all over the island. We've found old refrigerators out there, even an old boat trailer. Without the Coast Guard out there to watch over the place, the environment of that little island is going to take it on the chin" (Orlando Sentinel 1988: paras. 6–7). This is a recurring theme throughout Egmont Key's history: who is watching the island?

Throughout the twentieth century, tourism on Egmont Key sought to balance public interest with environmental protection, but the site has been plagued by overtourism and lack of sufficient management, topics that are explored more fully in chapter 4. Restrictions on development have helped protect the island's fragile ecosystems and historical sites. Yet the incredible appeal of Egmont Key, coupled with a lack of regulations on visitation, have negatively affected the island's flora, fauna, and historic sites. Nesting grounds are often disturbed by tourists, and the heritage sites fall further into ruin, falling victim to poor maintenance and vandalism. The twenty-first century has seen a continuation of these themes with the increased presence of sea-level rise and more virulent storms, such as the back-to-back hurricanes of the fall of 2024 that dealt the island infrastructure and ecosystems a devastating blow.

Tourism Today at Egmont Key: From Quarantine to Closure

Egmont Key transitioned from a government military site and quarantine camp to a public park in the latter part of the twentieth century. It is interesting to note that in the twenty-first-century quarantine touched the island yet again, but in this case, it was for those looking for outdoor recreation during the COVID-19 outbreak from 2019 to 2021. During the height of the pandemic, particularly before vaccines were made available, people were encouraged to congregate with others only in outdoor spaces. Tourism at indoor locales such as museums and aquariums dropped off or was forbidden, while it spiked at outdoor destinations, especially in Florida, which had fewer restrictions than other states. The number of visitors at Egmont Key during this period exceeded pre-pandemic levels, as people desperate to connect with nature and other people flocked to the island, overwhelming the few Florida Park Service staff assigned to monitor activities.

In the post-pandemic period, after 2021, tourism has boomed at Egmont Key, and Florida in general with over 143 million visitors in 2024. People now travel to the island with personal boats, rented boats and jet skis, ferries, charters, and even a wandering kayak sometimes. Hubbard's Marina runs the official

Figure 5.1. Passengers disembarking from a Hubbard's Marina ferry trip to Egmont Key during the pandemic in 2020, overseen by Captain Josh "Zip" Zipser. By permission of Brooke Hansen.

ferry to the island multiple times a day (see 5.1.) New marine tour companies were founded that focus only on excursions to Egmont Key. There are over two dozen marine tour operators taking patrons to Egmont Key with little or no oversight regarding the education given to people before disembarking into the island with its delicate ecosystems and vulnerable wildlife. No permits are necessary if the tour boats do not land on the island. They are able to come within feet of the sand and unload their guests who can then roam the island. During the summer months, the boats are side to side and stacked tightly along the west and east side of the island. One visitor, who maintains a blog called *Florida Rambler*, noted (Gross 2025: paras. 1–3):

> I had always imagined Egmont Key, an island in the mouth of Tampa Bay, to be a place far from the crowds: remote, wild and natural, and it has always intrigued me.
>
> We loved our day on Egmont Key, but it wasn't what we expected. It's a popular destination for people arriving both by ferry and private boat, so it isn't empty . . . and it is far from deserted. . . . But be prepared, because while plenty of people may be on the island, Egmont Key is remote. It has no cars, no drinking water and no bathrooms. You must arrive by boat and, no, you can't camp overnight.
>
> If you take a ferry, your ticket will be $40 to $70 depending on which you choose, so this isn't an inexpensive outing.

With its nature tourism appeal, fragile ecosystems, consistent overcrowding, and lack of enough supervision to monitor tourism impacts, a sustainable tourism approach is necessary and long overdue for this small island at the mouth of Tampa Bay. By adopting sustainable tourism practices, we can begin to create a future for Egmont Key that honors the island's dynamic and sometimes painful history and contextualizes it within its remarkable natural surroundings. This is the perspective we took in the Egmont Key Project that commenced in 2018. Through the Participatory Action Research framework that guided the project (discussed at length in Chapter 6), we had many discussions with land managers and nonprofit conservation groups working on the island, including the Egmont Key Alliance and their president at the time Richard Sanchez, who partnered with us on many projects. In addition, we taught classes and organized training workshops (most of which occurred on-island) on sustainable tourism, interpretation, and heritage at risk. We have involved hundreds of students, some as year-long interns, and have logged countless hours on Egmont Key as researchers and observers of tourism.

Some dramatic events happened toward the end of 2024 that brought the need for a sustainable tourism approach into sharp focus, especially to evaluate the impacts of climate change and how to foster resilience on this small island. Hurricanes Helene and Milton delivered a one-two punch to Egmont Key in September and October, destroying many parts of the island, littering debris everywhere, and precipitating the closure of the island to visitors. These powerful storms, among the strongest ever recorded as climate change fueled their strength, did what the global COVID-19 pandemic could not: force the closure of the island in late 2024. Sustainable tourism can be a guiding philosophy to help Egmont Key build back better from the devastation these storms wrought.

What Is Sustainable Tourism?

Sustainable tourism was one of the central themes of the Egmont Key Project from the outset, in addition to addressing heritage at risk with digital technologies and recovering invisible histories. UN Tourism, a leading international agency, defines sustainable tourism as "tourism that takes full account of its current and future economic, social and environmental impacts, addressing the needs of visitors, the industry, the environment and host communities" (UN Tourism 2025: para.1). Put simply, sustainable tourism aims to support the triple bottom line of people, planet, and prosperity. While many assume that sustainable tourism is just about environmental issues such as carbon reductions, biodiversity preservation, and pollution reduction, the human lens is equally as important. The people part of the tripartite agenda includes those working in tourism and the cultures upon which most tourism is based, including cultural heritage.

Sustainable tourism is now the guiding framework for whole countries like Slovenia, Australia, Palau, and most European countries. These regions have robust government-run programs for assistance with sustainable practices, certifications, and awards that have been aligned with global standards set by the Global Sustainable Tourism Council and other leading organizations such as the World Sustainable Hospitality Alliance, World Travel and Tourism Council, and UN Tourism. All these efforts are in sync with the United Nations Sustainable Development Goals (SDGs), around which many sustainable tourism efforts have rallied, such as the Tourism for SDGs platform (United Nations World Tourism Organization n.d.).

Formed in 2015 as a new platform rising out of the UN Millennium Development Goals, the SDGs entail a:

> Shared blueprint for peace and prosperity for people and the planet. . . . At its heart are the 17 Sustainable Development Goals (SDGs), which are an urgent call for action by all countries—developed and developing—in a global partnership. They recognize that ending poverty and other deprivations must go hand-in-hand with strategies that improve health and education, reduce inequality, and spur economic growth—all while tackling climate change and working to preserve our oceans and forests. [United Nations n.d.: para. 1]

Recognizing that tourism is one of the world's largest industries, the 17 goals include specific targets focused on tourism and all have direct applicability to Egmont Key. These include:

SDG 8.9 is part of Decent Work and Economic Growth. This target is specifically about promoting sustainable tourism and encouraging policies to create jobs and promote local culture and products through tourism. This is relevant to Egmont Key as sustainable tourism could support local jobs (e.g., through heritage interpretation and conservation tours) while preserving cultural heritage.

SDG 11.4 can be found under the umbrella of Sustainable Cities and Communities and aims to strengthen efforts to safeguard the world's cultural and natural heritage. This has been a main SDG from the inception of the Egmont Key Project and is directly applicable to Egmont Key's eroding military ruins, lighthouse, Indigenous history, and endangered species, all of which are at risk from climate change and overtourism.

SDG 12.b focuses on developing sustainable tourism monitoring tools to assess tourism impacts. This might include conducting carrying capacity studies, evaluating human-species interactions, or even just getting a better count of the actual visitors to the island. Egmont Key needs improved visitor monitoring systems, data collection, and management plans to reduce human impact on wildlife and fragile habitats.

SDG 14.7 specifically focuses on protecting Life Below Water and how to responsibly reap economic benefits from marine resources, especially for small island developing states (SIDS) and coastal areas. Egmont Key could be an example of sustainable marine-based tourism like eco-friendly boating and wildlife viewing. The reduction of plastics could also be encouraged to meet the metrics of this SDG target as well as SDG 12 which specifically targets the plastics crisis.

While strong in many other parts of the world, sustainable tourism and the SDGs are less well known in the United States, perhaps because there is no ministry of tourism as other countries have that often lead these efforts. There are notable policies and examples, however, such as the National Travel and Tourism Strategy developed by the US Department of Commerce. While there are four pillars of the national agenda (including promoting the United States as a tourist destination), the fourth one is to Foster Resilient and Sustainable Travel and Tourism with one overarching goal and seven specific strategies, all of which are highly relevant to Egmont Key (US Department of Commerce 2022: 39):

GOAL: Reduce travel and tourism's contributions to climate change and build a travel and tourism sector that is resilient to natural disasters, public health threats, and the impacts of climate change. Build a sustainable sector that integrates protecting natural resources, supporting the tourism economy, and ensuring equitable development.

STRATEGY 1: Ensure underserved communities can receive disaster assistance and develop greater institutional capacity.

STRATEGY 2: Support communities in resiliency planning.

STRATEGY 3: Reduce travel and tourism's carbon emissions.

STRATEGY 4: Support nature-based solutions for climate mitigation and adaptation.

STRATEGY 5: Protect natural assets to ensure travel and tourism resources for the future.

STRATEGY 6: Build a sustainable tourism ecosystem in the United States.

STRATEGY 7: Provide timely data on climate-related events and natural disasters.

Other noteworthy efforts in the United States include actions by destination marketing organizations (DMOs) to transition their scope of practice from just marketing or selling destinations to managing and even stewarding them. The Hawai'i Tourism Authority is of note here and could provide a blueprint for Florida and other locations. They legislatively dismantled their statewide DMO and resurrected it as a Destination Marketing and Management Organization (DMMO) to include the management piece along with the marketing. More than that, they refocused their organization on stewardship, cultural inclusion and celebration, and sustainable and regenerative tourism. The latter concept takes sustainability one step further to focus "on the net benefit of the visitor economy to a destination, looking at the social and cultural benefits" (Hawai'i Tourism Authority n.d.: 3). Destination stewardship is becoming more of a focus globally and has made it way to Florida Gulf Coast with both DMOs and conservation organizations increasingly promoting this powerful lens (Hansen 2022), including Visit St. Pete/Clearwater and Keep Pinellas Beautiful.

A shift in thinking has occurred globally when it comes to sustainable and regenerative tourism prompted by COVID-19. Before the pandemic brought tourism to a grinding halt in 2020, tourism numbers had reached an all-time high in many destinations, including Florida. Record numbers of people were traveling, and many regions of the world had become dependent on tourism as the main economic driver. With the economic benefits also came numerous negative effects such as overtourism, strain on vulnerable ecosystems, massive amounts of emissions from travel by air and cruise ship, pollution, and excess waste (Dodds and Butler 2024; Lenzen et al. 2018; Wood 2017). Tourism's long hiatus from 2020 to 2022 provided a space for many aspects of one of the world's largest industries to be re-evaluated. The cessation of air pollution, animals reinhabiting once busy tourism sites, and reflections on places getting a break from people gave many food for thought (Coll 2020; Cooper and Nagel 2021). Movements to build back better gained momentum (Spenceley et al. 2021). The World Economic Forum, in their 2021 Travel & Tourism Development Index Report (2022), stated that "building back better" is vital for travel and tourism to reboot with inclusivity, sustainability, and resilience as key components. This has become known as Build Back Better (BBB) in sustainable tourism (Nhamo at al. 2020), although one could argue for a Build Forward Better (BFB) credo as the point is to not go back to business as usual but forge a new sustainable and regenerative tourism paradigm.

The BBB (or BFB) movement in global tourism emphasizes restructuring the industry in a way that promotes sustainability, resilience, and inclusivity. Key goals include reducing carbon emissions and plastic waste, enhancing community engagement, and ensuring that tourism development benefits local economies. Other practices often highlighted include promoting eco-friendly travel options, supporting local businesses, and protecting natural and cultural heritage sites. This approach aims not only to recover the industry but also to transform it into a more responsible and future-proof sector (Gössling et al. 2021). Every major survey of travelers since 2019 has indicated that they want more sustainable options in travel. All of this applies to Egmont Key, which in some ways has become a canary in the coal mine when it comes to why we need a BFB sustainable tourism approach. Tourism is predicated on Egmont Key's unique cultural heritage, white sand beaches, endangered species, and island experiences. With half the island already gone from the effects of climate change and other anthropogenic forces, the sands where visitors recreate are literally washing away, with the 2024 hurricanes taking another bite out of the disappearing island. The remaining beaches are often littered with trash washing in on the west side from the Gulf and the east side from Tampa Bay. Building better forward means documenting and addressing these issues.

Egmont Key: A Case Study for Sustainable Tourism

The sustainable tourism paradigm is highly applicable to Egmont Key, and in fact is much needed. It is an island microcosm representing the challenges facing tourism globally. Issues plaguing the small key include overtourism, inadequate signage, ineffective interpretation, vandalism, infrastructural issues, waste management (there are no bathrooms or trash receptacles), and the lack of consistent Wi-Fi connectivity. Land managers report frequent incidences of visitors trespassing in the restricted National Wildlife Refuge area, and wildlife harassment is an ongoing struggle during the nesting seasons for birds and sea turtles. With increased tourism pressures and the continual loss of land, these species may disappear from the island. Some took a major hit with the of hurricanes of 2024 leading to reports of many dead gopher tortoises, a federally protected species. As of 2025, the full impact of the storms on the island's species has not been completed.

The gopher tortoise is an appropriate metaphor for Egmont Key. Like this island itself, it is endangered and its popularity with tourists leaves it at risk. Visitors, delighted by their frequent presence, often get too close and sometimes try to feed the slowly rambling reptiles, despite many signs placed around the island warning people not to touch them (see 5.2). We have witnessed the

Figure 5.2. One of many signs at Egmont Key warning visitors not to touch or harm the gopher tortoises, a third-degree felony. By permission of Brooke Hansen.

tortoises attempting to eat candy wrappers that visitors carelessly left at the picnic grounds. The gopher tortoise population at Egmont Key is considered unique and significant for several reasons. They are an insular population, meaning they were geographically isolated from mainland tortoise populations. If one is sick and has to be taken for care on the mainland, it cannot be returned back lest it introduces new diseases. Because of this, we have sometimes dubbed Egmont Key the "Galapagos of Tampa Bay" and in fact former Park Ranger Dave Ferdon did refer to the island as a mini-Galapagos (Thompson and Thompson 2012). Many have wondered how the turtles got there in the first place (both the gopher and the box turtle), given the distance from the mainland. Rita Youngman (Seminole) suggested that early Indigenous inhabitants may have brought them out there as an additional food source so there may be a connection with the ancestors of the Seminole Tribe of Florida adding to the tortoise's mystique (Roa 2025).

The gopher tortoise population on Egmont Key has historically been among the densest in Florida. As a keystone species, gopher tortoises dig burrows that provide shelter for over 350 other species. On Egmont Key, these burrows are critical for wildlife that may not have many other shelter options due to the island's limited vegetation and structures. The gopher tortoises of Egmont Key are also at high risk due to climate change. Egmont Key is rapidly eroding due to sea-level rise and storms thus reducing habitat for the tortoises and the species that depend on them. This makes the population an important indicator of climate vulnerability. The tortoises at Egmont Key have seen many storms through the years and have had positive survival rates as they create burrows with a chamber that can hold an air pocket until waters recede. Hurricane Helene in 2024 however brought record storm surge that may have overwhelmed the small creatures. Interestingly, and perhaps a metaphor of resilience, there are reports of dozens of gopher tortoises that were swept by the storm surge from Egmont Key to the mainland at Fort De Soto Park and Pinellas County Beaches (Tracy 2025). For a creature that is purported to not be able to swim, this in an incredible feat indeed.

SUSTAINABILITY AND COMPREHENSIVE CONSERVATION PLANNING: FROM CLIMATE VULNERABILITY TO VISITOR SERVICES

There are many issues that need to be addressed with a sustainable tourism approach, including the climate vulnerability at Egmont Key. Coastal tourism is a huge sector of global tourism and the centerpiece of Florida tourism. It is also the area most vulnerable to climate change threats, especially sea-level rise and the impact of hurricanes. Given the prominence of human occupation along the west Gulf Coast, adaptation and resiliency planning are major concerns and are being addressed at municipal levels across the region. Tourism is embedded in these municipalities (cities and counties), but more specific planning for the resilience of this sector is needed. Beach replenishment and renourishment have been ongoing for many years at Pinellas County beaches and at Egmont Key (discussed at greater length in Chapters 4 and 7), but a more holistic resilience plan for the tourism industry has not been conducted nor an evaluation of the impact of loss of coastline on the tourism industry. The Tampa Bay Regional Planning Council's Regional Resiliency Action Plan, created for a seven-county area along the Gulf Coast, scarcely mentions tourism, the area's number one industry (Tampa Bay Regional Planning Council 2023).

Climate change and its effects on Egmont Key have been included in other planning documents, specifically the Tampa Bay Refuges Comprehensive Conservation Plan (CCP). Published by the US Department of the Interior Fish and Wildlife Service Southeast Region in 2010, the lengthy document includes many important sections to ensure conservation and sustainable tourism across the three National Wildlife Refuges in the area: Egmont Key, Pinellas, and Passage Key (USFWS 2010). The CCP included biological and ecosystems assessments, an evaluation of visitor services, public comments, and proposed plans of action. Many pages were devoted to climate change and its impacts, not only to the viability of the island itself but also to the species that call it home. It is projected that bird species could decrease by almost a quarter and that sea-level rise will further endanger an already threatened ecosystem.

The CCP also mentions the need to address carrying capacity but lays out no clear plan to conduct a study on how much public use the island can sustain or how many commercial tour operators can reasonably be accommodated. Carrying capacity refers to an estimate of the number of users a recreation resource or facility can accommodate and still provide a high-quality experience and preserve the natural integrity of the site. Park rangers on the island have reported an increase in tourism during and after the pandemic, sometimes overwhelming the one full-time park ranger to keep eyes on multiple parts of the island. Rangers report constant issues of trespass into the portion of the refuge that is closed to visitors. There have been no studies of how visitor numbers affect the experience at the island either. To carry out such research, funds need to be allocated and partners, such as academic institutions, can be brought in to facilitate the on the ground research component. First, the range of activities at Egmont Key needs to be evaluated. These include beach use, swimming, snorkeling, diving, kayaking, boating, fishing, and hiking. Then the land and water use requirements for each activity relative to available resources needs to be determined to evaluate the environment's capacity for recreational activities without sustaining damage. This is an important step in preventing overtourism and maintaining balance between native wildlife communities and human visitors. Exceeding carrying capacity also puts the built heritage, in this case the remnants of historic Fort Dade, at risk from further damage.

The 2010 CCP also has multiple sections on improving visitor services with bathrooms, better interpretation, and more staff, although they state that they have no Visitor Services Plan. In the comment section of the plan, many people expressed the immediate need for restroom facilities on Egmont Key. Restrooms on Egmont Key should be a top priority with over 200,000 visitors each year and growing. Self-composting toilets might be ideal but may not be feasible due to the possibility of tropical storm or hurricane tidal surges. While the CCP indeed states that restroom facilities are needed on Egmont Key, it also mentions that proposed projects will only be implemented based on the availability of limited fiscal resources. Given that the report was published in 2010 and fifteen years have gone by and there are still no bathrooms at Egmont Key, it seems that fiscal issues need to be addressed by USFWS. Other comments for the 2010 plan encourage USFWS to explore the implementation of green energy solutions (e.g., solar panels for electricity, hot water, desalination, etc.) and that all the refuges should work toward being carbon neutral. It is disappointing that some of the great recommendations that would have enhanced sustainability at Egmont Key were not able to be implemented and the CCP has not been updated since 2010, leaving gaps in the ability to promote sustainable and responsible tourism on the island by the primary land managers.

TOURISM, RED TIDE, AND PLASTIC POLLUTION AT EGMONT KEY

There are of course many tourism issues to be addressed at Egmont Key, from the aforementioned biodiversity vulnerability and carrying capacity issues to problems related to widespread environmental threats such as red tide and plastic pollution. Red tide is a harmful algal bloom caused by the rapid growth of *Karenia brevis*, a microscopic alga that produces toxins harmful to marine life and humans. At Egmont Key, red tide can lead to massive fish kills, disrupt coastal ecosystems, and reduce visitation due to unpleasant odors and respiratory irritation for beachgoers.

Although red tide has been affecting Florida for decades, recent blooms are some of the worst in documented history, including the 2018 infestation (Weisberg et al., 2019) and the 2021 bloom. The 2018 red tide along the Florida Gulf Coast beaches lasted for months and accounted for significant economic losses from tourism decline and business closures (Bechard, 2019). State and local agencies have since mobilized to find better methods to track it and warn the public about the health issues. Island visitors can now consult the FWC Daily Sample Map (https://gis.myfwc.com/redtidecurrentstatus/) to find updates on locations with the highest concentrations and respiratory alerts so they can avoid those places and choose areas with less contamination. The algal infiltrations are likely exacerbated by climate change and agricultural chemical contamination, such as the Piney Point gypsum stack spill of March 2021, which released over 200 million gallons of contaminated water containing nitrogen and phosphorus into Tampa Bay (Bausback and Miller 2021). After the Piney Point spill, one of the worst red tides in decades ensued and surrounded the waters at Egmont Key. Monitoring is key to documenting the problem and mobilizing solutions. In addition to water samples collected by multiple agencies, surface monitoring is also important to assess the scope of the issue and its impact on tourism.

Another major pollutant found on Egmont Key and throughout the region's waters and beaches is plastic. A University of South Florida research study estimates over 4 billion pieces of microplastics in Tampa Bay (McEachern et al. 2019). The pandemic worsened this situation with a shortage of solid waste and recycling workers and the influx of personal protective equipment (PPE) into the watershed. There have been many reports of increases in plastic pollution around the globe prompted by factors related to COVID-19 (Abbasi et al. 2020; Alfonso et al. 2021; Silva et al. 2021). During the pandemic, members of the tourism industry from the Pinellas County beaches region noted some of the worst plastic pollution they have seen in years at locations such as Clearwater Beach, a repeat winner of the best beach in America. A weeklong cleanup during October 2021, organized by Ocean Allies, Amplify Clearwater, Visit St. Pete/Clearwater, and the Florida Restaurant and Lodging Association, among others, produced over 6,000 pounds of litter. We had a group of students from USF participate, and they picked up over 1,000 cigarette butts in less than two hours. After the hurricanes of 2024, the beaches of Egmont Key were littered with plastic debris, including many garbage bins, parts of boats, furniture, house insulation, and other items that were from the mainland, with some of it attributed to the wreckage of infrastructure on the island itself (discussed in detail in Chapter 8). If left unabated, the accumulation of synthetic debris will render Egmont Key and the Gulf Coast beaches unappealing to both locals and visitors, not to mention uninhabitable to the marine and terrestrial life found within.

As part of the Egmont Key Project featured in this book, we conducted a pilot project that used geoinformatics technologies in the form of terrestrial scanning and 3D capture to assess the scope of plastic pollution and red tide at Egmont Key in 2020 when both pollutants were battering Egmont's shore with dead fish and copious amounts of plastic debris (Hansen et al. 2022). While many digital capture devices and platforms are now available, this pilot project used the Matterport 360 to visually capture beach pollution at Egmont Key. With Matterport as one of the more prominent 3D technologies used in the real estate industry, with a recent push for adoption in the tourism and hospitality sectors, it seemed a logical choice to test it for applicability in documenting and conveying sustainability issues at a popular tourist site. The Pro 2 camera and iPhone 11 were used for the scans and 360 captures at Egmont Key. Benefits of the platform include its ease of transport, affordability, and annotation capabilities with tags (called Mattertags) and 360 captures that can be inserted into the virtual models.

The student interns took 3D scans of beach sites while also collecting as much trash as possible to conduct an inventory and typology of the collection (see Table 5.1). They took the base model created with the Matterport platform and annotated it with Mattertags to provide information about red tide and

Table 5.1. Trash Found During a Two-Hour Cleanup Event at Egmont Key

Types of trash	*Number of items found*
Rope	2
Sanitary napkins	1
Aluminum cans	6
Face masks	1
Plastic bottles	40
Plastic flossers	8
Foam	50
Smoking debris	250
Alcoholic beverage bottles	18
Plastic straws	12
Plastic cutlery	3
Chapstick	4
Bottle caps	12
Fishing items	18

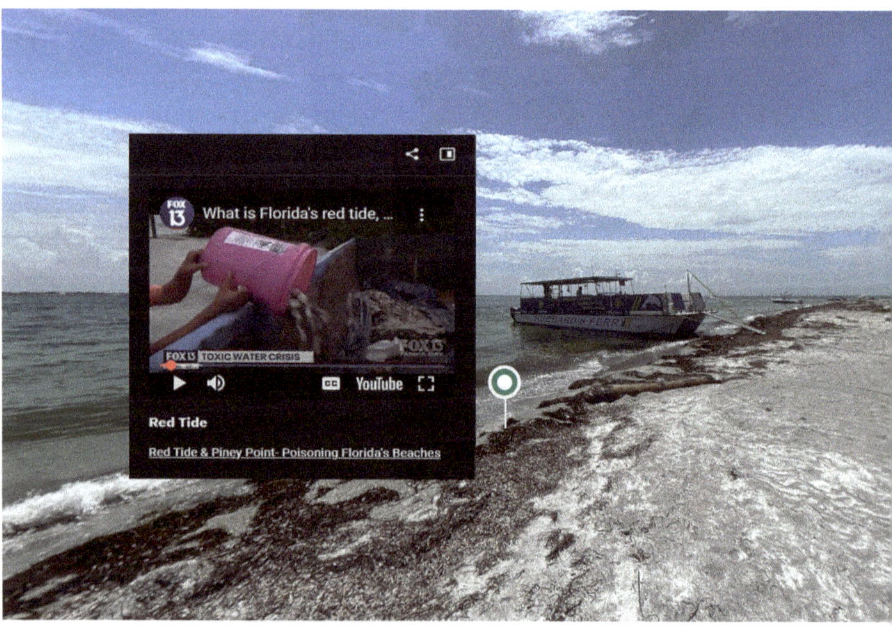

Figure 5.3. Screenshot of Egmont Key Pollution Matterport model. By permission of Brooke Hansen.

plastic pollution while aligning these issues with the SDGs, especially SDG 14 Life Below Water and SDG 12 Responsible Consumption and Production. The project yielded a fully annotated model that could be shared as a link (see 5.3) and was used in multiple presentations.

ENHANCING INTERPRETATION AT EGMONT KEY TO FOSTER SUSTAINABLE TOURISM

The stories, lessons, and warnings of Egmont Key need to be interpreted and shared if we are to heed the island's teachings. Whether addressing sustainable tourism issues such as red tide, plastic pollution, the rising seas, disappearing shores, or the unique natural and cultural heritage at Egmont Key, there needs to be effective on- and off-island interpretation available to share this information in an engaging way to visitors, locals, stakeholders, and the industry (Archi et al. 2023). As discussed throughout much of this book, the Egmont Key Project aimed to use virtualization technologies, public outreach, various extended reality prototypes, and educating many students and professionals to do just this—to better tell the Egmont Key stories. With the island disappearing, there is a pressing need to document the remaining cultural heritage and ecological habitats on Egmont Key and uncover the hidden histories of the many significant episodes of cultural occupation before they are lost forever to sea-level rise and erosion. These histories are the cornerstone of sustainable cultural heritage tourism at Egmont Key.

The field of interpretation is essential to accomplishing this agenda. Interpretation is the art and science of communicating meaningful connections between people and places, often used in heritage and environmental settings to reveal deeper understanding and significance. The National Association of Interpretation and the US National Park service offer various levels of training and certification in interpretation. Applying this lens to Egmont Key is essential to ensure its layered histories, cultural relevance, and unique biodiversity are conveyed to the public in compelling ways that inspire awareness, stewardship, and action in the face of climate change and other threats.

Digital technologies such as 3D laser scanning, photogrammetry, and virtual reality in conjunction with more traditional forms of public outreach and publication are crucial to creating interpretive tourism products that can be used by hotels, tour operators, and destination marketing organizations. These digital products can be used to develop sustainable tourism practices at Egmont Key that are sensitive to the island's complex cultural histories and ecological fragil-

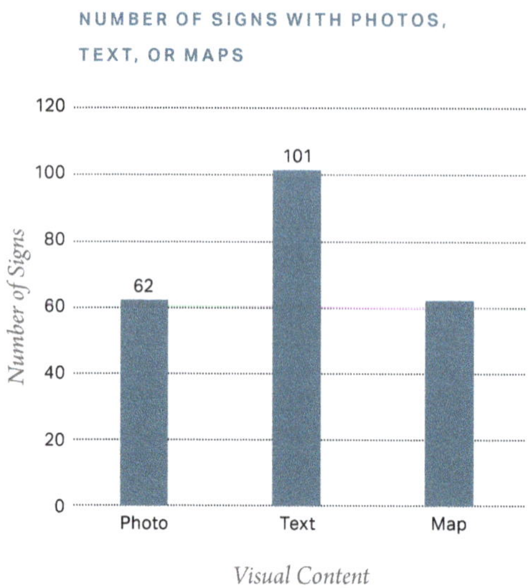

Chart 5.1. Typology of signage inventoried at Egmont Key, 2020. Chart created by Brooke Hansen, University of South Florida.

ity. Our goal is to scale up these pilot projects (discussed at greater length in Chapter 6) for full implementation in educational and tourism venues throughout Florida and beyond. These efforts will continue to engage multiple communities and organizations, such as the Seminole Tribal Historic Preservation Office and the Florida Public Archaeology Network's Heritage Monitoring Scouts program, to fully represent the diverse histories at Egmont Key, monitor the environmental threats that the island faces, and provide impactful education to visitors.

As part of the Egmont Key Project, we have engaged in research on the interpretation currently available on the island for visitors. While there are very informative displays in the reconstructed Guardhouse from the Fort Dade period, the building is rarely opened. As for the rest of the signage that is placed around the island, there are many examples of effective and engaging interpretation about bird species and nesting sites. Other signs are in disrepair, or their messaging is not effective at guiding the desired behaviors. To evaluate the on-island signage, we embarked on a research project with our students to inventory all the accessible signs on the island in 2020, documenting their size, materials they were made from, messaging, and current state regarding readability and durability. About 170 signs were inventoried and the distribution of those that were text, picture, or map based was assessed (see Chart 5.1).

Signs that warn people not to bring pets on the island were spread throughout the island and clearly visible (see 5.4), although most of them were destroyed in the fall 2024 hurricanes. Other signs are clearly in need of updating (see 5.5). The signage to keep people out of the National Wildlife Refuge is posted at regular intervals, but there is a different issue regarding these. When interpretive signs are meant to guide or dictate visitor behavior, they need to indicate *why* people should not engage in the forbidden behavior—in this case trespass (5.6). If there

Figure 5.5. Signage at Egmont Key that needed to be updated. Interestingly, this sign washed away in the hurricanes of the fall of 2024. By permission of Brooke Hansen.

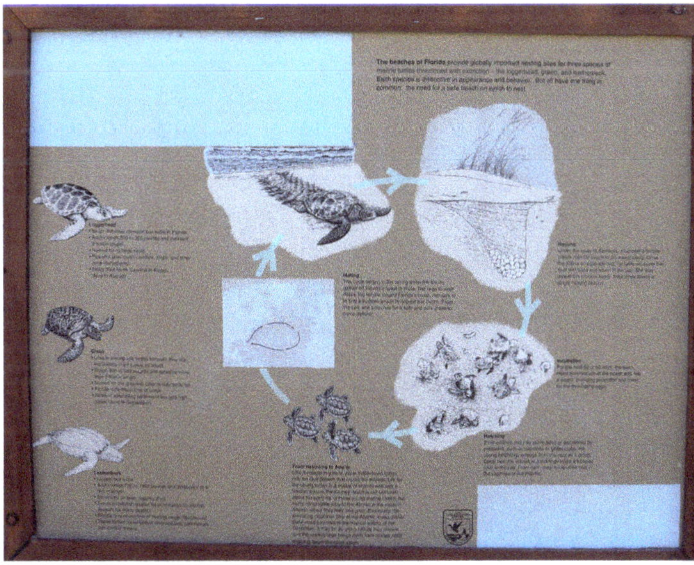

Figure 5.4. To safeguard nesting birds and turtles, no pets are allowed on the island, and these signs are placed around the island and are clearly visible. By permission of Brooke Hansen.

Figure 5.6. Signage to keep people out of the National Wildlife Refuge part of the island. By permission of Brooke Hansen.

were some additional descriptions here about nesting birds, endangered species, and how intrusion would affect them, these signs would be more effective. Park rangers routinely find people entering into the refuge—by land and sea (and in one unusual case by helicopter). We have offered several times during the Egmont Key Project to coordinate with the various land managers at Egmont Key and procure grants to update and improve signage, but an agreement on that collaboration has not been secured to date. The issue of the signage took on a new gravity after the 2024 hurricanes when many of the signs on the island were damaged or went missing.

The on-island interpretation through signage is in need of updating to reflect the important, and invisible, histories of Egmont Key, including the incarceration of the Seminole people in the mid-1800s. As described in Chapter 6, we embarked on many interpretive projects in the Egmont Key Project and produced an interactive touchscreen, virtual reality (VR) tour, and augmented reality tour prototype, in addition to giving many presentations, hosting workshops, and sharing the project to audiences around the world.

Destination Stewardship at Egmont Key

With all the issues facing Egmont Key, and the challenges that land managers face with staffing and funding, it is important to recognize the contributions of the many community groups, organizations, colleges, universities such as ours, and policymakers that have stewarded Egmont Key and will continue to do so in the future. Key protectors have included the Egmont Key Alliance (that for many years functioned as the citizen support organization for Egmont Key State Park), Friends of the Tampa Bay National Wildlife Refuges (which also produced an educational film about the island called *Where Birds Can be Birds* [Friends of the Tampa Bay National Wildlife Refuges 2022]), Eckerd College Turtle Trackers (which monitors nests on the island), the Tampa Bay Estuary Program (which conducts research on the sea grass beds around Egmont Key), Keep Pinellas Beautiful (which has organized ecotours of the island and trash cleanups), Take MAR (which has carried on the Egmont Key Alliance after a reorganization in 2022), and many more groups. We will all continue to work together to promote the ecotourism credo for tourism on the island: take nothing but pictures, leave nothing but footprints (see 5.7). Better yet we will add the regenerative tourism credo to this for everyone to leave Egmont Key better, cleaner, and more resilient than they found it.

Figure 5.7. The ecotourism credo to leave nothing but footprints near Battery Charles Mellon on Egmont Key. By permission of Brooke Hansen.

Conclusion: Egmont Key as a Global Lesson in Sustainable Island Tourism

Egmont Key offers a profound case study for rethinking sustainable island tourism. It is not only a microcosm of the challenges facing fragile destinations around the world, but also a poignant symbol of resilience, interconnection, and urgency. In many ways, it is a canary in the coal mine—its rapidly eroding shoreline and compromised ecosystems forewarning of what lies ahead for other island and coastal regions if more integrated, sustainable, and adaptive tourism strategies are not enacted. Egmont Key's intertwined legacy of militarism, colonialism, environmental change, and now tourism must be approached holistically if we are to preserve its remaining assets and harness its power as an educational tool for sustainable futures.

The lessons learned from Egmont Key underscore the importance of integration—between land and marine management, federal and state agencies, nonprofits, academic institutions, local communities, and marine tour operators. These stakeholders must work together in coordinated and transparent ways to design and manage regenerative tourism experiences. Egmont Key, like many islands in the Caribbean, the Pacific, and across the world's coastal zones, lacks a central tourism management authority. This absence has allowed unchecked visitation, inconsistent messaging, and insufficient monitoring of environmental impacts. Perhaps the island needs a destination stewardship council to better bring together the many key protectors that have worked to safeguard and interpret Egmont Key.

The island's challenges mirror those faced by small island developing states (SIDS), which are disproportionately affected by climate change despite often contributing least to global emissions. Egmont Key's circumstances—coastal erosion, habitat loss, marine pollution, overtourism, and heritage degradation—resonate far beyond Florida. In this way, Egmont Key can serve as an accessible case study for implementing the principles of the Glasgow Declaration on Climate Action in Tourism, leveraging sustainable marine tourism, engaging with the SDGs (especially 8.9, 11.4, 12.b, and 14.7), and fostering climate-resilient heritage preservation (United Nations World Tourism Organization 2021). Egmont Key's designation as part of the National Wildlife Refuge System and its status as a Florida State Park already provide some frameworks that can be built upon. However, these must be updated and strengthened through meaningful collaboration and regular reassessment—particularly the 2010 Comprehensive Conservation Plan, which has not kept pace with current threats or opportunities.

Ultimately, Egmont Key is a disappearing island that demands our attention—not only as a site of layered histories and irreplaceable biodiversity, but also as a mirror reflecting the fragility of many other destinations around the globe. Its deterioration is not inevitable; it is a call to action. Through destination stewardship, digital heritage preservation, participatory research, and community engagement, Egmont Key can remain a teaching ground and a beacon for sustainable tourism transformation. By listening to what the island is telling us—about resilience, mismanagement, climate urgency, and untold histories—we can respond not with despair, but with vision and responsibility. Egmont Key reminds us that the sands may be shifting beneath our feet, but the future is still ours to shape.

References Cited

Abbasi, S. A., A. B. Khalil, and M. Arslan. 2020. Extensive Use of Face Masks During COVID-19 Pandemic: (Micro-) Plastic Pollution and Potential Health Concerns in the Arabian Peninsula. *Saudi Journal of Biological Sciences* 27(12): 3181–3186. https://doi.org/10.1016/j.sjbs.2020.09.054.

Alfonso, M. B., A. Arias, M. C. Menéndez, A. C. Ronda, A. Harte, M. C. Piccolo, and J. E. Marcovecchio. 2021. Assessing Threats, Regulations, and Strategies to Abate Plastic Pollution in LAC Beaches During COVID-19 Pandemic. *Ocean and Coastal Management* 208 (July 1) 105613. https://doi.org/10.1016/j.ocecoaman.2021.105613.

El Archi, Y., B. Benbba, M. Kabil, and L.D. Dávid. 2023. Digital Technologies for Sustainable Tourism Destinations: State of the Art and Research Agenda. *Administrative Sciences* 13(8), 184. https://doi.org/10.3390/admsci13080184.

Bausback, E., and B. Miller. 2021. A Rundown of the Piney Point Wastewater Leak. Florida Museum, April 14. Updated April 25, 2022, https://www.floridamuseum.ufl.edu/earth-systems/blog/a-rundown-of-the-piney-point-wastewater-leak/, accessed June 15, 2022.

Bechard, A. 2019. Red Tide at Morning, Tourists Take Warning? County-Level Economic Effects of HABSo on Tourism Dependent Sectors. *Harmful Algae* 85: 101689. https://doi.org/10.1016/j.hal.2019.101689.

Booking.com. 2019. Booking.com Reveals Key Findings from Its 2019 Sustainable Travel Report.https://globalnews.booking.com/bookingcom-reveals-key-findings-from-its-2019-sustainable-travel-report/, accessed June 15, 2020.

Coll, M. 2020. Environmental Effects of the COVID-19 Pandemic from a (Marine) Ecological Perspective. *Ethics in Science and Environmental Politics* 20: 41–55. https://doi.org/10.3354/esep00192.

Cooper, D. H., and J. Nagel. 2021. Lessons from the Pandemic: Climate Change and COVID-19. *International Journal of Sociology and Social Policy* 42(3–4): 332–347. https://doi.org/10.1108/IJSSP-07-2020-0360.

Dodds, R., and R. Butler. 2024. 30 Years of Sustainable Tourism Policies: A Reflection on Success and Failure. In *Tourism Policy-Making in the Context of Contested Wicked Problems: Sustainability Paradox, Climate Emergency and COVID-19*, edited by Christof Pforr, Markus Pillmayer, Marion Joppe, Nicolai Scherle, Harald Pechlaner, pp. 17–29. Emerald, Leeds, UK.

Friends of the Tampa Bay National Wildlife Refuges. 2022. Where Birds Can Be Birds—The Remarkable Refuges of Tampa Bay. YouTube, June 8. https://www.youtube.com/watch?v=Cp_l_-ld-m8, accessed January 13, 2026.

Gössling, S., D. Scott, and C. M. Hall. 2021. Pandemics, Tourism and Global Change: A Rapid Assessment of COVID-19. *Journal of Sustainable Tourism* 29(1): 1–20. https://doi.org/10.1080/09669582.2020.1758708.

Gross, B. 2025. Five Things to Love About Egmont Key in Tampa Bay. *Florida Rambler*, April 22. https://www.floridarambler.com/tampa-bay-getaways/egmont-key-state-park/, accessed June 15, 2025.

Hansen, B. 2022. Keep America Beautiful Affiliates: Leading Stewardship Partnerships in Florida. *Destination Stewardship Report*—Autumn 2022 October–December 3(2). https://www.gstcouncil.org/destination-stewardship-report-2022-q4-vol3-issue2/.

Hansen B., S. Annis, S. Vorce, J. Coates, and A. Farr. 2022. Virtualization Technologies for Sustainable Tourism: Adapting the Matterport 360 Platform to Showcase the UN Sustainable Development Goals in Tampa Bay, Florida. In *The Green Institute: Working Papers*, May 12, 2022, pp. 1–10. https://greeninstitute.ng/visualization-technologies-for-sustainable-tourism-tampa-bay-florida.

Hawai'i Tourism Authority. N.d. Hawai'i Island Destination Management Action Plan. Hawai'i Tourism Authority. https://www.hawaiitourismauthority.org/what-we-do/destination-management/island-of-hawai-i/, accessed April 2, 2025.

Knetsch, J., and N. Wynne. 2011. *Florida in the Spanish-American War*. History Press, Charleston, South Carolina.

Lenzen, M., Y. Y. Y. Sun, F. Faturay, Y. P. Ting, A. Geschke, and A. Malik. 2018. The Carbon Footprint of Global Tourism. *Nature Climate Change* 8(6): 522–528. https://doi.org/10.1038/s41558-018-0141-x.

McEachern, K., H. Alegria, A. L. Kalagher, C. Hansen, S. Morrison, and D. Hastings. 2019. Microplastics in Tampa Bay, Florida: Abundance and Variability in Estuarine Waters and Sediments. *Marine Pollution Bulletin* 148: 97–106. https://doi.org/10.1016/j.marpolbul.2019.07.068.

Nhamo, G., K. Dube, and D. Chikodzi. 2020. *Counting the Cost of COVID-19 on the Global Tourism Industry*. Springer, Cham, Switzerland. https://doi.org/10.1007/978-3-030-56231-1.

Orlando Sentinel. 1988. Island in the Stream: Egmont Key Has Been a Fort, a Refuge, a Prison. It Has a Wild Past. Its Future Is Up for Grabs. *Orlando Sentinel*, April 24, updated July 29, 2021. https://www.orlandosentinel.com/1988/04/24/island-in-the-stream-egmont-key-has-been-a-fort-a-refuge-a-prison-it-has-a-wild-past-its-future-is-up-for-grabs/, accessed January 15, 2025.

Roa, R. 2025. Egmont Key Is More Fascinating Than We Could Ever Imagine. The Skinny, WMNF. https://www.wmnf.org/egmont-key-is-more-fascinating-than-we-could-ever-imagine/, accessed January 30, 2025.

Rogelj, J., M. den Elzen, N. Höhne, T. Fransen, H. Fekete, H. Winkler, R. Schaefffer, and M. Meinshausen. 2016. Paris Agreement Climate Proposals Need a Boost to Keep Warming Well Below 2°C. *Nature* 534(7609): 631–639. https://doi.org/10.1038/nature18307.

Salinero, M. 2009. Budget Cuts Could Imperil Island Beauty. *Herald Tribune*, January 6. https://www.heraldtribune.com/story/news/2009/01/06/budget-cuts-could-imperil-island-beauty/28685188007/, accessed January 15, 2025.

Sanchez, R. 2025. *Egmont Key: Stories from Eyewitnesses to History*. Self-published. https://floridahistory.shop/ols/products/egmont-key---stories-from-the-eyewitnesses-to-history.

Silva, A. L. P., J. C. Prata, T. R. Walker, A. C. Duarte, W. Ouyang, D. Barcelò, and T. Rocha-Santos. 2021. Increased Plastic Pollution due to COVID-19 Pandemic: Challenges and recommendations. *Chemical Engineering Journal* 405: 126683. https://doi.org/10.1016/j.cej.2020.126683.

Spenceley, A., S. McCool, D. Newsome, A. Báez, J. R. Barborak, C. J. Blye, K. Bricker, and others. 2021. Tourism in Protected and Conserved Areas amid the COVID-19 Pandemic. *Parks* 27(March): 103–118. https://doi.org/10.2305/IUCN.CH.2021.PARKS-27-SIAS.en.

Tampa Bay Regional Planning Council. 2023. Regional Resiliency Action Plan, accessed May 15, 2025. https://tbrpc.org/about/services/resiliency-planning/rrap/

Thompson, D. H., and C. Thompson. 2012. *Egmont Key: A History*. History Press, Charleston, South Carolina.

Tracy, K. 2025. Hurricane Helene Storm Surge Relocates Dozens of Egmont Key Tortoises to Fort De Soto. Fox 13 News, April 1. https://www.fox13news.com/news/hurricane-helene-storm-surge-relocates-dozens-egmont-key-tortoises-fort-de-soto, accessed April 1, 2025.

United Nations. N.d. The 17 Goals. https://sdgs.un.org/goals, accessed January 15, 2025.

UN Tourism. 2025. Sustainable Development. https://www.untourism.int/sustainable-development, accessed January 15, 2025.

United Nations World Tourism Organization. 2021. The Glasgow Declaration on Climate Action in Tourism. https://www.unwto.org/glasgow-declaration-climate-action-in-tourism, accessed January 15, 2025.

United Nations World Tourism Organization. N.d. Tourism for SDGs. Retrieved from https://tourism4sdgs.org/, accessed January 15, 2025.

US Department of Commerce. 2022. *National Travel and Tourism Strategy*. Retrieved from https://www.commerce.gov/sites/default/files/2022-06/National-Travel-Tourism-Strategy.pdf, accessed January 15, 2025.

US Fish and Wildlife Service. 2010. Comprehensive Conservation Plan: Tampa Bay Refuges. May. Southeast Region, Atlanta, GA. https://iris.fws.gov/APPS/ServCat/Reference/Profile/168154, accessed January 15, 2025.

US Fish and Wildlife Service. N.d. *Egmont Key National Wildlife Refuge*. Retrieved from https://www.fws.gov/refuge/egmont-key, accessed June 1, 2025.

Weisberg, R. H., Y. Liu, C. Lembke, C. Hu, K. Hubbard, and M. Garrett. 2019. The Coastal Ocean Circulation Influence on the 2018 West Florida Shelf *K. brevis* Red Tide Bloom. *Journal of Geophysical Research: Oceans* 124(4), 2501–2512. https://doi.org/10.1029/2018JC014887

Wood, M. E. 2017. *Sustainable Tourism on a Finite Planet: Environmental, Business and Policy Solutions*. Routledge.

World Economic Forum. 2022. Travel & Tourism Development Index 2021: Rebuilding for a Sustainable and Resilient Future. May 24. https://www.weforum.org/publications/travel-and-tourism-development-index-2021/in-full/4-3-building-back-better/, accessed January 15, 2025.

Wright, C. E. 1970. As Florida Roars into the Seventies. *New York Times*, January 4. https://www.nytimes.com/1970/01/04/archives/as-florida-roars-into-the-seventies.html, accessed January 15, 2025.

6

Egmont Key as a Living Learning Laboratory

Participatory Action Research Meets Digital Heritage

LAURA K. HARRISON AND BROOKE HANSEN

The Egmont Key Project (EKP) integrates Participatory Action Research (PAR) and applied digital heritage methodologies to document, interpret, and reflect on at-risk cultural heritage (Harrison 2019). This chapter highlights how the EKP project unfolded at Egmont Key—an island with an important but often overlooked history. The approach combines lidar scanning of existing heritage structures, the design of interactive exhibits using virtual and augmented reality technologies, the strengthening of community partnerships, and the delivery of professional development workshops and courses for emerging heritage and sustainability professionals. The findings demonstrate that action-oriented digital heritage research, when combined with community collaboration, serves as a powerful tool to highlight invisible, intangible, and lesser-known histories, digitally archive sites that may be lost to natural and anthropogenic effects, and engage diverse audiences in sustainability and conservation efforts.

Egmont Key: Heritage, History, and Fragility

As discussed in Chapter 2, the earliest human presence on the island was that of Indigenous peoples, who visited periodically for hunting and fishing. By the eighteenth century, European cartographers arrived in Tampa Bay and set about mapping the island and its environs, beginning with the Spainard Don Francisco Maria Celi in 1757. In the nineteenth century, human engagement on Egmont Key intensified. The Tampa Bay Pilots Association began using the island as a base of operations in the 1850s (formalizing the association in the 1880s), and the first lighthouse was erected in 1848 to support growing maritime activity in the region. This lighthouse was promptly destroyed by a hurricane the same year (1848), and a new lighthouse with thicker walls was built to replace it in 1858. In 1849, the US Army surveyed the island and neighboring Mullet Key, recommending that they both be retained for miliary purposes, which indeed occurred from this time up until World War II.

From 1856 to 1858, the US Army constructed and oversaw a prison camp on Egmont Key, where they forcibly held Seminole men, women, and children under the watch of armed guards. This was part of a broader attempt to expel the Seminole from their ancestral lands during the Seminole War and represented the last gasp of Indian Removal in the United States. No physical remains of the prison camp exist, but its presence is recorded in oral histories of the Tribe (as discussed in Chapter 3), as well as some archival documents referring to the purchase of wood to be used in the construction of a palisade, and firsthand accounts describing the imprisonment of the Seminoles. Many Seminole descendants think it is likely that there is, or was, a mass grave on the island at some point. Most archival documents of the time dehumanize the Seminole and thus any deaths that may have occurred at the prison camp were mostly omitted or documented solely by the weight of their bones rather than by name, a topic discussed more extensively in Chapter 3.

During the Civil War, Egmont Key was held by the Union and became a haven for individuals fleeing enslavement. By 1898, the Spanish-American War erupted, and military leaders were quick to identify Egmont Key as a strategic defensive location. The island was swiftly militarized with the construction of a series of disappearing gun batteries and underwater mines, designed to make Tampa Bay impregnable to any ship. Although the Spanish-American War only lasted six months, fears of a maritime invasion persisted, propelling the construction of Fort Dade, a bustling fort that housed up to 300 soldiers on Egmont Key, and grew to include such specialized sites as a hospital, morgue, stable, bakery, power plant, and firehouse. These sites were interconnected with a transportation network made up of brick roads, a dock, and over 1,300 feet of narrow-gauge railroad tracks. Fort Dade was decommissioned in 1923, at which point the island became a forgotten hinterland in Tampa Bay. The advent of military aircraft rendered the seacoast defenses obsolete, and the departure of military personnel encouraged outlaws and rumrunners to seek shelter amid the many abandoned buildings. Eventually, the lawlessness caught the eye of authorities, who set the island ablaze in an effort to smoke out the squatters and put an end to the bootlegging.

The military returned to Egmont Key during World Wars I and II—using it as a site for target practice—but eventually after these wars the island fell out of use for military purposes. The US Fish and Wildlife Service (USFWS) took over and established a National Wildlife Refuge in 1974, and then the island was designated a Florida State Park in 1989, harkening a new era of recreation and tourism. These designations underline a key aspect of Egmont Key that was overlooked throughout its militarization: its unique ecological niche for nesting shorebirds, sea turtles, and other species whose habitats were coming under threat due to the explosive growth of Florida's coastal real estate and recreation markets in the mid- to late twentieth century.

Egmont Key's designation as a state park and National Wildlife Refuge initiated a new focus on stewarding the island's cultural and natural resources, which in turn drew attention to the fact that these resources were under threat due to unrelenting erosion causing habitats and heritage sites to wash away. Comparing historic maps of Egmont Key from the past several hundred years clearly shows that the island has lost over half of its landmass. The remaining land may soon disappear, as strong storms continue to intensify and batter the tiny island, washing it into the sea. Clearly, the need to research and understand the stories and lessons of Egmont Key are urgent, as the island continues to slip away. As shown in Chapter 7, the southern tip of the island shrunk significantly after being battered in 2024 by Hurricanes Helene and Milton with strong winds and storm surge, wiping out the entire Tampa Bay Pilots Association village, and threatening to erase what remains of its built and natural heritage. Egmont Key is thus a rich landscape that is disappearing, both figuratively and literally. Against this backdrop of loss and urgency, the Egmont Key Project seeks to document, preserve, interpret, share, and reflect on Egmont Key's layered histories before they vanish.

Overview of Participatory Action Research (PAR)

Many methodological and theoretical frameworks could have guided our work at Egmont Key to recover invisible histories, protect heritage at risk, utilize virtualization technologies, and foster sustainable tourism. These are all complex tasks with many frames and vantage points. With the project embedded in local contexts, a participatory approach was necessary and appropriate for the task. One paradigm well suited to engage the main stakeholders involved with Egmont Key is Participatory Action Research (PAR). PAR is a collaborative research framework that actively involves community members in the research process to address social, cultural, and environmental issues while fostering meaningful change. Unlike traditional research methods that position researchers as external observers, PAR emphasizes co-creation of knowledge, where participants are both subjects and contributors to the research. Not only were we spurred into action hearing about the little-known histories of Egmont Key—including the Seminole imprisonment—but this was in our own backyard. We live in the Tampa Bay region and work at an AAU (Association of American Universities) university where it is expected that we combine innovative research with education and service, all the while training the next generation to be global citizens beneficially contributing to society.

With the pressing needs associated with Egmont Key to reveal untold stories of incarceration and a disappearing island in mind, we formulated a research plan to engage key partners in a PAR-centered approach. This is particularly effective in applied projects that seek to uncover invisible histories, protect heritage at risk, and develop community-led climate action initiatives. By integrating local knowledge, lived experiences, and academic expertise, PAR fosters deep connections between researchers and communities, ensuring that research findings are relevant, actionable, and rooted in the priorities of those directly impacted. It is widely used in fields such as Indigenous studies, cultural heritage preservation, and environmental justice, helping to amplify marginalized voices, inform policy decisions, and inspire grassroots activism for sustainable, long-term transformation (Nared and Bole 2020; Watkins 2020; Wells 2015).

The multiyear project (still ongoing at the time of this writing), simply titled the Egmont Key Project (EKP), was envisioned and led by University of South Florida (USF) faculty Harrison and Hansen, who brought complementary research backgrounds. Volume co-editor Harrison, the director of Access 3D Lab, brought over 15 years of experience in museums and digital public heritage to the project. Her work, broadly speaking, focuses on visualization and virtualization in archaeology (Harrison and Gürbüz 2018), and the documentation of at-risk cultural heritage. Dr. Harrison's research in applied digital heritage (Harrison 2019) uses digital tools and techniques to solve real-world problems—such as increasing the accessibility of remote sites and collections and democratizing access to cultural heritage. She has also published on the importance of community-centered heritage work that "closes the loop" on digital heritage research by encouraging data sharing and reuse (Harrison 2022).

Volume co-editor Hansen began the EKP as the director of Sustainable Tourism at the USF College of Global Sustainability and several years in transitioned to the School of Hospitality and Sport Management and became the director of the Hospitality and Tourism Management Program. Before that she spent over twenty years on community-based projects with Indigenous people in the Haudenosaunee Nations of New York State and with Kānaka Maoli (Native Hawaiians) in Hawai'i restoring Indigenous landscapes, seeking reparations for land claims, and working for environmental and cultural justice (Hansen and Rossen 2017). Much of this work was carried out with a PAR orientation with participation of the educational institutions where Dr. Hansen was based, including Ithaca College and the University of Hawai'i at Hilo. At USF, there were many students interested in sustainability, and Dr. Hansen taught both undergraduates and graduate students who sought classes and professional training opportunities in the fields of sustainable tourism and heritage interpretation and management. Egmont Key proved an ideal living laboratory for the pedagogies of engagement explored in the trainings, workshops, and classes focused on the disappearing island, its invisible histories, and its many visitors.

During this project, we won grants, taught classes, conducted research, led professional development workshops, engaged with community partners, and presented our project for both academic and community audiences. Each of these activities was intertwined with the others; the research informed the teaching; the community partners informed the workshops; the outreach informed the research, and so on. This intertwined and cumulative process that is very circular in nature is characteristic of PAR and transdisciplinary endeavors that include multiple stakeholders. This chapter presents some highlights of research, community engagement, and professional development across multiple years of working together in the EKP. We discuss both the successes and challenges encountered in our work, with the aim of identifying best practices in participatory and applied digital heritage and sustainable tourism research while reflecting on key lessons learned.

The Egmont Key Project: Research Overview

Over multiple years of research, Egmont Key revealed itself as a living laboratory. Through repeated visits—first with the Seminole Tribe, then the Egmont

Key Alliance, and later with students, international colleagues, and Pilots—we gradually came to understand what the island is, what it once was, and what it might become. Our quest to deeply explore these questions of Egmont Key's past, present, and future became the catalyst for engaging with a wide range of community groups, academic partners, and land managers. We took a deep dive into the science of sea-level rise and erosion and explored ways to preserve the island's endangered heritage sites, using these inquiries as foundations for training early career heritage and tourism professionals through academic courses and workshops.

Our research began in 2018 with trips to the island and conducting background research on Egmont Key. Surprisingly, there were few works on the subject but many news articles, archival references, and websites discussing the island. Also at this time, the Seminole Tribe of Florida was overseeing the collection and curation of their oral histories of Egmont Key. That was not part of our primary research, and we functioned in a supportive role to their endeavors collaborating and sharing what we learned and receiving guidance from them. We also discussed at length with the Tribal Historic Preservation Office (THPO) how some of the interpretive platforms we wanted to use (such as a virtual reality tour, an interactive touchscreen, and an augmented reality experience) could highlight the stories the Tribe wanted told about their experiences and reflections on the island. Works from the THPO that we integrated included an ArcGIS Story Map, numerous articles from the *Seminole Tribune*, and a booklet produced by the Tribe in 2019 called *Egmont Key: A Seminole Story* (see Mueller and Boge n.d.). Each step in this process was led by conversations and consultations with the THPO and sometimes staff members at the Ah-Tah-Thi-Ki Seminole Museum.

Documenting At-Risk Cultural Heritage with Lidar Scanning

A key objective of the project that was planned from the start was to digitally preserve the island's extant cultural heritage sites with detailed as-built models, as it was clear that these sites faced immediate threats due to erosion and sea-level rise. Eventually, we would come to have a much deeper and more granular understanding of exactly where and when these effects would be felt (discussed in greater detail in Chapter 7), but initially our goal was simply to digitize these sites and archive them in case they were destroyed by the next hurricane. Because the Seminole prison camp no longer exists, we prioritized the island's surviving built heritage, which bears witness to its enigmatic and complex history. We started our digitization and virtualization project in 2019 after months of planning and came up with a creative solution to offset the cost of the scanning and transport to the island. We ran it as a professional development workshop, and charged a fee for participants that helped offset the cost of using Access 3D Lab's Faro Focus terrestrial lidar scanners. This model allowed us to complete detailed scans of the Lighthouse, Battery Charles Mellon, the restored Guardhouse, and the Lighthouse Cemetery, and established an incipient community of practice around digitally preserving cultural heritage. In subsequent years, we expanded our documentation to encompass additional built heritage sites—notably Battery McIntosh, the largest, most complex, and most vulnerable Spanish-American War fortification on the island.

Terrestrial lidar scanning was used in this project instead of photogrammetry because it is, on average, more accurate in variable lighting conditions. Although photogrammetry is a useful and lower-cost virtualization method, it is very sensitive to weather and environmental conditions. It can be challenging to produce photogrammetry models that transition from outdoor settings in bright natural light to dark, unlit indoor spaces—a scenario frequently encountered at the Spanish-American War batteries and the lighthouse. Lidar scanners, on the other hand, simply use laser pulses to calculate the position of surfaces, regardless of lighting conditions. While light and shadows are reflected in the RGB (red, green, blue) values assigned to individual points (measurements), liminal zones between light and dark are easily documented. Furthermore, photogrammetry of Egmont Key's cultural heritage sites would have required blending two datasets; an aerial mission capturing building exteriors from a drone, and a terrestrial mission capturing the interiors on foot. Permitting requirements within the National Wildlife Refuge strictly limit the use of drones, making this option more logistically challenging than lidar scanning. In addition, placing terrestrial scanners on top of buildings captures roof data, allowing the models to be visualized from any vantage point. These 3D datasets can be viewed from any angle, including a top-down perspective often mistaken for a drone flight.

DIGITIZING THE LIGHTHOUSE

The 2019 lidar scan of the Egmont Key Lighthouse was completed in three days with a team of USF students (6.1). Our research team obtained a permit to scan the building's exterior as well as the interior, which is normally closed

Figure 6.1. Digital slice of the 3D terrestrial lidar scan of the lighthouse. The scan has been incorporated into many public presentations, increasing access to a structure that is closed to the public. The model also serves as a detailed digital archive of a structure threatened by storms, erosion, and sea-level rise, a topic discussed in greater detail in Chapter 7. A shows the overall scan of the lighthouse and surrounding buildings; B shows a cutaway slice; and C shows a detail. Image created by Elliot Alvarez, Access 3D Lab, University of South Florida.

to visitors as it is managed by the US Coast Guard. We used a Faro Focus x330 scanner with 1/4 resolution and 4× quality parameters, capturing 126 scans and 23.17 GB of raw data. The repetitive geometry of the interior spiral staircase, with 88 identical iron steps radiating around a central pole, presented a challenge, because lidar registration algorithms rely on finding correspondences between geometrically similar planes to align the project. In other words, unique geometry is helpful for registering a project, whereas repetitive, identical geometry (like lighthouse stairs) can cause errors, because the software can't tell the difference between say, the fifth step and the sixtieth step. This often results in misalignment—which is immediately obvious to the researcher as the project looks like an abstract rendition of the scanned site, rather than a realistic digital surrogate. To address the problem of the lighthouse's interior uniformity, our team incorporated the use of target spheres; white objects 150 mm in diameter with a magnetic base. Spheres were placed around the scan

Figure 6.2. Orthophotos of Battery Charles Mellon, showing (*A*) the side view facing west, and (*B*) the top view. Note the circular gun emplacements visible from the top view. Image created by Laura Harrison, Access 3D Lab, University of South Florida.

environment at irregular intervals. The unique placement helped streamline the processing workflow by allowing our processing software (Faro Scene) to properly differentiate between the lighthouse steps, despite their repetitive geometry.

DIGITIZING BATTERY CHARLES MELLON

Battery Charles Mellon, a gun battery structure from the Spanish-American War, is one of Egmont Key's most critically endangered heritage sites. It lies just meters from the island's volatile northwest corner—a dynamic area of erosion that has been the subject of many sand emplacements over the years as the water of the Gulf of Mexico encroach on its historic walls. The fort contains three gun emplacements along with a freestanding "dynamo" power generator and several interior rooms that were used for artillery storage. The entire structure is built out of locally made concrete, in which seashells were used as aggregate. The walls were painted with a tar-like black paint, to protect them from the elements—a coating that was standard for seacoast defenses of the era, but which has degraded steadily due to a lack of conservation or restoration over the years.

Vandalism of the site is also rampant, with many names carved into the concrete and paint. In one semi-subterranean room originally used to store 8-in shells, root intrusion has caused both structural and water damage. The terrestrial lidar scan of Battery Charles Mellon focused on fully documenting the entire interior and exterior of the building, with special attention to recording its overall condition and its many vulnerabilities including crumbling concrete, fading paint, structural damage, and graffiti. Over five days, the project collected 130 lidar scans, comprising 24.48 GB of data that were processed in Faro Scene at USF's Access 3D Lab. Research deliverables, which were shared with land managers, include geometrically corrected orthophotos (6.2) and scalar images (6.3) that are a useful tool for site monitoring, conservation, and public outreach.

DIGITIZING THE LIGHTHOUSE CEMETERY

The Lighthouse Cemetery, located a short distance southwest of the lighthouse, was documented primarily for archival and storytelling purposes (6.4). Although it contains a few dozen white wooden crosses that pique the interest of visitors, these are simply replicas. Human remains from the cemetery were disinterred and reburied in other cemeteries in 1912, a topic discussed in greater

Figure 6.3. 3D point cloud of Battery Charles Mellon. Top image (*A*) shows a scalar view of Battery Charles Mellon, illustrating the transition from intensity map to RGB colorization. The bottom image (*B*) shows a colorized point cloud. Terrestrial lidar scans like this have an average distance accuracy of +/- 4 mm, providing a high-resolution archival record for monitoring site conditions and guiding preservation planning. Image created by Laura Harrison, Access 3D Lab, University of South Florida.

Figure 6.4. USF team members use Faro Focus terrestrial lidar scanners to preserve the memory of the many lives lost on Egmont Key. Image created by Laura Harrison, Access 3D Lab, University of South Florida.

detail in Chapter 2. The Lighthouse Cemetery is not the only place on Egmont Key associated with death and burial; archival records refer to another cemetery on Egmont Key, toward the south end of the island, though its location is not known, and it may have already washed into the sea. Likewise, as discussed in Chapter 3, oral histories from the Seminole Tribe refer to a mass grave that once existed on the island. The purpose of scanning the Lighthouse Cemetery with lidar was to memorialize the site and make a 3D visualization that would serve as a reminder of the deaths caused by disease, war, and violence against Indigenous people on the island. The digital archive that our team created will survive, even if Egmont Key itself disappears. The Lighthouse Cemetery was fully documented in 17 scans, comprising 3.63 GB of data.

DIGITIZING BATTERY MCINTOSH

Battery McIntosh, another gun battery defense structure from the Spanish-American War, is a critically endangered cultural heritage site on Egmont Key that was the focus of a terrestrial lidar scanning project as well as the subject

Figure 6.5. The condition of the concrete at Battery McIntosh in 2022 was poor, with cracks and fading paint. Image created by Laura Harrison, Access 3D Lab, University of South Florida.

of a comprehensive coastal heritage risk assessment described in Chapter 7. Our team received a grant from the Archaeological Institute of America Steinmetz Fund to complete the work. Constructed out of concrete, Battery McIntosh is the largest historic structure still standing on Egmont Key, with two gun emplacements perched atop a labyrinth of interior artillery storage rooms. The southern portion of the building contains an open channel used to hoist artillery up to the top deck. Open metal beams in this area have been exposed to the elements for over a century, leading to water intrusion that is weakening the structural integrity of the concrete almost to the point of collapse. Like other heritage sites on the island (with the singular exception of the Fort Dade Guardhouse), Battery McIntosh has never been conserved or restored (6.5). This site, too, has been the target of graffiti. The land managers have addressed it by covering it with the paint they have at hand, leading to a patchwork mosaic of various colors.

The terrestrial lidar scanning digitally documented the structure's interior and exterior, as well as the beach to the west of the structure. The building once sat at the center of the island but is now perilously close to the encroaching

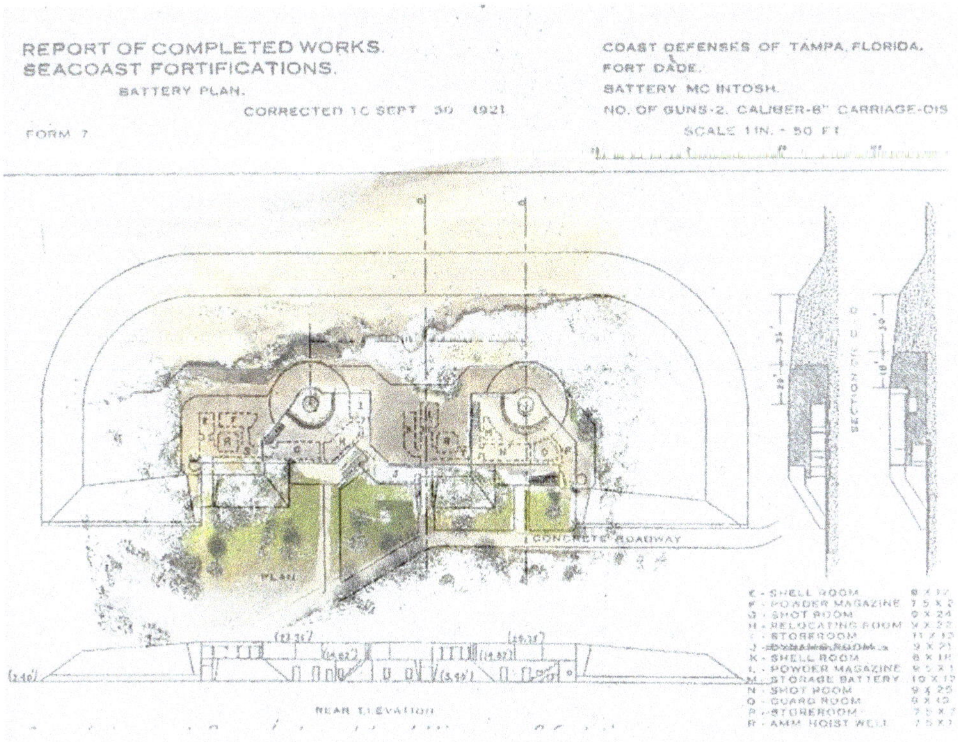

Figure 6.6. Composite image showing archival drawing of Battery McIntosh from 1921 overlaid atop geometrically corrected and colorized 3D image of Battery McIntosh (orthophoto). This image shows areas in which the 1921 drawing differs from the structure as built. Image created by Laura Harrison, Access 3D Lab, University of South Florida.

waters of the Gulf of Mexico. Our team collected 181 scans and 33.52 GB of raw data across 6 days of scanning, and processed the data in Faro Scene at Access 3D Lab. The results include a 3D point cloud, orthophotos overlaid with archival drawings (6.6), and detailed composite images comparing archival photos of the structure with the 3D scan from 2023 (6.7).

DIGITIZING THE TAMPA BAY PILOTS VILLAGE

In the aftermath of Hurricane Helene in 2024, our team received word that the island had been decimated by storm surge and violent winds. We traveled to the island with John Timmel, a retired Pilot, and Jack Timmel, the executive director of the Tampa Bay Pilots Association, to assess the historic cottage

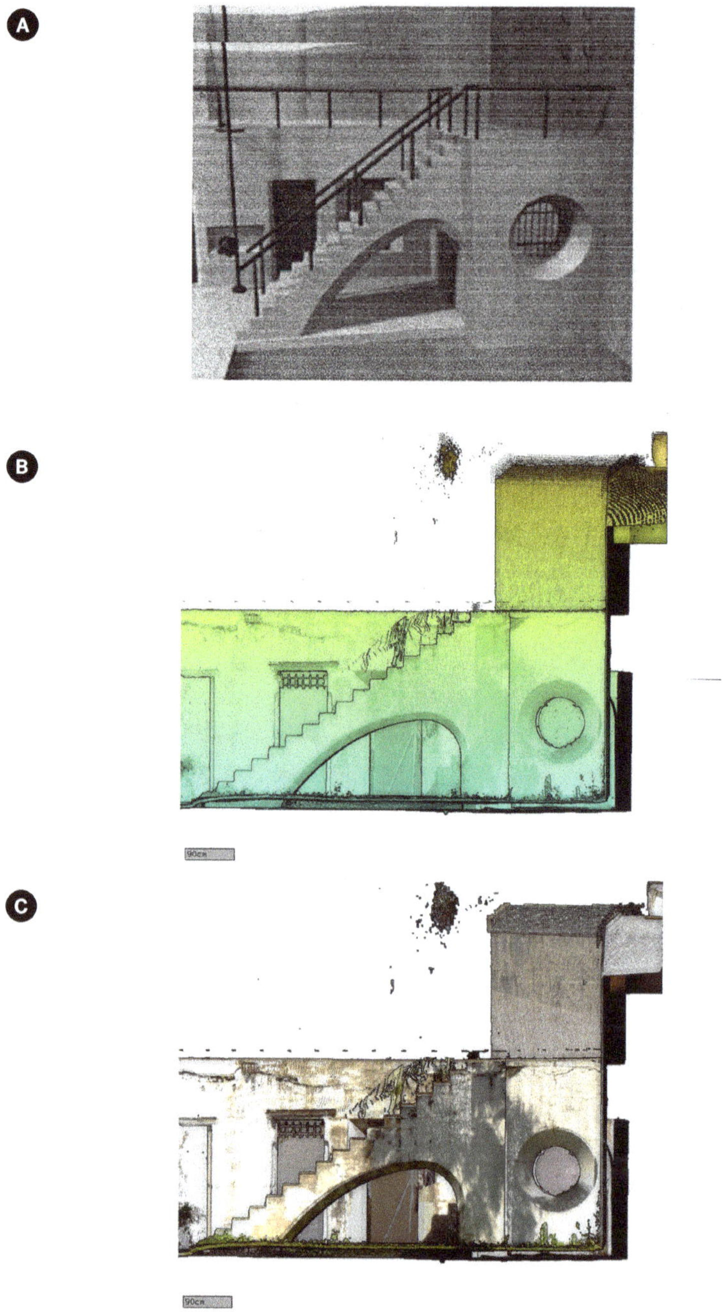

Figure 6.7. Composite image showing (*A*) historical photo of concrete staircase and railing, (*B*) point cloud colorized according to Z values, and (*C*) point cloud colorized by RGB values. Image created by Laura Harrison, Access 3D Lab, University of South Florida.

Figure 6.8. Scenes of destruction and devastation in the Egmont Key Pilots' village in the wake of Hurricane Helene, 2024. By permission of Laura Harrison.

they had used for decades in the Pilots' Village. The area consisted of multiple houses and infrastructure (docks, fuel tanks) to allow the Pilots to do their job, which is navigating ships into Tampa Bay. The village had an array of houses, the earliest one which was built around 1890, with most housing the Pilots and one for the US Fish and Wildlife Service (USFWS) staff, who also used the Pilots' boat dock. Hurricane Helene effectively destroyed the Tampa Bay Pilots Association village. The USFWS house was left uninhabitable. Without a dock to land and a base of operations their ability to have a presence on the island was made nearly impossible, except for occasional visits.

We proceeded to scan what was left of the historic homes in the village with Faro Focus terrestrial lidar scanners. With limited time and challenging conditions, our team collected 34 scans, and 12.07 GB of data, to document the devastation. Many of the historic cottages had been physically separated from their foundations, some shifting mere inches while others moved dozens of feet (6.8). One structure—a blue house—completely disappeared. It had washed out to sea (6.9). Our team returned to the island again in 2025 to document the aftermath of Hurricane Milton—a Category 3 hurricane storm with sustained winds over 100 mph. We collected a further 43 scans and 10.94

Figure 6.9. The blue house in the center was documented with a Matterport scan in 2021. It disappeared in 2024, as the storm surge from Hurricane Helene swept it out to sea. Other historic cottages in the village suffered heavy damage from the storm and Hurricane Milton, which impacted the island just 10 days later. The dock pictured here was also swept away in the storm. By permission of Laura Harrison.

GB of data, allowing us to create a composite image (6.10) showing how the Pilots' Village and command center quickly transformed from an orderly group of historic cottages into a nearly unrecognizable disaster zone in just one hurricane season. One house on stilts that made it through Helene was pushed off its foundation in the high winds of Milton.

Through systematic terrestrial lidar documentation, the EKP established a foundational digital archive of Egmont Key's surviving built heritage, capturing high-resolution structural and site data of the Lighthouse, Lighthouse Cemetery, military structures, and the Pilots' Village. This archive not only provides a durable resource for preservation planning and future research but also safeguards critical information about the island's endangered cultural heritage in the face of ongoing erosion, sea-level rise, and storm impacts. As these sites continue to change over time, the archive will serve as a reference point for future generations to study, interpret, and learn from the island's complex history.

Figure 6.10. Composite image showing damage to the Pilots' village in the aftermath of Hurricanes Helene and Milton in 2024. The colorized base map is derived from an aerial photo taken before the hurricane, showing two orderly rows of houses. The line drawings are an overview map derived from the terrestrial lidar scans, showing that many buildings were ripped from their foundations and moved large distances as storm surge swept through the area. The arrows show directional movement of the houses as a result of the storms. The one arrow pointing west indicates a house that was raised on stilts and not heavily impacted by storm surge from Hurricane Helene, but later was toppled from the stilts and fell down in the 100+ mph winds of Hurricane Milton. In the east row, the third building from the top washed completely out to sea during Hurricane Helene. This house is also pictured as it looked in 2019 in Figure 6.9. Map by Alex Fawbush, Access 3D Lab, University of South Florida.

Figure 6.11. The Matterport virtual tour of the Egmont Key Guardhouse contains multiple hot spots with further information about the exhibits. This tour, created during a professional development workshop, increases the accessibility of a museum that is almost always closed to the public. Image created by Laura Harrison, Access 3D Lab, University of South Florida.

Digital Storytelling with Interpretive Media

MATTERPORT SCANNING

In addition to digitally archiving Egmont Key's vulnerable built heritage sites with terrestrial lidar, our team leveraged Matterport scanning for digital storytelling and public outreach. In 2020 and 2021, we completed Matterport scans of the Coast Guard Museum, the Lighthouse, the Lighthouse Cemetery, the Pilots' Village and the Guardhouse, and in 2023 we rescanned portions of the Pilots' Village. These models were shared with stakeholders, and annotated with pertinent information and interpretation, to help compensate for the fact that these sites are often closed to the public or lack interpretive signage, making their histories invisible to the public. For instance, the Guardhouse—open only intermittently when volunteers are available—can now be explored virtually, while multimedia annotations add another layer of interpretation about the island's natural and cultural heritage (6.11). Similarly, the Lighthouse is never open to visitors, but the Matterport model provides an engaging way to navigate up and down the stairs and engage with annotations about several lighthouse keepers along the way, transforming hidden histories into an engaging, interactive experience. We also created a Matterport model to highlight issues of red tide and plastic pollution affecting the island (Hansen et al. 2022).

TOUCHSCREEN EXHIBIT

With funding from the USF Creative Scholarship Grant, our team integrated the lidar and Matterport scans of the island with extensive archival research, resulting in the development of several interpretive products: a digital touchscreen exhibit called *Uncovering Egmont Key's Hidden History,* a virtual reality experience called *Egmont Key VR Tour,* and an augmented reality experience called *Step into History.*

The digital touchscreen exhibit was a collaborative project with student assistants, Samantha (Sam) Vorce, Sophia Annis, Johnny Cheng, and Melody Yin, who carried out interviews about Egmont Key's history with Egmont Key Alliance President Richard Sanchez and historian Bruce McCall. The team also engaged in extensive archival research, along with April Min (co-author of Chapter 2) to bring narrative depth to the exhibit. The touchscreen itself was purchased with grant funds from the Florida Humanities Council, and the user interface was designed and deployed with the Intuiface platform. Our team engaged in collaborative storyboarding to distill the digital touchscreen exhibit down to several key place-based storytelling pathways: the Guardhouse, Battery Charles Mellon, the Lighthouse, Ecology, and a Seminole Story. Each of these pathways contained subcategories. For instance, the lighthouse had a gallery of archival documents, stories from three noted lighthouse keepers, and a navigable, annotated 3D virtual tour derived from the Matterport model, and the ecology section had subsections for key protectors (organizations involved with the protection and preservation of the island), key threats, and key animals.

The touchscreen exhibit was completed during the onset of the COVID-19 pandemic, so our plans to deploy it to pop-up at museums in the Tampa Bay area were put on hold. Eventually, we were able to bring it to several outreach events in Tierra Verde and on the USF campus, where it has been integrated into the curricula of many courses and highlighted during innumerable lab tours (6.12).

Figure 6.12. Melody Yin, Sophia Annis, and Johnny Cheng with the Egmont Key digital touchscreen exhibit at Access 3D Lab. By permission of Laura Harrison.

VIRTUAL REALITY TOUR

Virtual reality (VR) is an immersive simulation of a 3D image or environment that can be interacted with by a person using a headset and hand controllers. It provides a virtual place-based experience enriched with multimedia to engage the senses in multimodal storytelling. The impetus for developing the *Egmont Key VR Tour* was to increase public knowledge and understanding of the island's cultural and natural heritage and inform users of the many threats that the island faces in the form of erosion, sea-level rise, and overtourism. We also wanted to highlight some of the island's invisible and lesser-known histories, which are not included in the island's interpretive signage.

To accomplish this, our team downloaded Matterport 360 panoramas of the Lighthouse, Guardhouse, Battery Charles Mellon, and the beach to the west of Battery Charles Mellon from our Matterport cloud account. These files became a "base map" for the VR experience. Next, we created a storyboard for the experience (6.13) and used Pano2VR software to add multimedia annotations and interactivity to 3D Matterport panoramas (6.14). These annotations were derived from archival research and files shared with us via relationships with community stakeholders, partners, and colleagues including Neil Hurley, a

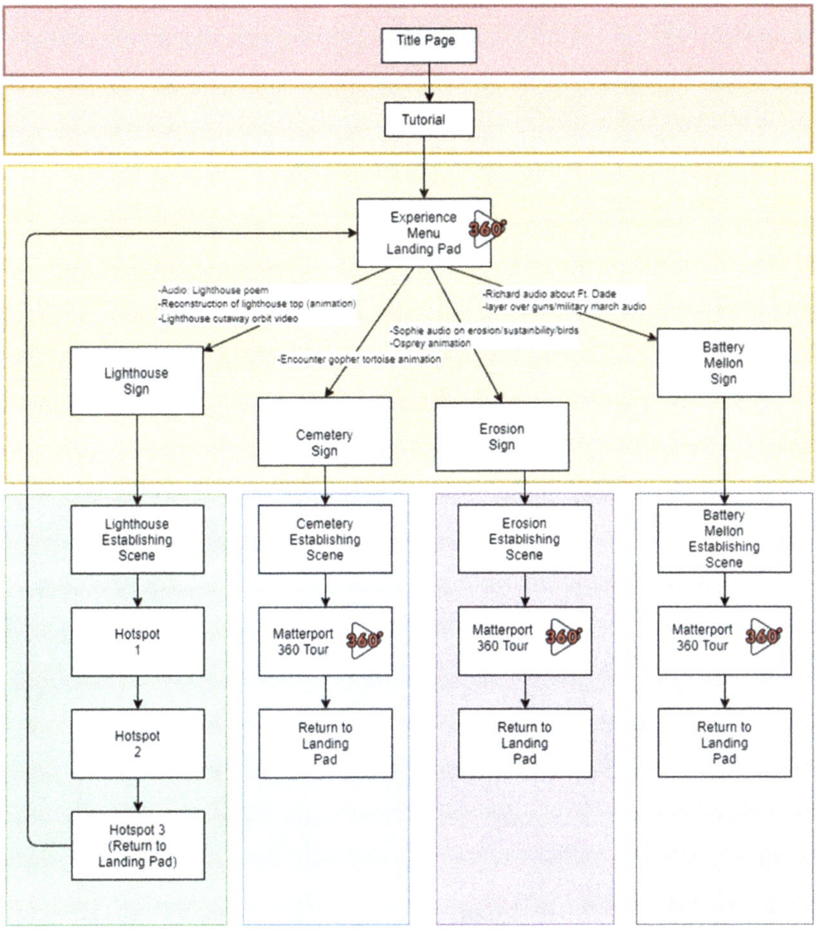

Figure 6.13. Draft storyboard of the Egmont Key virtual reality experience. Image created by Laura Harrison, Access 3D Lab, University of South Florida.

lighthouse expert and leader of the Egmont Key Lighthouse Artifact Survey, Egmont Key historians Bruce McCall and Richard Sanchez, and archival expert and lawyer April Min. Multimedia annotations included "The Midnight Hour," a poem written by a lighthouse keeper (see Chapter 2); a 1930s newspaper article with a photo of Fort Dade and the headline "GHOST CITY ON ISLAND TO BE POPULATED AGAIN"; an article from the *Seminole Tribune* about the canoe that was found on Egmont Key after Hurricane Dorian (see Chapter 2 and 3); archival photos of the Egmont Key Lighthouse before the top was

Figure 6.14. Scenes from the *Egmont Key VR Tour.* (*A*) Development of the application in Pano2VR. (*B*) Annotated model of Battery McIntosh discussing heritage at risk. (*C*) Rising seas encroach on Battery Mellon's western reaches. In this location, annotations discuss the many threats to natural and cultural heritage on the island with a newspaper referring to the Fort Dade "ghost town" and archival photos of a gun battery now underwater. (*D*) A photo of the Tampa Bay Pilots Association village after Hurricane Eta underlines the fragility of the island's cultural heritage. And (*E*) the entrance to Battery Mellon contains many white "hot spots" that, when clicked, present interactive content such as the map of erosion seen at the right. Image created by Laura Harrison, Access 3D Lab, University of South Florida.

Figure 6.15. The Egmont Key VR pop-up (*left*) and touchscreen display (*right*) at the USF Homecoming outreach event. By permission of Laura Harrison.

removed; and photos of Frederick Tresca, the lighthouse keeper from 1856 to 1860. Once the app was complete and all annotations were added, it was deployed directly from Pano2VR to VRTourviewer in the Oculus Quest 2 VR headset, where it was tested and then introduced to the public.

Once the VR app was developed, our team set about creating a "pop-up" VR lounge complete with a rug, chairs, side tables and a backdrop, and brought the experience to several outreach events (the USF homecoming at the Marshall Center, Discover the Island, and a tour of USF Access 3D Lab) (6.15). We secured Institutional Review Board (IRB) approval to conduct a user experience evaluation of the 80 participants who used the *Egmont Key VR Tour* across the three locations. We administered a survey to all participants and collated the results. Overall, participants reacted positively to the experience and pointed out some areas for improvement.

A key focus of our user study was evaluating the effectiveness of the VR tour as medium of public heritage communication and engagement. Toward this end, our team administered surveys to 80 participants at three separate events, recording basic demographic information as well as users' overall impressions of the experience and their suggestions for improvement. The events were a

DOES USING VR INCREASE IN LEARNING ABOUT HISTORY AND SUSTAINABILITY?

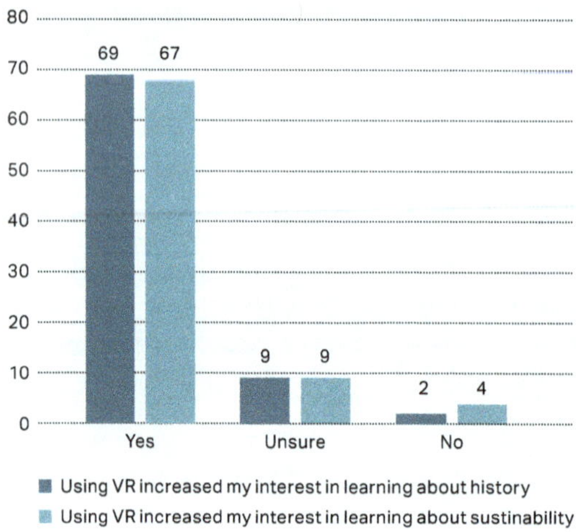

Chart 6.1. Egmont Key VR user survey indicating that the vast majority of users felt that the experience increased their interest in learning about history and sustainability. Chart created by Laura Harrison, Access 3D Lab, University of South Florida.

PEOPLE WHO RARELY PARTICIPATE IN CULTURAL EVENTS

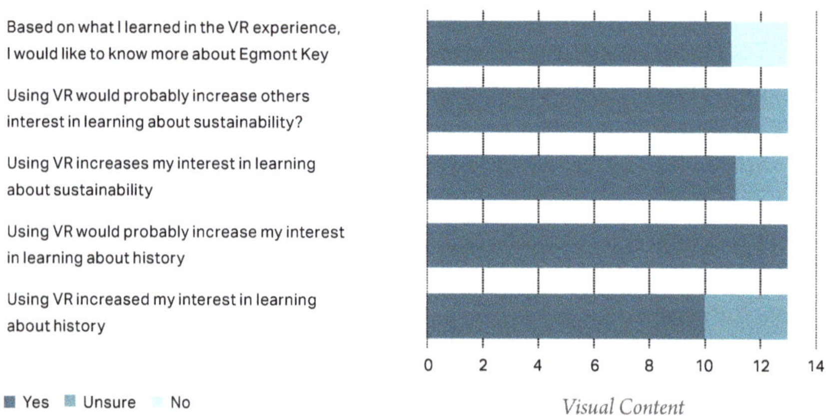

Chart 6.2. Egmont Key VR survey results, indicating that the experience increased interest in learning about history and sustainability, even for people who rarely participate in cultural events. Chart created by Laura Harrison, Access 3D Lab, University of South Florida.

student tour of Access 3D Lab, the USF homecoming event at the Marshall Student Center, and Discover the Island, a public outreach event on Egmont Key organized by our community partners the Egmont Key Alliance. The surveys were thus distributed across multiple ages and demographics, with mostly students at the lab tour, but a more diverse cross section of ages and backgrounds at the homecoming event and Discover the Island. One of our key findings from the entire study population was the strong affirmative response to the question of whether VR increased user interest in learning about history and sustainability (Chart 6.1).

One of the prescreening questions in the VR survey had to do with the frequency that users attended or participated in cultural events such as visiting museums or attending guided tours. Of our 80 users, 13 reported participating in such cultural activities just 0–1 times per year. The way that this "disengaged/disinterested" group responded to the VR experience was very enlightening. As shown in Chart 6.2, the overwhelming majority of these users expressed interest and engagement with history, sustainability, and learning about Egmont Key because of the VR experience. A particularly noteworthy finding is that 92% said they thought the VR experience would increase *others'* interest in learning about sustainability, and 100% thought the experience would increase *others'* interest in learning about history. This idea of whether users would recommend an experience to others aligns with the Net Promoter Score (NPS) (Reichheld 2003), a widely used metric in the business world used to measure customer engagement and satisfaction. In this case, the VR tour turned our "disengaged/disinterested" group into "promoters," or advocates who drive positive word of mouth and contribute to interest, growth, and adoption. Thus, the VR tour shows promising signs of becoming an integral part of growing a community of practice around preserving and protecting Egmont Key's heritage.

Another survey prescreening question identified first-time VR users, which was just over half of our survey population (n=44). We were very interested in how this group would respond to our user experience design questions, and whether they found the VR experience enjoyable and easy to navigate, or cumbersome and difficult. Our survey results indicate a high degree of overall satisfaction (Chart 6.2), with most users agreeing that the app worked the way they wanted it to work, they could easily navigate through the application, and that they found the application easy to use. The user experience design is directly tied to the communication of heritage stories, and the majority of first-time VR users also indicated that they knew more about Egmont Key after using the application (Chart 6.3).

Our team found the results from first-time users encouraging but also wanted to know more about specific pain points and highlights of the experience, so included a few open-ended questions to add some qualitative insights. When prompted to suggest improvements to the application, several users mentioned clumsy navigation, with comments such as "when you go into a room or beach, make it easier to go back by labelling the dots with 'back'" (User #6) and "I would suggest having an easily accessible menu to fast track you to one point instead of clicking through each previous point that you've been at" (User #20). Other critical comments related to the hardware, which can be difficult to use for people who wear glasses. User #22 mentioned "possibly adding an option to turn off the narrations. When walking back to an area, the auto narration still plays every time. This can potentially become disorienting. Also I was unable to use the software without my glasses, only contacts. When I searched online for this problem, other VR users w prescriptions with over -3.75 have the same issue." Other qualitative responses inquired about what users thought future Egmont Key VR experiences should include. User #41 mentioned wanting "3D representation of Egmont from various eras using CGI to recreate buildings and environments," and User #1 requested an "underwater edition to see what was eroded away. Maybe a form of reconstruction to show what it originally looked like."

AUGMENTED REALITY

Recent developments in information technology have enabled visitors to experience and appreciate cultural heritage sites beyond the constraints of time, space, and language. One such technology is augmented reality (AR), which overlays digital content onto users' surroundings, "allowing users to explore the surrounding environment by using mobile technologies" (Georgiou and Kyza 2017: 24). AR is a visualization technique that superimposes computer-generated data, such as text, video, graphics, GPS data and other multimedia formats, on top of the real-world view, as captured from the camera of a computer, a mobile phone, or other devices. In other words, AR can augment one's view and transform it with the help of a computer or a mobile device and thus enhance the user's perception of reality and of the surrounding environment (Harrison et al. 2025). Cultural heritage tourism is one of the most important areas served by the mobile application of AR, because AR can enhance tourists'

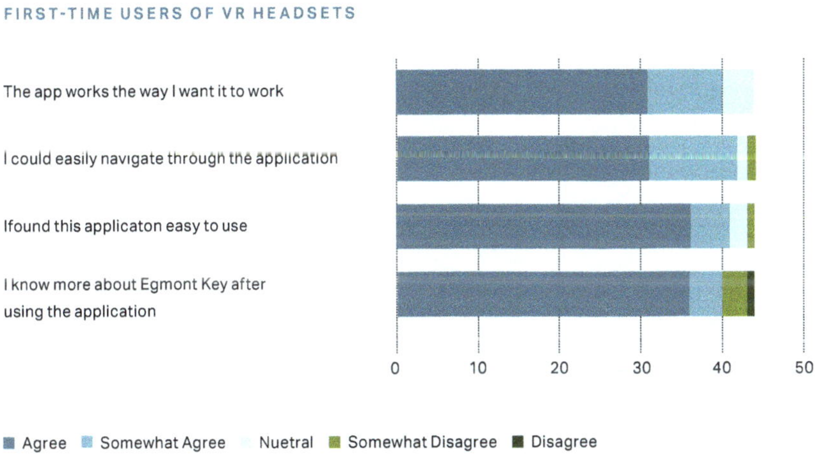

Chart 6.3. Reactions of first-time VR users to the Egmont Key VR experience. Chart created by Laura Harrison, Access 3D Lab, University of South Florida.

historical and geological knowledge and social awareness (Jung et al. 2015). Benefits of AR in terms of engagement, immersion, and attention make it a promising technology to engage visitors in a heritage tourism setting. Therefore, new and emerging digital technologies, such as AR, have been used for the enhancement of visitor experiences (Moorhouse and Jung 2017).

One of the key advantages of augmented reality (AR) is that it creates an engaging and interactive interpretive experience without requiring any physical alterations to the landscape, such as excavation or infrastructure installation. This makes AR an ideal tool for public heritage communication at protected and vulnerable sites like Egmont Key. With this in mind, our team developed *Step into History*, a prototype AR app designed to integrate locative media into the visitor experience at Egmont Key. Given that most of Egmont Key is a US National Wildlife Refuge, minimizing environmental impact was a priority for land managers and permitting officials. The app's development followed a process similar to that of touchscreen and VR applications, involving the curation of archival documents, creation of original 3D assets, user experience design, testing, deployment, and evaluation. This work was supported by a USF Creative Scholarship Grant focused on bringing Fort Dade's ghost town back to life. In the 1920s, park personnel deliberately set fire to the town in an effort to drive out bootleggers (see Chapters 2 and 4). Today, the remains of

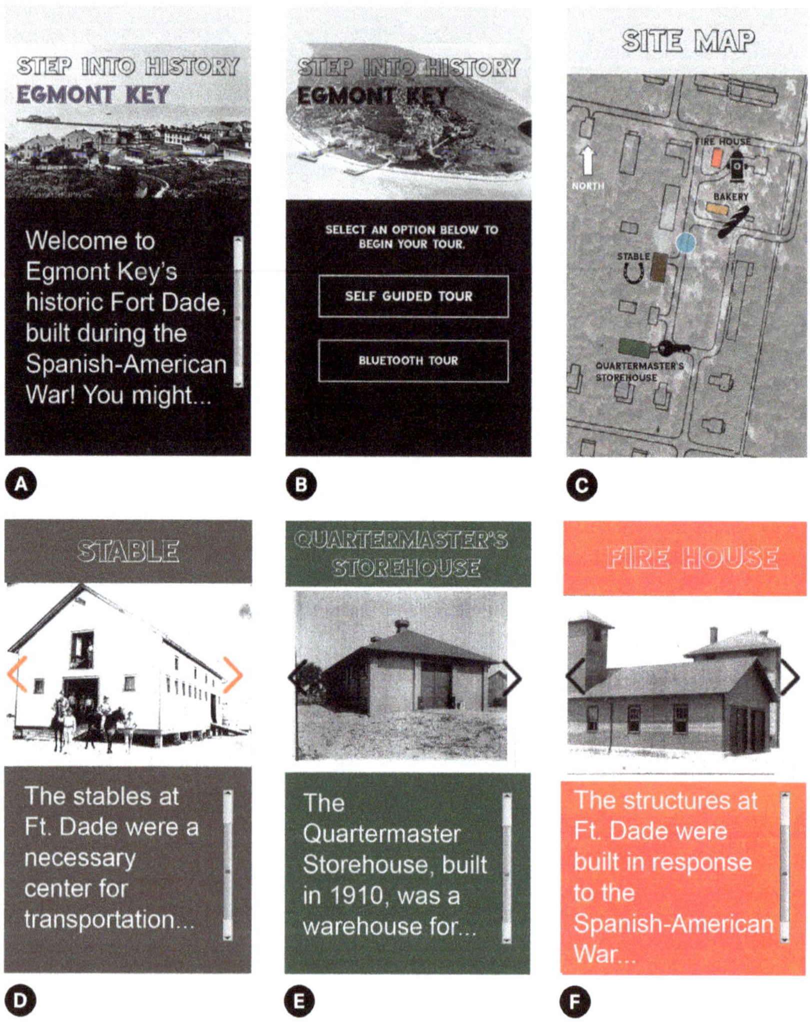

Figure 6.16. Design of the *Step into History* app. All users navigate through the initial sequence of the splash screen (*A*) and the home screen (*B*). If users choose self-guided tour, they see (*C*); otherwise, they choose Bluetooth tour and the interpretive information appears when they physically approach one of the sites on foot. Users can switch back and forth between the Bluetooth tour and the self-guided tour at will. Images D–F show the landing page for the Stable, Quartermaster Warehouse, and Fire Station, which each contain a gallery of archival photos and interpretive text coupled with an audio voice-over. The bakery, which contained a 3D reconstruction of the site visualized in place atop the building's decaying foundation, is described in greater detail in Figure 6.17. Image created by Laura Harrison, Access 3D Lab, University of South Florida.

Fort Dade consist of overgrown building foundations scattered along a well-preserved brick road network. *Step into History* allows visitors to experience this lost history through locative media and digital storytelling.

Step into History focuses on lesser-known aspects of Fort Dade's history, highlighting vignettes of daily life, which have received far less attention than the well-documented topics of military conflict and technology. The app focuses on four main sites within the ghost town: the Bakery, Stable, Fire Station, and Quartermaster Warehouse. Our team storyboarded the activity to present two modes of navigation through the content—one with a map that directed users from site to site, and one using Bluetooth sensors that automatically triggered the experience when a user got close to a site (6.16).

As a prototype, three of the hot spots contained simple 2D archival content such as historic photos and interpretive text/narration, but one hot spot became a test case for more interactive/immersive media content: the Bakery. We brought in archivist and historian April Min to uncover personal vignettes connected to the bakery, and after a few months of research into military records and archives she was able to uncover the incredible story of Julius the bugle-blowing baker (see Chapter 2). Julius Buren Tiedchen (1899–1944) joined the Army and was deployed to Fort Dade as a bugler—a position he held only briefly before being reassigned to the bakery. His daily tasks involved mixing dough in a large metal vat according to a specific Army recipe and baking it in a Middleburg oven. After several years at Fort Dade, Julius found himself working at the Federal Bake Shop on Central Ave. in nearby St. Petersburg, Florida, carrying on the legacy of his years at Egmont Key.

To bring the story of Julius the Baker to life in AR, our team referenced archival drawings of the bakery to create a 3D mesh in Unity that encompassed not only the building itself but also the dough-mixing trough and the Middleburg oven. An interactive visualization appeared in place—atop the overgrown foundation of the structure—when users approached the site. A USF graduate student was enlisted to create audio files for the app that included the story of Julius at the bakery.

Photos, maps, text, and audio files were given to Dr. Howard Kaplan at the USF Advanced Visualization Center, who programmed them into the prototype. The app was reviewed and tested multiple times to assess how it worked and if the Bluetooth triggers would launch the pages for each of the four locations featured. The first field test was successful, and the triggers launched the experience, including the pop-up overlay of the bakery building created from

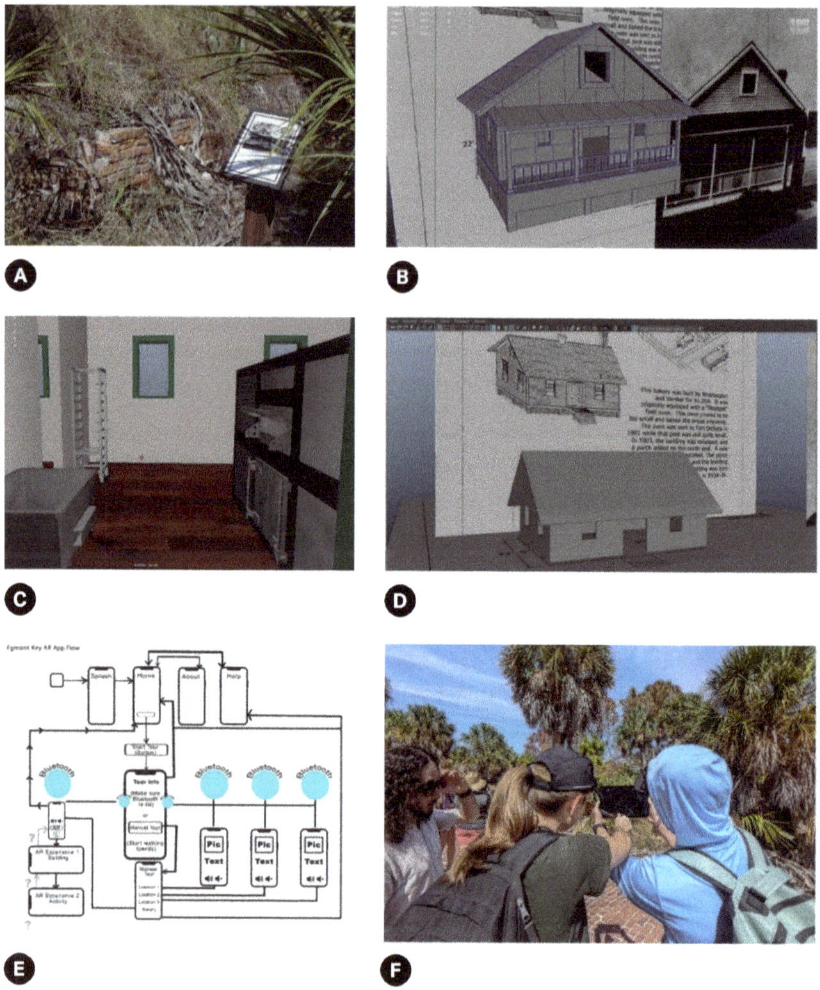

Figure 6.17. The Bakery was the highlight of the *Step into History* AR app. *A* shows the bakery as it appeared in 2023, reduced to an overgrown foundation with a simple sign nearby. *B–D* show the process of digitally reconstructing the site based on archival drawings in Unity. This reconstruction encompassed the buildings' exterior as well as interior elements, such as the Middleburg oven. *E* shows a storyboard for the app design, showing pathways between content, and *F* shows app testing on the island. Image created by Laura Harrison, Access 3D Lab, University of South Florida.

drawings provided to Dr. Kaplan's team (see 6.17: B and D). Two iPads were purchased for the project to assist with testing the app.

The AR experience itself begins with a tutorial and introduction. After users complete the tutorial, they launch the experience and explore the four locations at Fort Dade. The information includes a brief history, maps, archival photos, and audio descriptions. For the bakery, a rendition of the actual bakery house appears which can be explored, rotated, and entered.

The Egmont Key field test included volunteers from USF classes. Bluetooth triggers were placed at each of the four sites at Egmont Key, and participants were given iPads to explore the area with the app (see 6.17: F). The trigger launched a sound that signaled the initiation of the experience (e.g., a fire bell for the firehouse; horses whinnying for the stable). Following up on an earlier piece about the Access 3D Lab by Fox 13 News, several reporters accompanied the test group and wrote a story about the experience (Wilson 2023).

The test was a success and the triggers worked, in addition to the audio and real-time pop up of the bakery building over the site where the bakery was located (now a pile of rubble; see Chapter 4). After the experience, users were asked to fill out a survey (see Appendix A). The results were tallied by Access 3D Lab staff and showed an overwhelming positive response to the *Step into History* AR app. Results indicated that 92% of respondents affirmed that AR increased their interest in learning about history. The users found the application easy to use and navigate but noted that some improvements could be made in how the app worked. They suggested adding more locations, increasing the amount of supplementary information such as pictures, increasing the reconstructed building renditions (this one just had the bakery), and featuring more stories about the people who lived and worked there (only Julius Tiedchen the baker was included in the prototype). These were excellent suggestions and in line with the goals of the app prototype to develop a model of what could subsequently be created for Egmont Key in a full-blown professionally produced and publicly available app. Such an endeavor will require a much larger grant.

The establishment of a prototype allowed the research team to refine the characteristics and functionality of the app, in addition to documenting challenges such as the bright glare on the island at the Fort Dade building locations. The Bluetooth triggers worked but the experience would be enhanced if there was connectivity on the island, which currently has no Wi-Fi capabilities and intermittent cellular coverage. To fully deploy an app at this location would also include gaining federal, state, and local approvals to amend the signage or structures and permanently affixing small Bluetooth sensors to the signposts.

The Egmont Key VR and AR projects and prototypes created immersive digital experiences that make the island's cultural and natural heritage accessible while highlighting its vulnerabilities and lesser-known histories. Using Matterport scans, Pano2VR, Unity, and locative AR technologies, the team integrated archival research, multimedia annotations, and interactive storytelling to engage diverse audiences. User evaluations demonstrated strong interest and learning outcomes, including among participants not normally inclined to engage with cultural heritage. While the projects faced some shortcomings in terms of navigation, hardware limitations, and content scope, these efforts still provide a robust model for using immersive technologies to document, interpret, and communicate heritage in protected and fragile environments.

Professional Development Workshops and Academic Courses

The goals of the Egmont Key Project included digitally documenting the island and building interpretive products with the help of our partners. Through these activities we have been able to highlight invisible histories and better inform stakeholders about heritage at risk and coming impacts of erosion and climate change. Another goal, given our position in academia, was to engage Egmont Key as a living learning laboratory to teach students and colleagues about the many lessons the island has to offer. Toward this end we conducted four field schools, a three-credit graduate class called Applied Heritage and Sustainability Research at Egmont Key, and hosted numerous class visits at the Access 3D Lab (directed by chapter author Harrison) for students to learn about the EKP and see the products of the research. Hundreds of students experienced the VR tour, AR tour, and tried out the interactive touchscreen while learning about the many histories of Egmont Key. Chapter author Hansen uses the EKP as an extended case study in her Sustainable Tourism Practices undergraduate class where students also visit the Access 3D Lab each semester.

The field schools, run in 2019, 2021, 2022, and 2023, were operated as professional development workshops (Table 6.2) where participants paid a modest fee to help defray the costs of equipment use and travel to Egmont Key (an expense that increased each year as ferry transport prices rose). They were open to USF students and others interested in receiving training in digital technologies, heritage at risk, and sustainable tourism. The workshops focused on

Table 6.1. Summary of Egmont Key Workshops and Deliverables, 2019–2023

Year	Workshop title	Workshop deliverables	Technologies
2019	Applied Heritage & Sustainability Research at Egmont Key	Scanned Battery Mellon, Lighthouse, Cemetery	FARO Focus terrestrial lidar scanner
2021	Applied Heritage & Sustainability Research at Egmont Key	Scanned Guardhouse, Coast Guard Museum	Matterport
2022	Cultural Heritage & Climate Change Geomatics at Egmont Key	Scanned Battery McIntosh	FARO Focus terrestrial lidar scanner
2023	Geomatics for Heritage, Tourism and Sustainability Management at Ft. De Soto (Pinellas County); Career Forum: USF, FPAN, NPS, Riegl	Scanned Battery Laidley; Scanned and made 3D tour of Quartermaster Museum	FARO Focus terrestrial lidar scanner. DJI M600 drone; Matterport Pro2/ Pro3

technical skills and creating the digital assets described in the previous sections (lidar mapping, VR and AR tour prototypes, and Matterport digital twins), in addition to GIS components. With the completion of technical deliverables, including an edited Matterport model, and a reflection journal from what participants learned, they were able to earn a career-ready @Access 3D Gold Badge (see Fig. 6.18).

Participants from multiple universities and professional fields joined the workshops as guest speakers, which added depth to each workshop (see Fig. 6.19). In 2023, the research focused on the sister site to Egmont Key's Fort Dade, which is Fort De Soto in Pinellas County, built at the same time and just under two miles away across the Egmont Channel. Numerous partners were involved in providing expertise in the workshops, from the Egmont Key Alliance and the Florida Public Archaeology Network to the Seminole Tribal Historic Preservation Office. In 2023, we added a Career Forum with participants from the lidar industry (Riegl and Langan) and the National Park Service (6.20).

The impact of the workshops was evident in the evaluations provided by

Figure 6.18. Workshops participants receiving an @Access3D Gold Badge at Egmont Key upon completion of lidar fieldwork and technical training in geomatics technologies. The @Access3D Gold Badge is an applied technology certification developed at USF's Access 3D Lab. By permission of Laura Harrison.

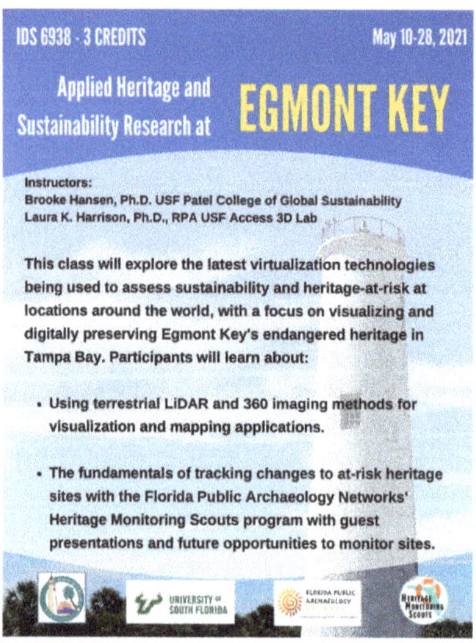

Figure 6.19. Flyer for the 2021course in Applied Heritage and Sustainability Research at Egmont Key. Image created by Laura Harrison, Access 3D Lab, University of South Florida.

Figure 6.20. Career Development Forum as part of the 2023 professional development training. Image created by Laura Harrison, Access 3D Lab, University of South Florida.

Figure 6.21. Participants in the 2019 Egmont Key professional development workshop. By permission of Laura Harrison.

participants (6.20). When asked "How did the workshop add to your professional skills? How might you use these skills in the future?" responses included:

> Yes, ground-based lidar inspired new potential applications in my current job.
>
> I am an archaeologist and can use aerial lidar to see ground contours. I can use drones and photogrammetry to better measure and present images of mounds.
>
> The workshop has fundamentally added new tools to my research that I can use to reconstruct ancient landscapes and cultural spaces and present that material to the public. It has also provided me with an opportunity to think of my research in more expansive ways to include applied elements related to sustainability and cultural heritage.
>
> The workshop added great skills in terrestrial lidar scanning & Matterport that I think will be beneficial in my career following USF.
>
> As a returning attendee, I loved the workshop. I think it's a fantastic introduction to incredible technologies that are excellent and valuable tools

> that aid in making you more employable. I'm hoping to utilize my expertise in climate mitigation and adaptation alongside GIS, Lidar, and Matterport to switch into a career focused on flood mapping and hazard mitigation.
>
> It made me aware of the capabilities and limitations of Matterport (photogrammetry) and Faro (terrestrial lidar) and their similarities and differences. I can easily see how they could both be useful methods of documenting an archaeological site.

In general, the workshops were very impactful for the participants who valued the opportunity to connect with peers, engage directly with at-risk heritage, and envision their future roles in preservation (6.22). Participants' feedback illustrates how the workshops demystified geomatics technologies and empowered them to engage directly with heritage documentation in a real-world context:

> I really appreciate the work you all put in to make this workshop successful. It quite literally changed my life and career aspirations, and for that I am so grateful. Hopefully next year I can return as someone working in the industry.
>
> I got to engage with both the equipment and the software in a hands-on approach to the material being learned. It demystified lidar for me which is what I wanted. I feel like I could, more or less, go out and work on a project using lidar. Obviously, there is more to learn, but I feel I have enough to go on now to where I could travel on the learning curve with greater ease as I actively engage in using the technology in research.

In 2020, with restrictions put in place by the global pandemic, a fully in-person professional training was not feasible, so we decided to offer it as a three-credit graduate class titled Applied Heritage and Sustainability Research at Egmont Key. The class was taught remotely with visits to the Access 3D Lab for equipment demos and a one-day site tour of Egmont Key. Given the inability to provide fully hands-on technology training, the focus was more on the pedagogies of cultural heritage, sustainable development, heritage at risk, and digital storytelling (Huggett 2015; Little et al. 2020; Silberman 2007; Tanasi 2020; Xiao et al. 2018). Framed through the lens of PAR, the course emphasized how engaged, collaborative inquiry can address heritage and sus-

Figure 6.22. Brooke Hansen and Richard Sanchez with 2021 workshop participants at Egmont Key. By permission of Laura Harrison.

tainability challenges. Topics included the role of international organizations and agreements (e.g., ICOMOS, ICCROM, UNESCO, UN SDGs), the case study of Egmont Key, Seminole perspectives, and how to best address preserving and protecting the island in the face of growing threats. Additional units addressed National Park Service interpretive training, GIS for site monitoring, and careers in heritage and sustainability.

One class project focused on evaluating if Egmont Key might qualify as a UNESCO World Heritage Site as a means of providing greater recognition and conservation. The conclusion was that it does indeed meet the qualifications, but with the submerging landscape and assets already underwater, it might be better served as National Marine Sanctuary. Other activities performed by the class included assessment of the Tampa Bay Refuges Comprehensive Conservation Plan (discussed at length in Chapter 4) and discussion of what should be included in a revised sustainable management plan.

To enliven the class and connect with key stakeholders, guest speakers were incorporated from the Egmont Key Alliance (EKA), Seminole Tribe of Florida Tribal Historic Preservation Office (THPO), and the Florida Public Archaeology Network (FPAN). For a comparative case study from another area with vulnerable coastal heritage sites, we invited Ellie Graham from the Scotland Coastal Archaeology and the Problem of Erosion project (SCAPE), who had already been collaborating with FPAN (Graham et al. 2019; Graham and Hambly 2020). Scotland has over 11,000 miles of coastline (Florida has over 8,000) and thousands of archaeological sites and critical infrastructure that prompted the formation of SCAPE. Noting their common agendas, FPAN teamed up with SCAPE to learn best practices, technology recommendations, and geospatial data management systems. It was very beneficial for the students in the class to learn about these global collaborations and protocols for documenting heritage at risk.

Student reflections on the course engaged with several key themes, including the importance of combining Indigenous perspectives, digital storytelling and sustainability, heritage at risk/disappearing heritage, professional career development, and global connections (Table 6.2). It was particularly gratifying to see students engaging with not only the course readings and assignments but also developing a nuanced understanding of Egmont Key integrating perspectives from guest speakers and site visits. One student noted that while cultural heritage, sustainability, and technology may initially seem distinct, they are deeply interconnected—a key theme of the course and indeed the overall Egmont Key Project. In addition, the hands-on experiences with professionals from FPAN, THPO, SCAPE, and the Seminole Tribe of Florida (STOF) provided networking opportunities for students and insight into potential career pathways. Many students articulated a newfound understanding of how their interests in sustainability, heritage, and digital technologies could converge in meaningful potential career pathways in the heritage, tourism, and sustainability sectors.

The impact of the training did seem to contribute positively to the participants' careers as the alumni from the workshops and class went on to secure professional positions—often with recommendation letters written by the research team—at organizations including the Nature Conservancy, the Advisory Council on Historic Preservation, the National Marine Sanctuary Foundation, Audubon, and Kind Traveler (an organization devoted to sustainable travel). One student went on to work in disaster resiliency planning with The Federal Emergency Management Agency (FEMA), while another became the sustainability manager for a coastal tourism city located about 40 minutes boat ride from Egmont Key. Notably, a participant from the 2023 cohort, Alex Fawbush, went on to gain employment at the Access 3D Lab where he carries out duties that include collecting 3D scan data and processing digital heritage

Table 6.2. Student Feedback from Applied Heritage and Sustainability Research Course

Course themes	Student feedback
Indigenous Heritage	The perspectives and values of indigenous groups must be integral in the development of plans to conserve heritage by involving those communities in the projects and assessing their views on the need for the project.
	The cultural heritage of these people needs to be incorporated in tourism planning and management since tourism is a mechanism to teach and share.
	The course clarified and deepened by understanding of the differences between tangible and intangible heritage, especially through the engagement with the STOF and Egmont Key. What an opportunity to be able to hear from Tribal members and THPO directly! That experience, along with some of the analytical reading, made me realize how much intangible heritage I was missing. Tying this to my interest in tourism in marine and coastal environments, this will be extremely important for me to remember and consider given that 40% of the world's population lives within 100 km of a coastline.
Digital Storytelling and Sustainability	This course comprehensibly demonstrated the intersections between cultural heritage, sustainability, and visualization technologies. Although at first these concepts appeared to be independent of each other, each field supports the other in various ways that have been incorporated in research and preservation projects around the world.
	Cultural heritage practices involve remembering and honoring people and events in past so that future generations may learn from them, appreciate them, and connect with them. In a similar way, sustainability encourages the conservation of the natural and cultural environment that has characterized our planet for so long, so that these environments may continue to thrive and that humanity may use and care for them responsibly in the future.
	The ideologies underlying cultural heritage and sustainability indicate a responsibility to people and the environment, both in their past and future forms.
	Climate change is a major threat, but so is over-tourism, the introduction of invasive species, and the lack of protections in place for vulnerable local populations. Fortunately, technology is making it easier to combat these challenges every day.

Table 6.2. continued

Course themes	Student feedback
Heritage at Risk/ Disappearing Heritage	The trip out to Egmont Key provided so many examples of lost cultural heritage. While there are many visitors who have some knowledge of the island's history, there are many more who have no clue. This class has helped me better understand what it means to lose cultural history from our world, and the consequences of losing that heritage. The preservation of cultural heritage was not at the forefront of my global sustainability thought processes, however the trip to Egmont Key, as well as the information discussed about the loss of Seminole Heritage helped me better understand what it means to focus on saving cultural heritage. Creating the visitor's center would be a great way to increase education on the history of Egmont Key, while it is also important to preserve the natural habitats for the native species.
Careers in Heritage and Sustainability	This course provided insight into some of the skills necessary to pursue a career in the fields of cultural heritage, digital archeology, and sustainable tourism. Even as someone who has had interest and some entry level experience in GIS applications, I had not studied advanced visualization technologies. I think one of the many valuable takeaways from this course was the introduction to the different laser scanners and photogrammetry tools. I also found the introduction to the section 106 requirements and hearing about how that can translate to internship opportunities to be highly valuable information. One of the best opportunities this course provided was real-world experience through our work on Egmont Key and the interaction with people working in the field such as FPAN, THPO, STOF, and SCAPE. These were educational experiences as well as networking opportunities. Being able to review successful grant applications was also very helpful. This class really opened my eyes to how sustainability and heritage can intersect, especially career-wise. I knew that I wanted to try and find a career that touched on the environment and in my personal life I also care a lot about learning about and preserving heritage. I love the idea of working somewhere similar to a THPO (or even at a THPO) to help preserve heritage and help bridge the communication gap between different cultures. Especially on projects like Egmont Key, these two passions really go hand in hand. This course helped me find more of a direction to go in.

Course themes	Student feedback
Global Connections	Ellie Graham from the University of St. Andrews in Scotland, presented to the class what technology has made possible in Scotland. Most notable is the Wemyss 4D Caves website, which offers an online tour of the Wemyss caves so that people can virtually visit the caves without harming them in any way. SCAPE, the organization Ellie works for in Scotland, has also developed a system where locals can send in information and pictures of potential archaeological sites using their cellphones. This allows SCAPE to have access to all of Scotland and evaluate potential sites, without having to use the funding to travel to the sites. On top of preserving funding, this process involves locals in discovering and protecting history, allowing them to be part of the process rather than outsiders.

datasets, refining workflows, and conducting archival and interpretive research on heritage topics. He is also a co-author of Chapter 7 in this book.

Workshops, trainings, courses, and partnerships have driven much of the research and teaching in the Egmont Key Project. Despite the challenges of the pandemic to the educational components of the project, the opportunity it provided to have a credit-bearing class with deeper scholarly explorations and guest speakers was valuable. As of the writing of this book, the education continues with the work from the EKP integrated into classes, ongoing internships at the Access 3D Lab, and plans for future professional training workshops at both Egmont Key, Fort De Soto, and other comparable sites regionally and globally. The lessons that can be learned from the EKP also live on in the many presentations we have done on the project that will continue into the foreseeable future.

Regional, National, and International Engagement: Professional and Public Outreach with the Egmont Key Project

Participatory Action Research (PAR), a key foundation for the theory and praxis of the EKP, emphasizes not only collaborative inquiry and education but also the sharing of findings to diverse audiences to promote understanding and

Figure 6.23. Tabling with the VR pop-up experience, Discover the Island hosted by the Egmont Key Alliance at Egmont Key. By permission of Brooke Hansen.

real-world change. Presenting to academic peers is important, of course, along with making sure community members, policymakers, residents, and visitors also get to learn, reflect, and take action. Toward this end, since 2018, we have done over 40 presentations at formal academic conferences, universities in other countries, educational festivals (6.23), history centers, museums, civic clubs, business chambers of commerce, retirement communities, and even a history happy hour and local car show (the Tierra Verde Classic Car Show).

While local audiences certainly got to be part of this public outreach, especially though the support of a Florida Humanities Council grant (discussed below), people around the country and world also got to learn about the disappearing island at the mouth of Tampa Bay. Of note are the international presentations where the tiny island's lessons were shared with audiences in England, Spain, Italy, Estonia, and Serbia (6.24). These efforts help bridge the gap between scholarship and action to foster broad engagement, enhance education, build communities of practice, and create greater awareness of invisible histories, heritage at risk, and the application of digital technologies. We took the mandate of PAR quite literally to share research far and wide (Table 6.3).

The impetus for the EKP began with creating more public awareness about

Figure 6.24. Chapter author Brooke Hansen (*left*), Laura Harrison (*right*), and USF student Jack West at the Green Destinations conference in Tallinn, Estonia, with two presentations on Egmont Key. By permission of Laura Harrison.

Figure 6.25. Tabling and outreach at the American Indian Arts Celebration (AIAC), Big Cypress Reservation, November 2018, with chapter author Laura Harrison and Bobby Henry (Seminole). By permission of Brooke Hansen.

the Seminole story at Egmont Key (and then grew to include many other topics). We began working with the Seminole THPO right away to plan how we could best help them tell the Egmont Key story. We brought information on the USF part of the Egmont Key Project to the Big Cypress Reservation and tabled at the well-attended 21st Annual American Indian Arts Celebration in 2018 (6.25). This was followed by meetings with the THPO both at Big Cypress, Egmont Key, and USF.

One of the ways we were able to promote education in collaboration with the THPO was through a Florida Humanities Council grant that enabled us to do a series of three webinars (COVID-19 prevented us from carrying out the in-person presentations that were originally planned at three different sites). The first two webinars featured our presentations about the EKP and the research products to date, along with speakers from FPAN (Jeff Moates) and the Egmont Key Alliance (Richard Sanchez). The third webinar was titled "Seminole Perspectives on Egmont Key" and included speakers Aaron Tommie (Seminole Tribe of Florida), Dave Scheidecker (Seminole Tribal Historic Preservation Office), and Quenton Cypress (Seminole Tribe of Florida).

This presentation shed light on the little-known Seminole chapter of Egmont Key's history and heritage and moving stories were shared about resilience, survival, and pride that continue to resonate among the Tribe (discussed at length in Chapter 3). Webinar attendees filled out evaluation forms of the presentations. One guest remarked, "[I am] horrified at the ignorance of those people who don't know about the current population of Seminole people. Glad to hear about the interaction with the Tribe. I have known about the history of Egmont and other sites; it's been ingrained in my experience of Florida due to my interests. I hope to attend more in future." Others felt compelled to act. One person asked, "Please let us know how we can participate in spreading this awareness in SW Florida." Likewise, another attendee remarked "Thanks all for speaking so powerfully about this site. What can the average person do to spread the message that Tribe still exists?" These comments and others reveal that this project successfully met our goal of raising public awareness and understanding of Egmont Key and the enduring presence of the Seminole people.

An interesting global connection that occurred was with Serbia. At the inception of the EKP, Hansen was already engaged in sustainable tourism projects at cultural heritage sites in Serbia in collaboration with various offices and programs in the country. This led to creating a space for cross-country collaborations on sustainability, tourism, and the use of virtualization technologies that involved the expertise of both Hansen and Harrison. We received a US Embassy Serbia University Partnership grant in 2022 titled "Imersivne tehnologije za kros-kulturni razvoj turizma: SAD i Srbija na putu ka digitalnoj transformaciji" (Immersive Technologies for Cross-Cultural Tourism Development: US and Serbia on a Pathway to Digital Transformation).

The grant, a partnership between USF and the University of Novi Sad, enabled the exchange of faculty, students, and research projects at both locations, in Florida and Serbia. In Serbia, we gave presentations on the EKP and digital technologies, including hands-on demos of scanning technologies by Harrison at the Museum of Vojvodina in Novi Sad. When the University of Novi Sad faculty and students traveled to Florida, they were able to immerse themselves in the EKP with tutorials at the Access 3D Lab on the equipment and research products to date (interactive touchscreen, VR tour, digital twins, and TLS scans). They were also given a tour on-site at Egmont Key so that they could connect the research process with the in-situ reality of carrying out this kind of project on a remote island only accessible by boat. In the evaluation of the exchange, one of the Serbian students noted,

> Dr. Harrison introduced to us her lab and some projects she is working on; we had a chance to scan the entire room with the Faro Focus 3D laser scanner, to scan some artifacts and our professor Dr. Miroslav with a 3D scanner too. In the lab of Dr. Harrison, we saw their research as a good example using 3D scanners in a project to protect the wildlife refuge Island Egmont Key that is disappearing. It was a pleasure for me and I was honored to visit a place like the Egmont Key because of all the story behind it.

Another Serbian student commented,

> As the first observation I would like to mention Egmont Key and the usage of 3D scanners for protection and making VR access to some of the main buildings on the island. 3D projections of the ruined buildings are one of the best practices for keeping cultural and natural heritage alive. Since my country is landlocked, I had a special experience visiting Egmont Key.

Part of the grant deliverables included webinars where students from both universities attended, which ended up including almost 20 classes from USF and the University of Novi Sad. We presented on our work in the EKP to hundreds of students from our own university and in Serbia. The evaluations done on the webinars were overwhelmingly positive and students mentioned gaining a better understanding of cultural heritage tourism, digital technologies, invisible histories, and sustainable tourism. Another culmination of the grant, this time in the Phase Two continuation, was a 2024 international conference called "STRENGTH: Strengthening Sustainability Communication in Tourism, Hospitality, and Event Industries." We presented the EKP research and also the digital heritage preservation work that we had done during the trips to Serbia at cultural heritage and ecotourism sites in the country.

Our commitment to community engagement extended beyond the presentations, pop-up virtual reality and touchscreen exhibits, and tabling; we also collaborated with journalists and media figures from many outlets to share our work on digital heritage and sustainability. The first major news story to come out about the project covered the lidar scanning of the lighthouse and our collaboration with the Seminole Tribe (Guzzo 2019). Other media features followed and highlighted the virtualization and sustainable tourism aspects of the EKP (Smith 2021a, 2021b). A significant amount of news coverage integrated Seminole voices and perspectives, particularly Emerald Morrow's piece on Channel 10 News WTSP (Morrow 2019). Later coverage included TV segments, radio shows (Roa 2025), and media articles that presented our work alongside more Seminole perspectives, such as the three-part series featured in *The Marjorie* that covered threats to the island, the USF EKP, and words from two Seminole youth (Hamilton et al. 2022). We traveled to the island with the article's authors and young Seminole Tribe of Florida members Mahala Billie Osceola and Carmello Shenandoah. The article includes sections written by Mahala and Carmello about their thoughts. Shenandoah wrote:

> With time, Florida's history with the Seminole Tribe of Florida is being forgotten, for better or worse. The Seminole Tribe has a long history in Florida, and everyone should be able to learn about it. Whether or not it is appropriate to conserve places like Egmont Key is a subject of debate. Even though it will be controversial, the historic property does not need to be physically protected. Because of the great advancements in technology, it is now possible to make a virtual duplicate of the place. The real location is still being claimed by nature. The University of South Florida has been working on a 3D lab of the key with the Seminole Tribe of Florida, and it is skillfully done. Learning in the 3D lab made it easier

Table 6.3. Egmont Key Project International, National, and Regional Outreach and Community Engagement

Title	*Location*
INTERNATIONAL	
Presentation at Computer Applications in Archaeology conference	Oxford, UK
Presentation at European Association of Archaeologists conference	Rome, Italy
Presentation at University of Belgrade	Belgrade, Serbia
Presentation at Viminacium	Stari Kostolac, Serbia
Presentation at Serbian Chamber of Commerce	Belgrade, Serbia
Presentation at Green Destinations conference	Tallinn, Estonia
Presentation at STRENGTH conference	Novi Sad, Serbia
Presentation at Global Sustainable Tourism Council conference	Seville, Spain
Egmont Key virtual reality tour, Museum of Vojvodina	Novi Sad, Serbia
NATIONAL	
Presentation at Archaeological Institute of America annual meeting	New Orleans, LA
Poster at American Anthropological Association annual conference	Tampa, FL
Presentation at Society for American Archaeology annual meeting	Virtual
REGIONAL	
Pop-up touchscreen exhibit at Tierra Verde Classic Car Show, USF Homecoming, Access 3D Lab	Tierra Verde, FL
Pop-up touchscreen exhibit at the Egmont Key Alliance 30th Anniversary event, Tampa Bay Watch	Tierra Verde, FL
Pop-up virtual reality experience at Hope Spot event	Dunedin, FL
Outreach and tabling at American Indian Arts Festival	Big Cypress Reservation, FL

Table 6.3. continued

Title	*Location*
Tabling and outreach at the Florida State Fair	Tampa, FL
Outreach, tabling, and virtual reality tour at Discover the Island (Egmont Key Alliance event)	Egmont Key, FL
Presentations for Florida Humanities Council series with THPO, Egmont Key Alliance, and FPAN	Virtual
Presentation at Hope Spot Gala	Dunedin, FL
Presentation at GIS day at Big Cypress Reservation (Seminole Tribe of Florida)	Big Cypress, FL
Presentation at Time Sifters public archaeology group	Sarasota, FL
Presentation at Bradenton Yacht Club	Bradenton, FL
Presentation at Westminster Suncoast Retirement Community	St. Petersburg, FL
Presentation at Westminster Palms Retirement Community	St. Petersburg, FL
Presentation at the Tampa Bay Sea Kayakers Club	St. Petersburg, FL
Presentations on the Hubbard's Marina Egmont Key ferry	Tierra Verde, FL
Presentation at St. Petersburgh Museum of History "Happy Hour with the Historian" speaker series	St. Petersburg, FL
Presentation at Green Drinks at Gasparilla Distillery and Cocktail Bar	Tampa FL
Presentation at Tidally United conference	Pensacola, FL
Presentation at Tidally United conference	Fort Myers, FL
Presentation at Synergy Summit for Cultural Heritage and Tourism	Fort Lauderdale, FL
Presentation at Tampa Bay History Center with partners from THPO and Egmont Key Alliance	Tampa, FL

to see the environment and comprehend how climate change is affecting Egmont Key. (Osceola and Shenandoah 2022: para. 10)

This kind of broad engagement and sharing of knowledge, stories, the products of research, and diverse perspectives is inherent to the PAR approach, and we will continue to promote this as one of the most valuable ways academia can both advance knowledge, promote real-world societal benefits, and contribute to human well-being.

Conclusion

The Egmont Key Project is a model of how Participatory Action Research, digital heritage methodologies, and community dialogues can document heritage at risk, while simultaneously creating new ways to understand the past and its implications for the present and future. In bringing together these methodologies, the Egmont Key Project advances an action-oriented, community-engaged, and digitally enhanced perspective on heritage management and preservation. The Egmont Key Project reflects the iterative cycle of PAR, where research informs teaching, community partners guide workshops, and outreach reinforces research. By employing terrestrial lidar scanning to digitally preserve built heritage, developing immersive VR and AR experiences to enhance public understanding of heritage and sustainability, and offering innovative courses and workshops, the EKP became an integral part of a community of practice centered on digitizing and reflecting on the disappearing island.

The key problem that spurred all of this work was the dual threat to invisible histories at a disappearing island. As sea-level rise and erosion accelerate the physical loss of Egmont Key's built environment, many of its significant but overlooked narratives—such as the legacy of Seminole imprisonment during Indian Removal—also risk being forgotten. Digital heritage tools played a crucial role in confronting this loss and erasure. Lidar scanning created high-resolution records of Egmont Key's at-risk built environment, while VR and AR experiences helped bring the island's layered past and intangible histories to life for diverse audiences. By centering Indigenous voices and collaborating with a multitude of stakeholders, the project aimed not only to preserve the site's tangible heritage but also to highlight historically marginalized perspectives that are often absent from mainstream narratives.

A key lesson learned from this project is that while digital tools can enhance heritage preservation, their success depends on meaningful community engagement and interdisciplinary collaboration. The intertwined nature of our research, teaching, and outreach reinforced that no single discipline or methodology can adequately address the complexities of heritage at risk. Partnerships with community organizations, Indigenous groups, and sustainability experts ensured that our multiyear project evolved and remained relevant and impactful. At the same time, challenges such as navigating differing stakeholder priorities, technical limitations, and tight funding underscored the importance of adaptability and ongoing dialogue. Ultimately, the Egmont Key Project demonstrates that digital heritage and PAR are most effective when they are iterative, inclusive, and responsive to both the needs of communities and the realities of environmental and historical change.

Beyond research and preservation, the EKP has demonstrated the power of hands-on training and professional development. Through workshops, field schools, and university courses, the project has trained hundreds of students and professionals in digital heritage techniques, equipping them to translate the lessons learned at Egmont Key to careers in heritage management, tourism, and sustainability at heritage sites around the country and the world.

The EKP's public engagement strategy, which included pop-up VR exhibits, digital touchscreen storytelling, and participation in community events, reinforced the importance of making research accessible to multiple audiences. Whether at academic conferences, historical societies, or local outreach events, sharing findings with a broad cross section of the public has deepened awareness of community perspectives on the disappearing island. The island is beloved by locals who often share memories of childhood visits decades ago, before some of the gun batteries were underwater. For them, and many others, the loss of its heritage is deeply personal. We've found that visualizations of Egmont Key's disappearing heritage resonate strongly with the local community. This approach aligns with the principles of PAR, which prioritize both knowledge creation and mobilization to drive meaningful change.

The urgency of preserving Egmont Key's disappearing heritage was underscored by the devastating impact of Hurricanes Helene and Milton in 2024, which destroyed historic sites across the Tampa Bay region, including parts of Egmont Key. These storms reinforced the critical need for proactive digital documentation, as lidar scans, Matterport models, and immersive media (VR and AR) became some of the only remaining records of structures and landscapes that no longer exist. The loss of physical heritage due to extreme weather events highlights the growing role of digital tools and techniques in safeguarding cultural memory against climate change. Beyond preservation, these technologies also serve as powerful storytelling devices, ensuring that communities can continue engaging with their histories even as the physical spaces transform or disappear.

Moving forward, the lessons learned from the EKP can serve as a model for other at-risk heritage sites globally. The project draws attention to the need for continued collaboration between academics, Indigenous communities, government agencies, and nonprofit organizations to address pressing issues of heritage preservation, climate change, and sustainable tourism. By integrating digital tools, community engagement, and interdisciplinary research, the future of heritage management can be both technologically innovative and deeply rooted in cultural and environmental stewardship.

References Cited

Georgiou, Y., and E. A. Kyza. 2017. The Development and Validation of the ARI Questionnaire: An Instrument for Measuring Immersion in Location-Based Augmented Reality Settings. *International Journal of Human-Computer Studies* 98:24–37.

Graham, E., and J. Hambly. 2020. A Tale of Two Fishing Boat Graveyards. *International Journal of Nautical Archaeology* 49(1): 107–41. https://doi.org/10.1111/1095-9270.12393.

Graham, Ellie, Tom Dawson, and Steve Liscoe, with contributions by Peter Dick. 2019. The Newshot Island Boat Graveyard: An Assemblage of Nineteenth-Century Vessels on the Clyde. *International Journal of Nautical Archaeology* 48(1): 151–171. https://doi.org/10.1111/1095-9270.12332.

Guzzo, P. 2019. They Can't Turn Back Waves, but USF and Seminoles Are Preserving Egmont Key in Digital Form. *Tampa Bay Times*, May 17. https://www.tampabay.com/florida/2019/05/17/they-cant-turn-back-waves-but-usf-and-seminoles-are-preserving-egmont-key-in-digital-form/, accessed July 15, 2025.

Hamilton, A., H. Brown, and R. Burton. 2022. Island Impermanent: Part II: Safeguarding a Touchstone. *The Marjorie*. https://themarjorie.org/2022/10/03/safeguarding-a-touchstone/. accessed April 1, 2025.

Hansen B., S. Annis, S. Vorce, J. Coates, and A. Farr. 2022. Virtualization Technologies for Sustainable Tourism: Adapting the Matterport 360 Platform to Showcase the UN Sustainable Development Goals in Tampa Bay, Florida. In *The Green Institute: Working Papers*, May 12, 2022, pp. 1–10. https://greeninstitute.ng/visualization-technologies-for-sustainable-tourism-tampa-bay-florida

Hansen, B., and J. Rossen. 2017. Activist Anthropology with the Haudenosaunee: Theoretical and Practical Insights from the Two Row Wampum Renewal Campaign. *Anthropology in Action* 24(3): 32–44. https://doi.org/10.3167/aia.2017.240304

Harrison, Laura. 2019. A Roadmap to Applied Digital Heritage. *Studies in Digital Heritage* 3:1, 40–45. https://doi.org/10.14434/sdh.v3i1.27552.

Harrison, Laura. 2022. Closing the Loop on the Digital Data Lifecycle: Reviving a Salvage Archaeology Dataset. In *Critical Archaeology in the Digital Age*, edited by Kevin Gartski, pp. 79–96. UCLA Cotsen Institute of Archaeology Press, Los Angeles.

Harrison, Laura K., Howard Kaplan, Jennifer T. Matthews, and Eric Santiago. 2025. Making Meaningful Places: Augmented Reality for Digital Placemaking in Clearwater, Florida. *Journal on Computing and Cultural Heritage* 18:1, 1–21. https://doi.org/10.1145/3703916.

Harrison, L., and B. Hansen. 2020. Using Geoinformatics to Document Heritage at Risk and Climate Change at Egmont Key. *The Forum*, August 25. University of South Florida Institute for the Advanced Study of Culture and the Environment. https://usf.app.box.com/s/x861py9mogjk64wjj6kvtozrpvii614v, accessed April 1, 2025.

Harrison, Laura, and Aycan Gürbüz. 2018. A 3D Visualization of the Ancient Built Environment of Seyitömer Höyük, Turkey. In *Assyromania and More: In Memory of Samuel M. Paley*, edited by Friedhelm Pedde and Nathaneal Shelley, pp. 287–300. Zaphon, Münster.

Huggett, Jeremy. 2015. Digital Haystacks: Open Data and the Transformation of Archaeological Knowledge. In *Open Source Archaeology: Ethics and Practice*, edited by Andrew T. Wilson and Ben Edwards, 6–29. De Gruyter Open Poland, Warsaw. https://works.hcommons.org/records/417tm-08w30.

Jung, T., N. Chung, and M. Leue. 2015. The Determinants of Recommendations to Use Augmented Reality Technologies: The Case of a Korean Theme Park. *Tourism Management* 49:75–86. https://doi.org/10.1016/j.tourman.2015.02.013.

Little, Chris, Alexandra Bec, Brent Don Moyle, and Dale Patterson. 2020. Innovative Methods for Heritage Tourism Experiences: Creating Windows into the Past. *Journal of Heritage Tourism* 15(1): 1–13. https://doi.org/10.1080/1743873X.2018.1536709.

Mueller, Bradley, and Alyssa Boge (editors.) N.d. *Egmont Key: A Seminole Story*. Seminole Tribe of Florida, Tribal Historical Preservation Office. Clewiston, Florida. https://stofthpo.com/egmont-key/.

Moorhouse, N., and T. Jung. 2017. Augmented Reality to Enhance the Learning Experience in Cultural Heritage Tourism: An Experiential Learning Cycle Perspective. *eReview of Tourism Research* 8. https://e-space.mmu.ac.uk/id/eprint/617555.

Morrow, E. 2019. "We're Still Here": Seminole Tribe Shares Dark History of Egmont Key. *10 Tampa Bay*, November 25. https://www.wtsp.com/article/news/local/pinellascounty/seminole-tribe-egmont-key/67-a6ee7a61-ceb9-45e6-a2cd-f699a7e72fd1, accessed March 31, 2025.

Nared, J., and D. Bole. 2020. Participatory Research on Heritage- and Culture-Based Development: A Perspective from South-East Europe. In *Participatory Research and Planning in Practice*, edited by J. Nared and D. Bole, pp. 107–119. Springer, Cham, Switzerland.

Osceola, M., and C. Shenandoah. 2022. Island Impermanent: On Egmont: Words from Tribal Members. *The Marjorie*. https://themarjorie.org/2022/10/03/on-egmont-words-from-tribal-members/, accessed April 1, 2025.

Reichheld, F. F. 2003. The One Number You Need to Grow. *Harvard Business Review* 81(12): 46–54.

Roa, R. 2025. Egmont Key Is More Fascinating Than We Could Ever Imagine. The Skinny, WMNF. https://www.wmnf.org/egmont-key-is-more-fascinating-than-we-could-ever-imagine/, accessed April 1, 2025.

Silberman, N. A. 2007. "Sustainable" Heritage? Public Archaeological Interpretation and the Marketed Past. In *Archaeology and Capitalism*, edited by Yannis Hamilakis and Philip Duke, pp. 179–193. Left Coast Press, Walnut Creek, CA.

Smith, J. 2021a. Seminole Tribe, USF Sustainable Tourism and USF Access 3D Lab Preserve History at Egmont Key. *83 Degrees Media*. https://www.83degreesmedia.com/features/seminole-tribe-and-USF-work-to-preserve-egmont-key-in-Florida072021.aspx, accessed April 1, 2025.

Smith, J. 2021b. USF Sustainable Tourism Team Reframes Visitor Experience to Help Save Egmont Key. *83 Degrees Media*. https://www.83degreesmedia.com/features/USF-Sustainable-Tourism-team-helps-Seminoles-save-Egmont-Key-Florida-072021.aspx, accessed April 1, 2025.

Tanasi, Davide. 2020. The Digital (Within) Archaeology: Analysis of a Phenomenon. *The Historian* 82(1): 22–36. https://doi.org/10.1080/00182370.2020.1723968.

Watkins, J. 2020. Heritage Preservation and Indigenous Communities in the United States: A Case for Community-Based Participatory Research. In *Communities and Cultural Heritage*, edited by Valerie Higgins and Diane Douglas, pp. 106–115. Routledge, London.

Wells, J. C. 2015. In Stakeholders We Trust: Changing the Ontological and Epistemological Orientation of Built Heritage Assessment Through Participatory Action Research. In *How to Assess Built Heritage? Assumptions, Methodologies, Examples of Heritage Assessment Systems*, edited by Bogusław Szmygin, pp. 249–265. International Scientific Committee for Theory and Philosophy of Conservation and Restoration ICOMOS, Paris, France.

Wilson, Mark. 2023. USF Preserves Egmont Key with 3D App as Barrier Island "Washes Away." https://www.fox13news.com/news/usf-preserves-egmont-key-with-3d-app-as-barrier-island-washes-away, accessed April 1, 2025.

Xiao, W., J. Mills, G. Guidi, P. Rodríguez-Gonzálvez, S. G. Barsanti, and D. González-Aguilera. 2018. Geoinformatics for the Conservation and Promotion of Cultural Heritage in Support of the UN Sustainable Development Goals. *ISPRS Journal of Photogrammetry and Remote Sensing* 142:389–406. https://doi.org/10.1016/j.isprsjprs.2018.01.001.

Appendix A

EGMONT KEY: AUGMENTED REALITY USER EXPERIENCE SURVEY

Thank you for taking the time to experience the augmented reality (AR) tour of Egmont Key. Please take a few moments and provide some feedback that will be used to further develop AR products. Note: the "application" refers to the experience and content in the AR app.

PLEASE TELL US A LITTLE ABOUT YOU BY CIRCLING THE CORRECT INFORMATION

Age: Please check the box of your age group.

- ☐ 18–20
- ☐ 21–30
- ☐ 31–40
- ☐ 41–50
- ☐ 51–60
- ☐ above 60

Gender:

- ☐ male
- ☐ female
- ☐ other
- ☐ prefer not to say

Length of time living in Florida:

- ☐ 0–5 years
- ☐ 10–20 years
- ☐ 5–10 years
- ☐ more than 20 years

Occupation:

Income:

- ☐ 0-$20,000
- ☐ $20,000–40,000
- ☐ $40,000-$60,000
- ☐ $60,000-$80,000
- ☐ $80,000-$100,000
- ☐ $100,000 and above

Education:

- ☐ high school/ GED
- ☐ some college
- ☐ technical/ vocational degree
- ☐ college degree B.A/B.S
- ☐ advanced college degree M.A./ M.B.A./Ph.D./ M.D.

I identify my ethnicity primarily as:

- ☐ Asian
- ☐ Black/African
- ☐ Caucasian
- ☐ Hispanic/Latinx
- ☐ Native American
- ☐ Pacific Islander
- ☐ Prefer not to answer
- ☐ Other:

PLEASE TELL US ABOUT YOUR EXPERIENCE WITH CULTURAL HERITAGE:

How many times a year on average do you visit a museum? ____________

How many times a year do you go to cultural events like festivals and guided tours?____

How many times per year do you volunteer at cultural heritage sites, parks, or museums? ____

PLEASE TELL US ABOUT YOUR EXPERIENCE WITH AUGMENTED REALITY AND THE APPLICATION:

I consider myself comfortable using digital technologies.

☐ agree ☐ neutral ☐ disagree
☐ somewhat agree ☐ somewhat disagree

Prior to this experience, have you used a AR application?

☐ Yes ☐ No

If Yes, have you used an AR app for (check all that apply):

☐ entertainment ☐ work ☐ other
☐ education ☐ navigation

If Yes, were your previous VR experiences:

☐ positive ☐ neutral ☐ negative

Using AR increases my interest in learning about cultural heritage:

☐ agree ☐ neutral ☐ disagree
☐ somewhat agree ☐ somewhat disagree

Would you tell a friend that AR is an interesting way to learn about cultural heritage?

☐ agree ☐ neutral ☐ disagree
☐ somewhat agree ☐ somewhat disagree

INDICATE YOUR LEVEL OF AGREEMENT WITH THE FOLLOWING STATEMENTS:

I found this application easy to use:

☐ agree ☐ neutral ☐ disagree
☐ somewhat agree ☐ somewhat disagree

I could easily navigate through the application:

☐ agree ☐ neutral ☐ disagree
☐ somewhat agree ☐ somewhat disagree

The app works the way I want it to work:

☐ agree ☐ neutral ☐ disagree
☐ somewhat agree ☐ somewhat disagree

PLEASE TELL US ABOUT THE HISTORIES OF EGMONT KEY AND THE MATERIALS PRESENTED IN THE APPLICATION.

I knew about cultural heritage sites on Egmont Key before using this application:

☐ agree ☐ neutral ☐ disagree
☐ somewhat agree ☐ somewhat disagree

I know more about cultural heritage sites on Egmont Key after using the application:

☐ agree ☐ neutral ☐ disagree
☐ somewhat agree ☐ somewhat disagree

I knew about the history of the Spanish-American War and Ft. Dade before using this application:

☐ agree ☐ neutral ☐ disagree
☐ somewhat agree ☐ somewhat disagree

I know more about the Spanish-American War and Ft. Dade after using the application:

☐ agree ☐ neutral ☐ disagree
☐ somewhat agree ☐ somewhat disagree

Before this experience, I knew that Egmont Key was washing away, endangering its heritage:

☐ agree ☐ neutral ☐ disagree
☐ somewhat agree ☐ somewhat disagree

I found the information on the history of Egmont Key easy to understand

☐ agree ☐ neutral ☐ disagree
☐ somewhat agree ☐ somewhat disagree

Based on what I learned in the AR experience, I would like to visit Egmont Key again:

☐ agree ☐ neutral ☐ disagree
☐ somewhat agree ☐ somewhat disagree

Based on what I learned in the AR experience, I would like to know more about Egmont Key's cultural heritage:

☐ agree ☐ neutral ☐ disagree
☐ somewhat agree ☐ somewhat disagree

If you agree, which topics would you like to learn more about?

Of the information presented in the application, what part did you find most interesting?

This is a prototype of a larger AR tour of Egmont Key—do you have suggestions to improve the application?

Future AR experiences for Egmont Key should include:

Did this application improve your experience visiting Egmont Key?

7

Shifting Sands and Rising Seas

Assessing Heritage at Risk with Lidar and GIS

LAURA K. HARRISON, STEVEN FERNANDEZ, AND ALEX FAWBUSH

In 2017, the Florida Trust for Historic Preservation named Egmont Key one of the state's 11 most endangered heritage sites (Florida Trust for Historic Preservation 2017). Maps and surveys dating back hundreds of years chronicle the island's continuous shrinkage, revealing that it has lost about half of its landmass in the last 150 years. Erosion remains a constant threat and is exacerbated by the currents around the Egmont Deep, strong storms, and the dredging of a nearby shipping channel. With the loss of land comes the loss of irreplaceable cultural heritage sites: Spanish-American War structures from Fort Dade, including Battery Page and Battery Burchsted, have already been reduced to ruins and are now popular offshore snorkeling destinations. Battery McIntosh, Battery Howard, the 1901 Power Plant/Mess Hall, and Battery Charles Mellon, originally built near the center of the island during the Fort Dade period (1898–1923), now sit perilously close to the shoreline, awaiting their fate. These sites may be lost in a matter of decades, as the land they are built on slips into the sea. Will we have done enough to preserve their memory when the inevitable happens?

Beach renourishment (also known as sand placement) provides a short-term solution for stabilizing the western shoreline and protecting heritage sites, but it comes with some drawbacks: it is costly, not environmentally neutral, and only lasts a few years before the sands are swept back out to sea. How can we better understand the ongoing tug-of-war between erosion and beach renourishment, to better plan if, when, and where sand should be placed in the future?

And how can we more accurately simulate the impacts of rising sea levels on heritage sites already vulnerable to erosion? Beach renourishment cannot guarantee the permanent stabilization of these sites. This chapter addresses these key questions with the goal of introducing a data-driven approach to understanding the threats facing coastal heritage. While Egmont Key's situation is unique as an island near a major shipping channel, it also reflects global challenges as heritage sites everywhere contend with rising seas, shoreline erosion, and human impacts.

The first case study examines Battery McIntosh, a structure from Fort Dade whose vulnerability makes it an ideal site for high-resolution modeling and mapping. We georeferenced a 3D terrestrial lidar point cloud of the fortification, applied National Oceanic and Atmospheric Administration (NOAA) sea-level-rise scenarios in Geographic Information Systems (GIS), and visualized how rising tides would impact the site. The results show that actions to digitally preserve Battery McIntosh are well justified, as the site may face irreversible damage and loss in the coming decades.

The second case study broadens the focus to the entire island. We used 3D aerial lidar data to model multiple sea-level-rise scenarios on aerial lidar scan data. The maps show areas that will remain above water and areas that will become submerged in the coming decades. The results underscore why we refer to Egmont as the disappearing island.

Our third case study considers the interplay between erosion and beach renourishment. We analyze a series of aerial lidar scans starting in 2007 and show where sand has been placed and where it has washed away over the ensuing decades. This dance between erosion and beach renourishment has resulted in a net loss of about 11 acres of land between 2015 and 2024, showing that beach renourishment is a temporary fix that slows but does not stop broader erosional processes.

The three case studies serve as guideposts for understanding the many environmental threats facing Egmont Key. They do not, however, consider the greatest existential risk facing the island: a future Category 5 hurricane making landfall. The devastation caused by Hurricanes Helene and Milton in 2024 underscores this risk. Although the methods presented in this chapter cannot prevent catastrophic loss from such an event, they represent proactive steps to record and interpret threats and can help guide decision-making around protecting heritage before irreversible damage occurs. The uncertain future of Egmont Key outlined in this chapter reinforces themes discussed elsewhere in the volume, including the importance of digitizing built heritage (Chapter 6), recording histories (Chapters 2–3), and developing interpretive content (Chapter 6) for at-risk sites. These approaches cannot prevent catastrophic loss but can ensure that knowledge, meaning, and memory endure even when sites face an uncertain future.

Mapping and Cultural Heritage

Accurate mapping and modeling are critical for assessing risks and guiding preservation efforts at vulnerable sites before irreversible damage occurs. Coastal mapping in the United States has a long history—from the pioneering surveys and heritage documentation carried out by the United States Coast and Geodetic Survey (USC&GS) to more recent digital innovations incorporating GIS, Global Positioning Systems (GPS), and lidar, all of which have progressively enhanced our ability to understand, preserve, and manage cultural resources situated on or near coastlines. The USC&GS, founded in 1807, is the predecessor of NOAA. For many years, it played a crucial role in mapping the nation's coastlines, conducting geodetic surveys, and producing nautical charts. In 1875, the USC&GS was involved in detailed surveys to support maritime navigation, which included documenting both natural and cultural resources along the US coasts, including in Florida. These early cartographic endeavors laid the groundwork for the systematic documentation of cultural heritage sites, a process that continued as USC&GS became part of NOAA in 1970. NOAA's historical shoreline maps, known as T-Sheets, are accessible to the public via an online database (NOAA 2020).

Since the 1990s, the digitization and georeferencing of paper maps by US federal agencies like NOAA and the United States Geological Survey (USGS) have revolutionized cultural heritage mapping. GIS has enabled researchers to overlay and integrate historical and modern datasets, providing new insights into landscape changes over time (González-Tennant 2016; Warner-Smith 2020). By the 1980s, advancements in Global Positioning System (GPS) technology significantly improved locational accuracy compared with traditional survey methods, facilitating more precise heritage documentation (Conolly and Lake 2006).

Recently, lidar technology has further transformed heritage research; introducing "big data" into the world of cultural heritage site preservation and coastal monitoring. These advances in technology have made it possible to

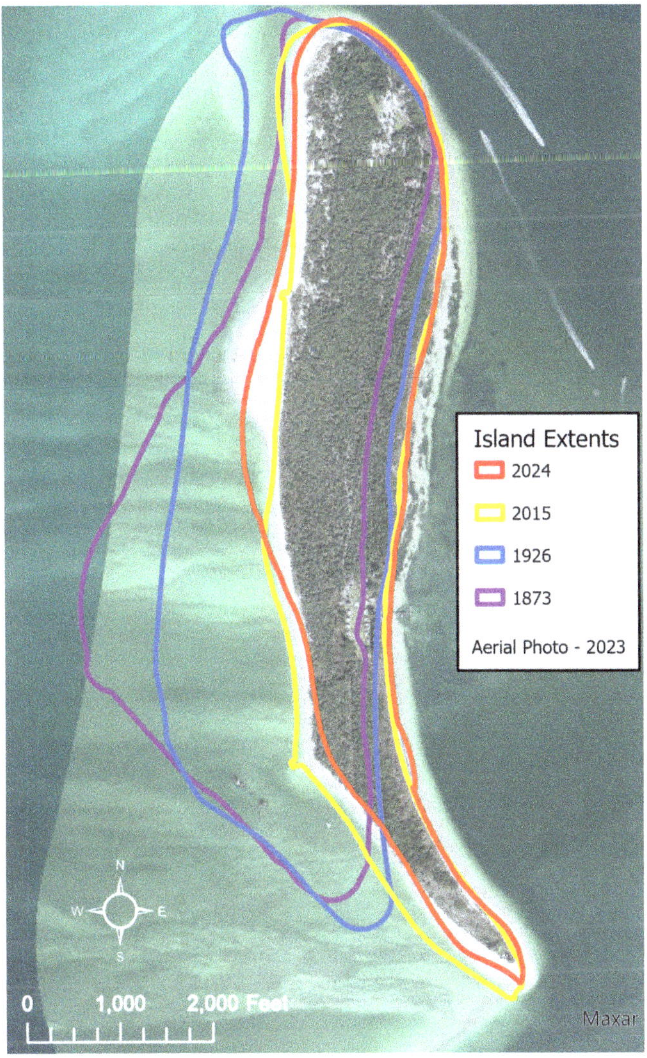

Figure 7.1. Changes in the Egmont Key shoreline between 1873 and 2024, based on historical maps, aerial photography, and lidar data. The 2023 aerial photo (*background image*) shows a semicircular expanse of beach sand along the western shoreline, which is largely flattened by 2024 (red line). This illustrates the temporary, shifting nature of replenished sand and highlights how artificially placed sand requires ongoing maintenance to counteract the powerful forces of erosion that threaten historic sites. Submerged historic sites Battery Page and Battery Burchsted are visible off the southeast of the island, in between the yellow (2015) and blue (1926) island extents. Map created by Steven Fernandez, University of South Florida.

accurately map change over time, as seen in 7.1, which shows how the shoreline of Egmont Key has shifted between 1873 and 2024. This map shows significant loss of land across the entire western side of the island, a progressive narrowing and lengthening of the southern point, and a slight eastward shift of the entire island. Better understanding how these shifting sands and the rising seas that accompany them threaten cultural heritage sites is the key focus of this chapter.

Aerial and Terrestrial Lidar for the Cultural Heritage Sector

Innovative technologies like lidar—an acronym for "light detection and ranging"—are enhancing the documentation of at-risk coastal heritage sites. Lidar was first conceived in 1958 by the aerospace industry, where it was used to measure the surface of the moon on the Apollo 15 mission (Cremons 2022). By the late twentieth century, use cases and applications expanded to include barrier island mapping, quality control of aeronautical parts, and medical equipment. By the twenty-first century, it became a mainstream method for flood plain modeling, transportation planning, coastal management, and many other domains. Lidar is also an in-demand technology in society at large, with recent integrations into consumer-oriented products like smartphones and self-driving cars. There are several use cases for lidar within archaeology and heritage, especially for the documentation of sites (Vinci et al. 2025), identification of sites hidden beneath canopies (Maté-González et al. 2022), and assessment of risks such as sea-level rise and erosion, discussed in the case studies below.

Lidar uses laser pulses to measure distances between a sensor and target surfaces, enabling the creation of highly accurate 3D models of topography, structures, and landscapes. Lidar scanners emit a laser pulse that captures the 3D position of an object or surface, called a point. Each lidar instrument uses a mirror to send out an array of laser pulses, collecting millions of points, which are individual 3D measurements. Points are aggregated together into a point cloud—a collection of millions, or even billions, of 3D measurements that together create an accurate representation of the surfaces of an object or environment. Point clouds of buildings, environments, and landscapes are powerful visual and analytical tools that can be integrated into GIS environments to aid in cultural heritage mapping, documentation, and site monitoring.

Lidar sensors can be configured in many ways. Terrestrial lidar scanners are mounted on a stationary tripod that sits on the ground, whereas aerial/mobile lidar scanners are affixed to a moving vehicle like a drone, helicopter, plane,

Figure 7.2. A USF team conducts a terrestrial lidar survey of Battery McIntosh, a Spanish American War fortification on Egmont Key's highly vulnerable western coast. Note the scanners placed on tripods around the survey site. By permission of Laura Harrison.

truck, or boat. Aerial lidar collects data from greater distances than its terrestrial counterpart, resulting in lower resolution, with an average point spacing of about 0.2–0.7 m (~ 8–24 in). It is mainly used for large-scale mapping of the earth's surface. Terrestrial lidar, on the other hand, operates at closer ranges with higher precision, making it better suited for digitizing buildings, architectural details, small landscapes, and archaeological features.

Within the cultural heritage sector, aerial lidar is commonly used to find and remap known sites, whereas terrestrial lidar is used for targeted, fine-scale documentation of individual buildings, neighborhoods, and landscape features (7.2; see Chapter 6 for examples from Egmont Key). Aerial lidar is available publicly and can often be downloaded for free, whereas most terrestrial lidar datasets require a researcher to physically conduct fieldwork at a site with their own instrument. This can present a barrier to entry, as lidar instruments cost tens of thousands of dollars, and obtaining site permissions is a complex process that often requires institutional affiliation. However, with each passing year, consumer-grade lidar makes its way into more personal electronics, expanding opportunities for terrestrial lidar scanning and public engagement with reality capture.

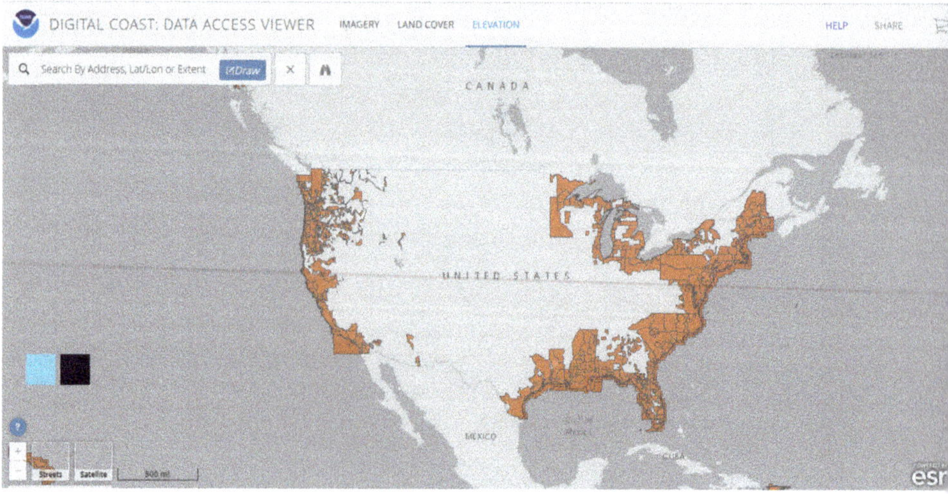

Figure 7.3. The NOAA Data Access Viewer (https://coast.noaa.gov/dataviewer/#/lidar/search/). From the National Oceanic and Atmospheric Administration website.

AERIAL LIDAR

Unlike traditional survey methods, aerial lidar can penetrate dense vegetation, uncovering hidden features such as building foundations, ancient roads, monuments, and earthworks (Bewley et al. 2025), making it especially valuable for identifying archaeological sites in forested or overgrown environments (Ringle et al. 2021). Aerial lidar has been valuable in mapping coastal changes and assessing flood risks to heritage sites. Beyond documentation, aerial lidar plays a crucial role in disaster risk assessment, aiding in the evaluation of vulnerabilities to hazards such as floods, earthquakes, and landslides (Cuca et al. 2023; Ikawa 2023). It is particularly useful in simulating disasters like storm surge and sea-level rise—essential for heritage management in coastal areas—by enabling predictive models that assess potential impacts on at-risk sites (Opitz and Herrmann 2018; Rouhani and Romão 2023).

At the World Heritage site of Skara Brae in Orkney, Scotland, aerial lidar has been used to monitor coastal erosion and evaluate the impacts of rising sea levels on the site's Neolithic structures (Dawson et al. 2020). Similarly, aerial lidar was used to assess the vulnerability of the Outer Banks in North Carolina by mapping coastal archaeological sites and geomorphological changes, enabling researchers to model the potential impacts of sea-level rise and storm surges

(Mallinson et al. 2011). These disaster risk assessments are enhanced when lidar data are imported and analyzed within a geospatial software environment.

The first publicly available aerial lidar data were produced by NOAA in the late 1990s and solely concentrated on the east coast barrier islands because they were the lands most vulnerable to erosion and hurricane damage. Because of widening use cases for lidar, data collection has expanded beyond coastal environments to include the eastern United States, portions of the Midwest, and the West Coast. NOAA aggregates and standardizes lidar datasets from around the country (7.3). Some geographical areas have been scanned more than once, which shows how landscapes and coastlines change over time. By 2023, the entire state of Florida had publicly available lidar data. The data used to generate the digital surface models (DSM) and digital elevation models (DEMS) in the case studies below were collected from flights in 2007, 2015, and 2024.

TERRESTRIAL LIDAR

Terrestrial lidar was first used in engineering and surveying, and by the late 1980s and early 1990s it was being used to create accurate "as-built" models of cultural heritage sites. The accuracy of terrestrial lidar is up to +/- 2 mm, and its high resolution makes it much more precise than aerial lidar. In many cases, it is better suited for mapping architectural details than aerial lidar, which is more useful at broader scales like landscapes, coastlines, and the earth's surface. Throughout the 2000s, terrestrial lidar became faster and more portable, resulting in a slew of new projects in the burgeoning field of digital cultural heritage.

Terrestrial lidar is an indispensable tool for documenting intricate details of archaeological and architectural features with millimeter-level precision, offering a level of accuracy that far exceeds that of aerial lidar and traditional mapping techniques (Guidi and Frischer 2020). This enables volumetric calculations, such as determining the volume of excavation units or assessing the mass of site components, which are critical for understanding construction techniques and site dynamics. Additionally, terrestrial lidar facilitates structural monitoring by providing baseline data for tracking changes over time, including deformation, erosion, or damage caused by environmental factors or human activity (Lercari et al. 2021). This capability is particularly valuable for condition assessments, where accurate and repeatable measurements are essential for identifying and addressing vulnerabilities at heritage sites.

One key strength of terrestrial lidar is capturing detailed data on architectural features, making it an important tool for assessing the structural integrity of heritage sites exposed to climate risks like earthquakes, floods, and extreme weather events. For instance, after the 2016 earthquake in Bagan, Myanmar, researchers documented 12 monuments using lidar technology to create accurate 3D models for conservation planning (Mezzino et al. 2017). In Pompeii, Italy, terrestrial lidar has been employed to monitor structural deformations and assess risks to the site's masonry. And a study focused on the Sarno Baths utilized terrestrial laser scanning to create detailed 3D models, facilitating the monitoring of facade deformations and informing conservation strategies (Monego et al. 2019).

The Notre Dame Cathedral in Paris was extensively scanned with terrestrial lidar, as part of a preservation effort led by art historian Andrew Tallon (2014). Tallon's work created an exceptionally detailed digital record of the cathedral, mapping its intricate Gothic architecture with millimeter precision. This dataset was invaluable following the devastating fire in 2019, serving as a blueprint for restoration and reconstruction. The high-precision archiving of sites that face a possibility of future damage or destruction is one of the most significant benefits of terrestrial lidar scanning within the cultural heritage sector.

In recent years, as heritage practitioners have become more accustomed to integrating terrestrial lidar into field projects, they have moved beyond site documentation to address complex challenges, such as digitally simulating the impacts of natural disasters on heritage sites (Rayne et al. 2023). For example, Lercari and colleagues (2021) explore how advanced remote-sensing technologies, including terrestrial laser scanning, photogrammetry, and GIS, provide insights into environmental threats and structural changes over time, enabling predictive modeling and proactive conservation strategies at Bodie State Historic Park in California. The interdisciplinary research approach emphasizes collaborative visualization through WebGL, making heritage site data more accessible to stakeholders and demonstrating how remote sensing can support adaptive management and resilience in heritage management. It also elevates the research profile of terrestrial lidar beyond mere site documentation and into the realm of analysis, site management, and protection, which is also a key goal of our work with lidar and GIS at Egmont Key.

GIS and Lidar for Climate Risk Assessment

Integrating GIS, terrestrial lidar, and aerial lidar into a multidisciplinary research framework provides a window to better understand how sea-level rise and erosion threaten cultural heritage near the coast. Coastal heritage sites are among the first places to experience the effects of climate change, and climate risk assessments and vulnerability studies show that sea-level rise will erode or destroy a massive number of archaeological sites in Florida and other low-lying areas in the coming decades. Indeed, coastal erosion driven by sea-level rise is already affecting Florida's cultural heritage, with thousands of sites facing imminent destruction, and many more already underwater (Miller and Murray 2018).

The White House Council on Climate Preparedness and Resilience in 2015 formed a task force to establish sea-level-rise scenarios to serve as a starting point for coastal preparedness planning and risk-management processes. Researchers at NOAA have identified Florida as the state most at-risk from sea-level rise, concluding that even a low-emissions pathway would result in an average of 1 ft of sea-level rise by 2100. A high-emissions pathway could result in as much as 8.2 ft of sea-level rise over the same timeframe (Figures 7.4 and 7.5). Understanding specifically how these scenarios will affect historic coastal structures requires the creation and analysis of a lidar-derived digital elevation model (DEM) in GIS.

LIDAR-DERIVED DIGITAL ELEVATION MODELS (DEMS)

Digital elevation models (DEMs) derived from lidar data are critical tools for tracking and monitoring coastal sites. Rising sea levels, strong storms, and other climate-related events lead to erosion or accretion, and these processes are measurable through DEMs. Comparing volumetric data from DEMs makes it possible to track shifts in sand dunes, coastal erosion, and changes to cultural landscapes over time. These measurements not only reveal physical transformations in landscapes but also show how environmental processes impact heritage sites. The integration of climate models with spatial data enhances predictive capabilities, aiding in disaster preparedness and heritage site conservation (Fatorić and Seekamp 2017). Studies have shown that such techniques are useful in assessing risks posed by climate change, particularly in coastal and vulnerable areas (Orr et al. 2021; Sesana et al. 2021).

Lidar DEMs are effective for tracking landscape-scale changes affecting cultural heritage sites, but their spatial resolution is limited. Climate modeling in GIS often incorporates aerial lidar data collected from airplanes, and as such, the models generated have a spatial resolution as low as 1 ft (7.6). In other words, it is possible to discern features in the landscape that are 1 ft or larger. Features smaller than 1 ft—such as architectural details of historic

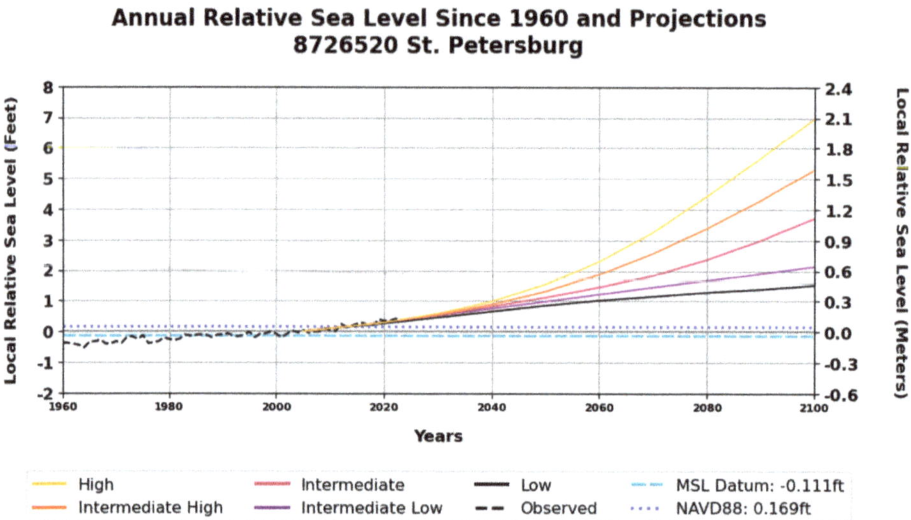

Year	NOAA2017 VLM	NOAA2017 Low	NOAA2017 Int-Low	NOAA2017-Intermediate	NOAA2017 Int-High
2000	0.00	0.00	0.00	0.00	0.00
2010	0.03	0.13	0.16	0.23	0.30
2020	0.06	0.30	0.36	0.49	0.62
2030	0.09	0.46	0.56	0.79	1.02
2040	0.11	0.59	0.72	1.08	1.41
2050	0.14	0.79	0.95	1.44	1.97
2060	0.17	0.92	1.15	1.87	2.62
2070	0.20	1.08	1.35	2.33	3.38
2080	0.23	1.21	1.54	2.82	4.20
2090	0.26	1.31	1.71	3.38	5.15
2100	0.29	1.44	1.90	3.90	6.17

Figure 7.4. NOAA's projections for sea-level rise between 1960 and 2100 (*top*) and 2000 and 2100 (*bottom*). The figures are calculated based on Station ID #726520 in St. Petersburg, Florida. Image from the National Oceanic and Atmospheric Administration website.

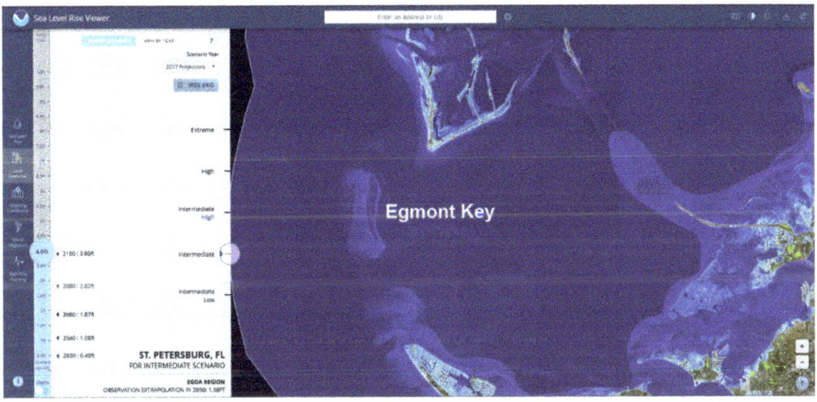

Figure 7.5. The 2026 NOAA Sea Level Rise Viewer is an online tool that visualizes potential sea-level rise and coastal flooding. It does not include Egmont Key, but shows how nearby Fort De Soto and Anna Maria Island would be impacted by rising seas. The NOAA Intermediate scenario for 2100 is pictured here, with underwater areas indicated in light blue. Image from the National Oceanic and Atmospheric Administration website.

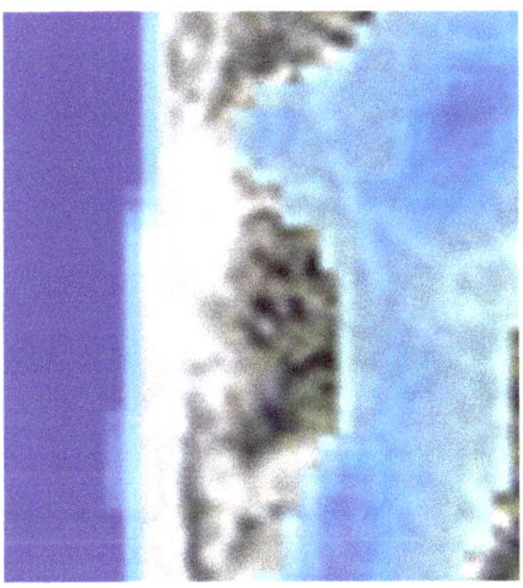

Figure 7.6. The 2023 NOAA Sea-Level Rise Viewer included Egmont Key. While useful for general observations, its resolution was too low to discern the details of landscapes and heritage sites such as Battery McIntosh, pictured here. This chapter describes a workflow to georeference a terrestrial lidar scan of the building and visualize NOAA sea-level rise scenarios on the 3D model in GIS, providing higher-resolution results. Image from the National Oceanic and Atmospheric Administration website.

buildings—are poorly defined. Aerial lidar doesn't have the resolution necessary to accurately track changes at such a fine scale; it is more suited to tracking macroscale changes in coastlines, dunes, and vegetation. Terrestrial lidar, on the other hand, captures excellent records of fine architectural details, but is often not georeferenced, hampering its ability to inform our understanding of how major climactic events damage heritage sites. Combining aerial lidar and terrestrial lidar offers a way to integrate the strengths of both methods while compensating for their weaknesses.

Modeling Sea-Level Rise at Battery McIntosh

The first case study in this chapter focuses on analyzing how rising tides will affect Battery McIntosh, a 1900 Spanish-American War fortification on Egmont Key's western shoreline. The battery is part of a network of coastal fortifications from the Fort Dade period (1898–1923), when the island was militarized to defend Tampa Bay from a feared foreign maritime invasion (a topic discussed in greater detail in Chapters 2 and 6). Fort Dade contains some of the best surviving examples of late-nineteenth or early twentieth-century artillery batteries in the southern United States, known as the Fourth System of seacoast defenses (Lewis 1970). These low-lying, camouflaged structures have disappearing guns and were designed to work in concert with underwater mines to ambush enemy ships. Each battery was strategically buried within a sand dune so as to remain undetected by passing ships. There are over 100 Fourth System forts in the southeastern United States; however, most of them are retrofitted from brick and mortar Third System forts, which stand out because of their characteristic tall vertical masonry walls. The artillery batteries on Egmont Key, including Battery McIntosh, are unique because they are one of only three purpose-built Fourth System seacoast defenses in existence. This network of camouflaged forts is considered the last major innovation in defense strategy before the advent of aircraft.

Battery McIntosh is located on Egmont Key's highly vulnerable western shoreline; most of the island's shrinkage over the past 150 years has been concentrated on this coast (7.7). Over the years, erosion, strong storms, and channel currents have swept the dune away, exposing Battery McIntosh's concrete facade to the elements and causing it to decay as water seeps into the structure's many cracks. As discussed in Chapter 4, the structure has never been restored or conserved. Other nearby structures built in the same era with similar design features have already collapsed in on themselves (Battery Howard), or have fallen into the sea (Battery Burchsted and Battery Page). Lidar and GIS analysis can show when sea-level rise may finally inundate the fort, or damage it beyond recognition. The following section chronicles the geomatics methods used toward this end.

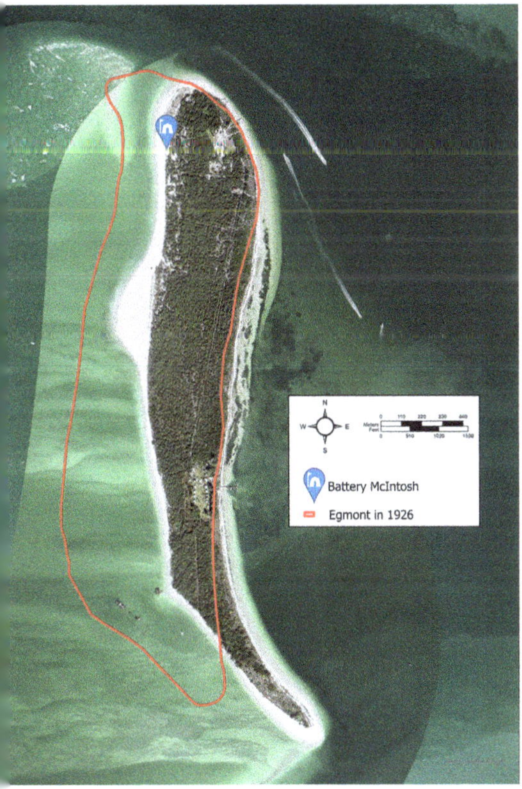

Figure 7.7. Aerial photo of Egmont Key from 2024 showing the location of Battery McIntosh. The 1926 boundary of the island is highlighted in red. Erosion poses an immediate threat to the historic structure. Map created by Alex Fawbush, Access 3D Lab, University of South Florida.

TECHNICAL WORKFLOW: LIDAR AND GIS FOR SEA-LEVEL-RISE ANALYSIS AT BATTERY MCINTOSH

The urgent need to document Battery McIntosh before it washes away compelled our team from the University of South Florida to analyze how rising seas might affect the structure with a combination of terrestrial lidar, aerial lidar, and GIS analyses. The fieldwork was integrated into the curriculum of a professional development workshop on cultural heritage and climate change geomatics led by chapter author Harrison (7.8). Over the course of five days, workshop participants completed a terrestrial lidar survey of the structure, focusing on complete documentation of all interior and exterior architectural details, along with mapping the beach to the west of the structure (7.7). The workshop participants used a combination of Faro Focus X330, S150, and Premium lidar scanners, which are similar instruments manufactured in different years from 2016 to 2021. The datasets from all three scanners are easily combined in Faro's Scene software. The scan plan emphasized an even point density of interior and exterior features. Resolution parameters were set to 4× quality and 1/4 resolution, with a combination of even-weighted and horizon-weighted metering to balance the exposure in interior and exterior settings (Table 7.1). A total of 181 scans were captured, resulting in 33.52 GB of raw data.

Figure 7.8. Chapter author Laura Harrison teaches workshop students how to effectively use a terrestrial lidar scanner to document Battery McIntosh's historic architecture and surrounding landscape. By permission of Laura Harrison.

LIDAR DATA PROCESSING

The lidar scans of Battery McIntosh were processed in Faro Scene software to generate as-built documentation intended to enable future research on the site, and the Fourth System of seacoast defenses, even if the structure itself cannot be saved. Individual scans were imported, aligned, cleaned, georeferenced, and exported in Faro Scene at USF Access 3D Lab (7.9). The entire post-processing workflow took approximately 280 hours. The project was sectioned off into the May and June workshop scanning (the entire structure) and the October scanning (a follow-up visit a week after Hurricane Ian). The May–June campaign focused on documenting Battery McIntosh and the beach to the west of the structure. The October campaign focused solely on the changes to the beach, west of the structure. The result was a fully aligned, cleaned, and colorized 3D point cloud of the structure as it appeared in 2023 (7.9)

GEOREFERENCING THE TERRESTRIAL LIDAR SCAN DATA

To fully simulate and visualize how sea-level rise will impact Battery McIntosh, it was necessary to georeference and decimate the terrestrial lidar point cloud. Both georeferencing and decimation can be thought of as forms of "prepro-

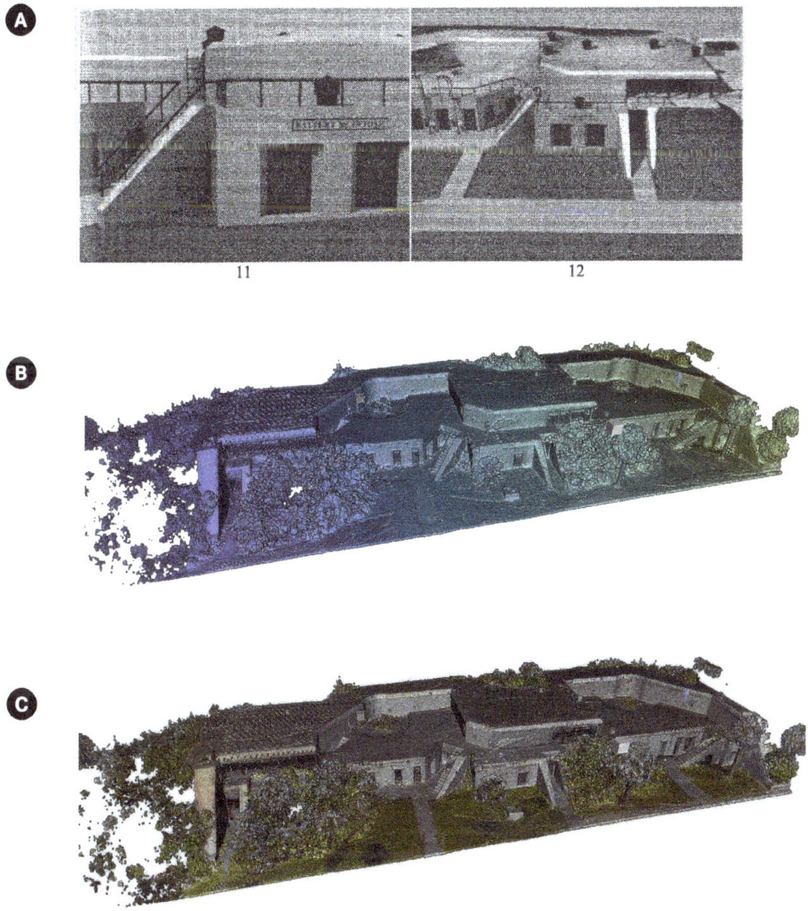

Figure 7.9. Composite image of Battery McIntosh showing (*a*) archival photo; (*b*) lidar point cloud colorized according to horizontal position (x values); and (*c*) lidar point cloud colorized according to RGB values. Image created by Laura Harrison, Access 3D Lab, University of South Florida.

Figure 7.10. Control points selected for georeferencing from an aerial photo (*left*) and terrestrial lidar (*right*). Note that points 1, 2 and 3 are identical in both images. Image created by Alex Fawbush, Access 3D Lab, University of South Florida.

cessing" the data to prepare it for sophisticated GIS analyses. Georeferencing refers to tying a visual digital product to a known global coordinate system. The resulting dataset must be decimated because ArcGIS is not optimized to handle such large, dense datasets. Point cloud decimation is a common practice when working with such high-resolution point clouds, as it reduces computation times and memory requirements by systematically removing a specified number of points (Bailey et al. 2020).

To georeference a terrestrial lidar scan in a remote area without known survey markers, it is necessary to manually identify correspondences between terrestrial lidar and aerial lidar (7.10). In other words, a researcher must compare an aerial with a terrestrial lidar scan of the same area, then identify at least three easily identifiable visual "landmarks" that will serve as control points. This method is relevant to other projects in similarly remote locations, where the lack of established survey benchmarks complicates direct measurement. For Egmont Key and many other locations in the United States, aerial lidar datasets are generated every few years and made available to download for free from USGS or NOAA.

Terrestrial lidar datasets must be captured manually during targeted fieldwork, whereas aerial lidar of large regions (e.g., entire the entire state of Florida) is captured periodically by government agencies and can be downloaded for free (it is also possible to collect specific aerial lidar datasets independently with a lidar sensor mounted on a drone, helicopter, or plane). With the aerial lidar data in hand, it is possible to create a digital surface model (DSM) of the area of interest. Taking a close look at this DSM—which typically has around 1-ft spatial resolution—allows the researcher to identify landmarks, such as right angles or corners of a building, which can become control points for georeferencing (7.9). The location and elevation of these landmarks are known as Z values. Each landmark also has X and Y values that represent its horizontal position along north-south and east-west axes. A minimum of three control points is necessary to accurately georeference a terrestrial lidar point cloud, and these points must be visible on both the DSM and marked as points in the terrestrial lidar point cloud.

A common challenge in this process is managing to identify control points that are visible in both the aerial lidar data (resolution approximately 1 ft), and the terrestrial lidar data (resolution approximately +/- 2 mm). Often, geometrically distinctive areas, such as corners or right angles, are helpful. This manual process is only needed in remote areas; if traverse points or survey markers are present—as is often the case in more urban areas—their legal description can be digitized and used for georeferencing. If there are no traverse points, however, it is necessary to manually identify landmarks to be used as control points. As a remote island, Egmont Key requires the manual type of georeferencing.

There are inherent limitations to georeferencing TLS data. The distinction between mapping-grade and survey-grade accuracy is critical here. Our project employs mapping-grade technology, which, while still high-resolution, adheres to the USGS map accuracy standards that allow for a resolution of approximately 1 ft. This is in contrast to survey-grade tools, which offer a much finer precision of 1 cm. This difference in resolution is important for understanding the limits of our current data in the context of the island's vulnerability to climate change and rising sea levels.

THE Z CONVERSION AND DECIMATION

The Z conversion ensures that the lidar scan is displayed not only in the correct position with respect to X and Y values but also at the proper elevation above sea level: the Z value. This workflow involves selecting three control points in the aerial lidar data within ArcGIS and identifying the same three corresponding points in the terrestrial lidar point cloud in Faro Scene. A Z

Table 7.1. Sample Formatting for XYZ Values (locational information) in Georeferencing Workflow

Control point	*X value*	*Y value*	*Z value*
1	156980.801	401970.788	9.091817
2	156971.722	401970.811	11.397095
3	156980.789	401966.442	7.339531

conversion is then applied to adjust for elevation differences between Faro Scene and ArcGIS. Establishing the Z value is critical to accurately simulating the impact of sea-level rise on a heritage site scanned with terrestrial lidar. The workflow involves calculating the difference between the Z value (elevation) of a control point in the aerial lidar DSM and the terrestrial lidar point cloud. The resulting value is the Z value for the project.

Once established for the first control point, the difference (Z value) is subtracted from the other two control points in the terrestrial lidar point cloud. This establishes vertical continuity across the entire dataset. The resulting Z values are then recorded in an Excel spreadsheet, with the three control points listed in successive rows and columns for the X, Y, and Z values extending from left to right (Table 7.1). The spreadsheet must be saved as a .csv file with general formatting to properly georeference the point cloud in Faro Scene.

To apply the Z conversion, open the project in Faro Scene, import the .csv reference points, and create a workspace-level cluster in the Explore tab. Add all scans and reference points to the cluster, then align it in the Registration tab. A pop-up will confirm the scans have shifted, and the updated X and Y coordinates should be close to those in Table 7.1. Finally, generate a project point cloud (PPC) to prepare for GIS export and decimation.

To decimate the PPC, go to the Explore tab, select Project Point Cloud, and choose Homogenize Point Density. Start with the default 1.5 mm to establish a baseline, then check the total point count in the Project tab. If the PPC exceeds 50 million points—too large for ArcGIS sea-level-rise analyses—increase the density value (e.g., 3 mm), regenerate the PPC, and recheck until the count falls below 50 million. This step is essential, as ArcGIS cannot display models that exceed the limit.

Once the PPC has been decimated to a usable size, it is ready to be exported from Faro Scene as an .e57 file and then opened in CloudCompare for conversion to a .las file. After opening the .e57 in CloudCompare, the PPC is selected in the table of contents and saved as a .las. Now that the PPC has been georeferenced, decimated, and exported as a .las file, it can be brought into ArcGIS.

IMPORTING GEOREFERENCED TERRESTRIAL LIDAR INTO GIS

Importing a georeferenced, decimated terrestrial lidar dataset in ArcGIS brings us one step closer to visualizing how sea-level rise will impact Battery McIntosh in the future. The technical workflow involves opening ArcGIS, then starting a New Project as a Local Scene (which can display 3D data on a local scale in a flat-world view). Each project must have a defined coordinate system, which is set by right-clicking the PPC .las file to access its properties, navigating to the coordinate system section, and selecting NAD 1983 (2011) StatePlane Florida West FIPS 0902 (Meters). The coordinate system is determined by the location of the project. While NAD 1983 (2011) StatePlane Florida West FIPS 0902 (Meters) is the correct system for Tampa, Florida it will not be appropriate for projects outside of the region. The visualization of the terrestrial lidar point cloud in GIS begins with the creation of a LAS Dataset (LASD) and the definition of the project's coordinate system. The PPC is then added to the LAS Files section, dragged into the Contents Pane, and colorized using RGB in the Symbology tab.

VISUALIZING SEA-LEVEL RISE IN GIS

The 2024 lidar-derived DEM was generated by integrating terrestrial lidar (TLS) scans with aerial lidar data. TLS scans were added to a new LAS Dataset in ArcGIS Pro, and the coordinate system was set to NAD 1983 (2011) StatePlane Florida West FIPS 0902. Aerial lidar data were then added to the same LAS Dataset, and any vertical offsets between TLS and aerial points were corrected to ensure consistent elevation values across the combined dataset. The points were then visualized and colorized. Finally, the LAS Dataset to Raster tool was used to interpolate the aerial and terrestrial lidar point clouds into a continuous surface, producing a high-resolution DEM that reflects both fine-scale details of Battery McIntosh captured with terrestrial lidar and broader topographical and coastal features recorded in the aerial lidar.

The workflow for modeling sea-level rise relies on this lidar-derived DEM. To map areas above and below projected future sea levels, the DEM must be reclassified by identifying elevation values within specific ranges. Using the

Reclassify tool or Raster Calculator in GIS, areas above and below defined thresholds can be assigned new values and visualized. For instance, in the NOAA 2080 High scenario (7.11), the threshold is 4.6 ft NAVD, which means that seas will rise to a level 4.6 ft above the North American Vertical Datum (NAVD) in 2080 if that scenario is realized. To show how this would impact Battery McIntosh, the DEM is reclassified to show areas above and below 4.6 ft NAVD. The reclassification isolates areas that would be inundated and areas that remain above water in this scenario (7.11). This result is a key step toward understanding exactly where and when the impacts of rising seas will impact a vulnerable heritage site on the coast.

RESULTS: RISING TIDES THREATEN BATTERY MCINTOSH

The georeferenced terrestrial lidar point cloud of Battery McIntosh, shown in 7.11, illustrates precisely how and where rising seas could impact the structure by 2080 under the NOAA High scenario. The terrestrial lidar data, with a resolution of 0.17 ft (5 cm), provides far greater detail than would be possible with aerial lidar analyses alone. It is also a substantial improvement in level of detail over the NOAA Sea Level Rise Viewer (7.6), which is better suited to provide a general overview of the scenarios than specific information tailored to an individual heritage site. Key architectural features are obscured in the NOAA viewer, but clearly visible in the terrestrial scan.

The inset in 7.11 highlights water rising to the fourth step of Battery McIntosh in the 2080 High scenario, illustrating exactly where and when sea-level rise will affect this site. 7.12 shows a 2D aerial photo of Battery McIntosh and shows how the NOAA High 2050 and High 2080 scenarios will impact the structure; again, the High 2080 scenario spells trouble. The message is clear: Creating a digital twin of this site, and continuing to monitor it, are essential in the coming decades, because by 2080 the site may be partially underwater. Indeed, if this scenario is realized, the rest of the island will also be mostly flooded, making future documentation and monitoring difficult if not impossible.

Island-Wide Sea-Level Projections at Egmont Key

The second case study in this chapter investigates the projected impacts of NOAA sea-level-rise scenarios (7.4) on the island as a whole, rather than on Battery McIntosh itself, by analyzing the aerial lidar-derived DEM from 2024 in ArcGIS. The focus of these analyses is not how rising seas will impact a specific

Figure 7.11. Visualization of the georeferenced 3D point cloud of Battery McIntosh, showing the NOAA High 2080 scenario. The inset image indicates the exact level of sea-level rise, with water rising to about the fourth step in the center staircase. Image created by Laura Harrison, Access 3D Lab, University of South Florida.

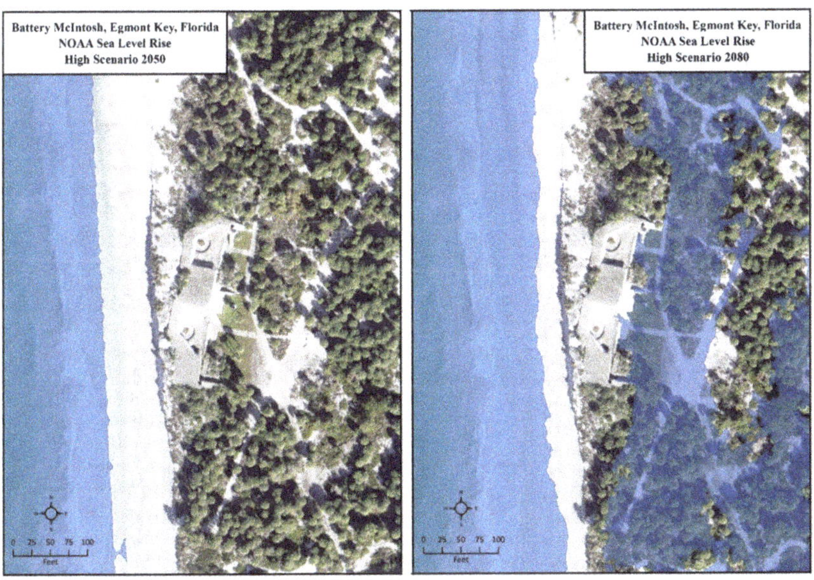

Figure 7.12. GIS map showing the projected impacts of sea-level rise on Battery McIntosh in the NOAA High 2050 Scenario (*left*) and the NOAA High 2080 scenario (*right*). Image created by Steven Fernandez, University of South Florida.

heritage site, but rather how much of the island will be inundated in different NOAA sea-level-rise scenarios.

PROJECTED IMPACTS OF SEA-LEVEL RISE IN 2080

If NOAA's intermediate scenario of 2.53 ft/0.77 m of sea-level rise is realized in 2080 (7.13A), the north end of the island may stay intact, but the interior of the island will flood as waters encroach over the small dune on the eastern shore. The bulge seen halfway down the western shoreline in 7.13A appears to be a large swath of land that would survive in this scenario, but this is deceiving. In fact, the island's natural shape is more rectangular than shown in the aerial lidar scan (7.13A and 7.13B), which was captured shortly after a major beach renourishment. Most sand emplacements on Egmont Key only last two to three years because of the intense currents in the area. This means that unless the beach is regularly replenished every few years, these artificially placed sands will wash back into the Gulf of Mexico. It also means that many of the cultural heritage sites that are situated along Egmont Key's northern and western shoreline (like Battery McIntosh) will experience a heightened risk if beach renourishment ever stops.

As beach renourishment at Egmont Key is tied to the dredging of the shipping channel into the Port of Tampa, there are many scenarios in which it could be halted—especially if it is no longer financially viable for the Port to continue dredging the sand and placing it on the island's western shore. Relying on beach renourishment as a heritage conservation strategy thus puts Egmont Key on shaky ground and shifting sands, literally and figuratively.

The situation for Egmont Key is more dire if the NOAA High scenario (7.13B) is realized in 2080. Here the island is submerged under 4.6 ft/1.4m of sea-level rise. Water has poured in over the eastern shore, and while it appears that a dune will form slightly inland from the western shoreline, in fact this ridge would likely be washed away by erosion (7.13B). Thus, for all intents and purposes, if the NOAA High 2080 scenario is realized, Egmont Key will be a memory rather than a destination.

PROJECTED IMPACTS OF SEA-LEVEL RISE IN 2120

The passage of time will do Egmont Key no favors. As seen in 7.14A, by 2120, rising seas may leave the island almost completely submerged, even in the NOAA Intermediate scenario (with 3.9 ft/1.2 m of sea-level rise). The dune on the north and west side of the island visualized in 7.14A is actually just artificial,

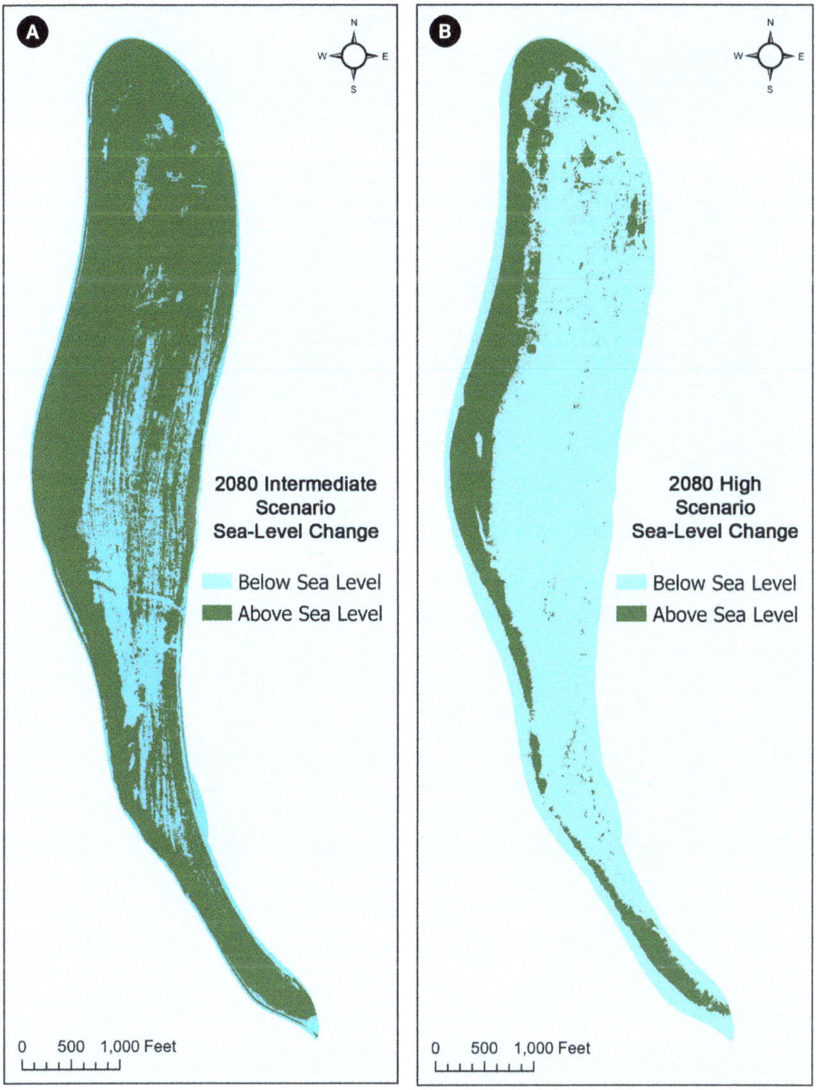

Figure 7.13. Map of Egmont Key showing the projected impacts of NOAA High and Intermediate scenarios in the year 2080. The models were created from a 2024 DEM and use scenarios from St. Petersburg Tide Level Station #8726520. Image created by Steven Fernandez, University of South Florida.

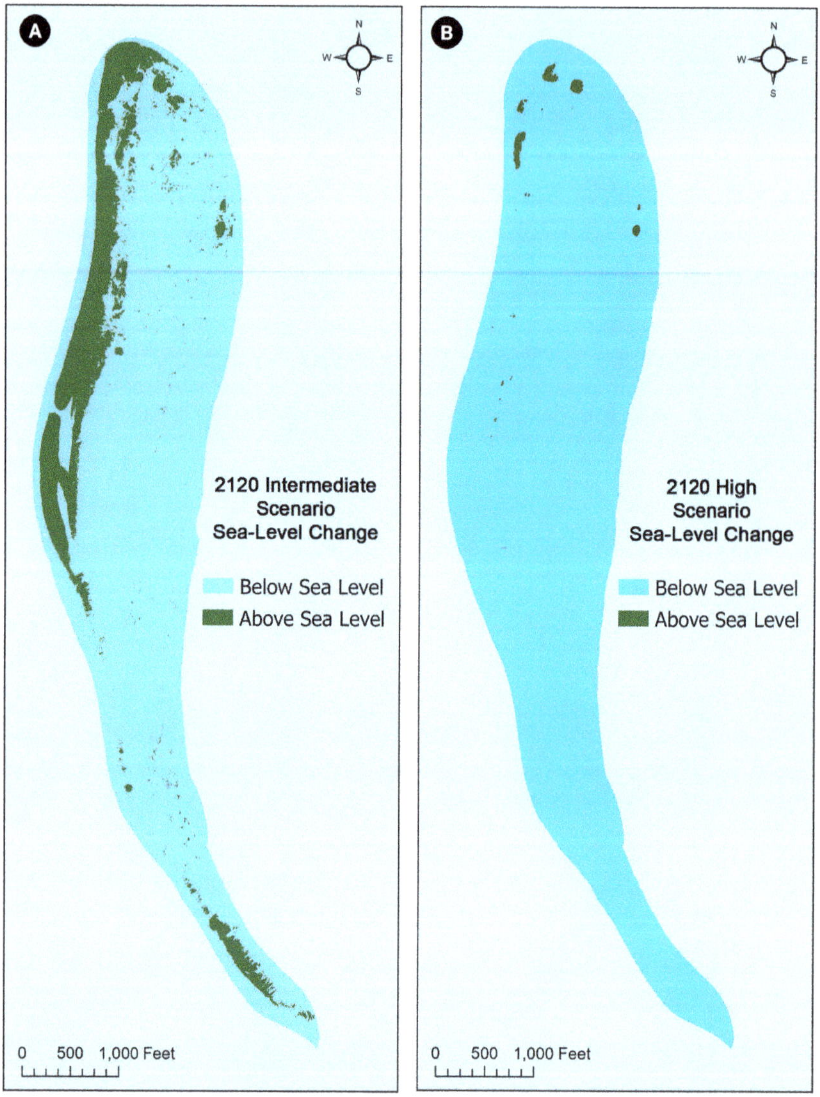

Figure 7.14. Map of Egmont Key showing the projected impacts of NOAA High and Intermediate scenarios in the year 2120. The models were created from a 2024 DEM and use scenarios from St. Petersburg Tide Level Station #8726520. Image created by Steven Fernandez, University of South Florida.

replenished sand. As the island sinks further into obscurity, beach renourishment is likely to come to a halt, so these sands will be long gone. That leaves just a few features of the island that would remain visible to boaters passing by—perhaps the top of the lighthouse, and the upper portions of Battery Mellon and Battery McIntosh, if they have not already given way to the currents and crumbled into the sea.

As we turn our attention to the High 2120 scenario, with 8.5 ft/2.6 m of sea-level rise, shown in 7.14B, it is clear that Egmont Key is all but a memory. The top of the lighthouse along with a few concrete remains of Battery Mellon and Battery McIntosh will still peek above the surface, visible to boaters and snorkelers who know where to look, but the island itself will have been reclaimed by the sea, and all that will be left of the disappearing island are memories and histories that will have been rendered invisible by rising tides.

The Ongoing Struggle Between Beach Renourishment and Erosion

Egmont Key is a testament to the ongoing struggle between natural forces and human intervention. Since 2000, the US Army Corps of Engineers (USACE) has carried out beach renourishment on the island every four to eight years, a process linked to the dredging of the Egmont Channel (7.15). While these efforts temporarily mitigate erosion, they do not halt the island's gradual loss to the sea that are propelled by incessant tides, winds, and storms.

According to a 2014 USACE news release, reusing dredged sand benefits Egmont Key's ecosystem by stabilizing the shoreline and protecting its historic and cultural resources (Maglio et al. 2015). Dredging project manager Milan Mora said, "We all recognized that if nothing is done, storms and wave action will continue eroding the shoreline and eventually destroy the historic structures" (UASCE 2014: para. 13). However, Mora also acknowledged the limitations of these efforts: "It's only a band-aid, but we'd like to continue to beneficially use the dredged sand to help preserve Egmont's cultural and natural environment as long as possible for future generations" (UASCE 2014: para. 14).

Egmont Key's erosion is not merely a function of rising sea levels but is closely linked to modifications and dredging of the Egmont Channel (Roberts and Wang 2012). A USF study by Tyler (2016) found that the rate of island-area reduction from 1942 to 2014 followed a linear trend. If not artificially maintained, the island could completely disappear by 2062—a finding that agrees

Figure 7.15. Beach renourishment underway at Egmont Key. Bulldozers move sand brought in from geotextile tubes. The work area is delineated with a safety barrier. By permission of Richard Sanchez.

with the analyses presented in Figures 7.13 and 7.14. Additionally, the beach renourishment projects have placed nearly 764,000 m^3 of fill on Egmont Key since 2002, but much of the dredged material is of low beach sand quality, requiring special permitting for use (Maglio et al. 2015; UASCE 2014). In addition, just putting sand back on an island does not an ecosystem make. Without the organic infrastructure of dunes, mangroves, and vegetation, placed sand is vulnerable to simply washing away again with nothing to keep it in place. Other recommendations for Egmont Key have included additional measures for beach stabilization with groins, submerged reefs, and seawalls (James et al. 2006).

Severe weather further exacerbates Egmont Key's instability. Between 2015 and 2024, Hurricanes Irma, Eta, Ian, Debby, Helene, and Milton impacted the island, causing extensive destruction and accelerating the erosion of the western shoreline. This period also saw significant beach renourishment efforts, which aerial lidar scans from 2015, 2017, 2022, and 2024 document in stark detail. Aerial lidar mapping and GIS document the tug-of-war between humans and nature, revealing that nature is winning: the island has shrunk from 286.8 acres in 2015 to 274.9 acres in 2024, losing 280,307 cubic feet of land (7.16 and Table 7.2).

The island's shifting sands and transformation are not uniform. The north-

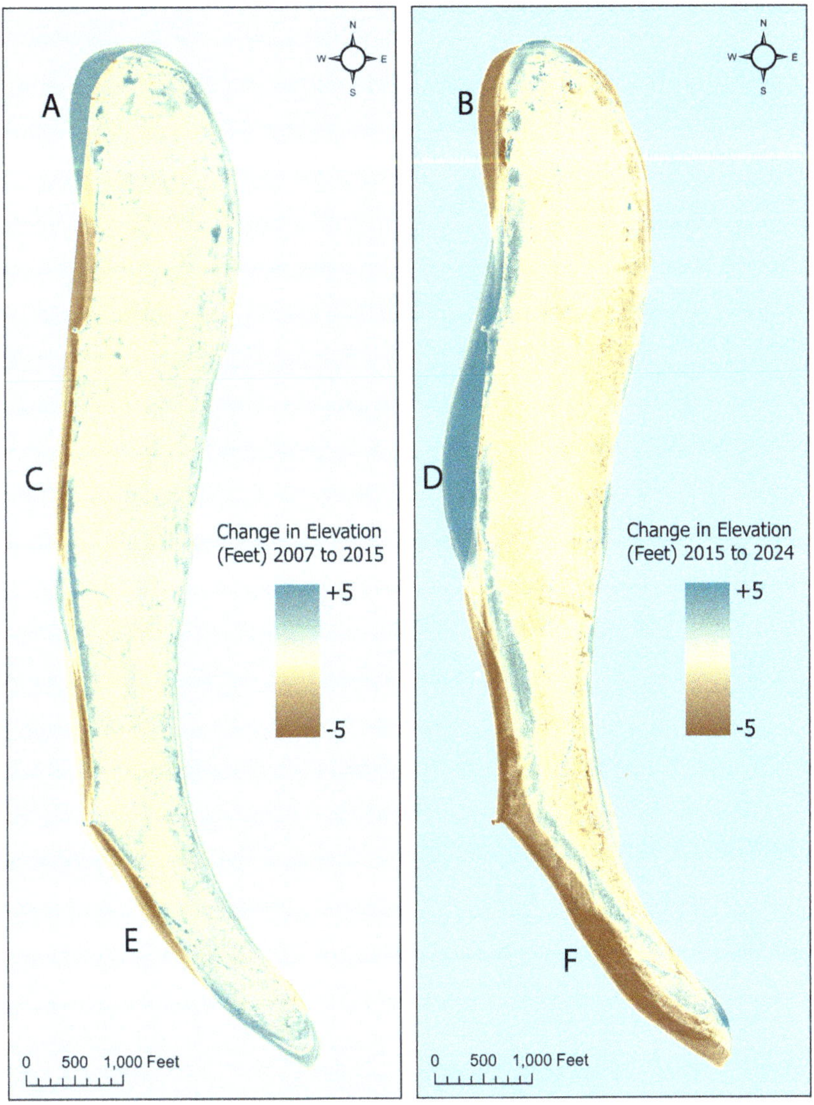

Figure 7.16. Aerial lidar map showing a comparison of digital elevation models (DEMs) from 2007 to 2024. The maps illustrate the constant interplay between nature (erosion) and human intervention (beach renourishment). Sand accretion is shown in blue, and erosion is shown in orange. All sand accretion on the western side of the island is due to targeted beach renourishment. Natural accretion occurs on a much smaller scale at the island's southeastern tip. The western shoreline experienced intense erosion between 2007 and 2015, highlighted in orange in the left image. These same processes will likely remove the renourished sand visible near the letter D in the right image. Map created by Steven Fernandez, University of South Florida.

Table 7.2. Erosion at Egmont Key (2015–2024) Measured in 2D Area (Flat Footprint), 3D Area (Surface Accounting for Elevation), and Volume (Cubic Feet)

	2D area (sq ft)	*3D area (sq ft)*	*Volume (cu ft)*
2015	12,494,533	12,565,440	41,110,892
Acres	286.8	288.5	n/a
2024	11,976,373	12,102,875	40,830,585
Acres	274.9	277.9	
Difference	-518,160	-462,565	-280,307
Difference (acres)	-11.9	-10.6	n/a

west corner of Egmont Key, where currents are strongest near the dredged shipping lane, has suffered the most substantial erosion. This trend is visible when comparing A and B in 7.16: A shows the results of beach renourishment on Egmont's northwest corner from 2007 to 2015, and B shows the erosion of that same sand back into the Gulf of Mexico between 2015 and 2024. A major beach renourishment project in 2024 is visible in the aerial lidar DEM from that year (7.16D). The 2024 aerial lidar DEM (7.16 between D and F) also shows a blue ridge along the west side of the island that is evidence of storm surge from Hurricane Helene and Hurricane Milton moving the beach sand farther inland. The island's southwest edge also continues a historical pattern of shrinkage dating back to the nineteenth century (7.16 between D and F). In this area, following the very active 2024 hurricane season, the southern portion of the island lost 350 ft of width, reducing to half its original size.

Egmont Key's cultural heritage is caught in the crosshairs of this battle between beach renourishment and erosion. The island's Spanish-American War fortifications are highly vulnerable to the forces of erosion, though paradoxically they also serve as a breakwater and provide limited beach stabilization (Tyler 2016). Additionally, the island's southern and western coasts are vital to nesting shorebirds and sea turtles, whose habitats shrink with each passing storm. Sandy Colbert of the Egmont Key Alliance encapsulates the precarious nature of the island's future, noting, "If nature has decided to work against the island by sea level rise and gulf subsidence, then we may have to resign ourselves to that eventuality. However, if man is found to be at fault, then we may well be able to pursue manmade solutions. For now, birds, turtles, and ghosts of soldiers and sailors long gone can still find a place to rest on Egmont Key" (Hoppe 2002: para. 1).

HURRICANES AND EROSION

The biggest existential threat facing Egmont Key is a future Category 5 hurricane making landfall on the island. While our lidar and GIS models cannot predict the exact form that destruction would take, it would certainly be catastrophic and would alter the timetables for inundation and erosion outlined above. Analyzing the effects of past hurricanes provides a glimpse at how strong storms affect the shoreline. In May 2022, our team completed a 3D scan of Battery McIntosh (also discussed in Chapter 6), including the beach to the west of the structure. Hurricane Ian hit Tampa Bay on September 28, 2022, and our team was able to return to Egmont Key on October 8, 2022, to rescan the beach and analyze changes in the volume of beach sand before and after the storm (7.17). A visual analysis of the beach didn't show any major erosion—the rotation of the hurricane caused onshore winds to batter the island's western shore, mitigating losses. But a comparison of the georeferenced DEMs of a 1295 m^2 study area before and after Hurricane Ian revealed that the beach immediately west of Battery McIntosh lost 385.6 m^3 of sand during the storm (7.18 and Table 7.3). Digital monitoring can thus reveal fine-grained changes in the island that are invisible to the naked eye.

Figure 7.17. Terrestrial lidar scan data overlay from May 12, 2022, and October 8, 2022. Image created by Laura Harrison, Access 3D Lab, University of South Florida.

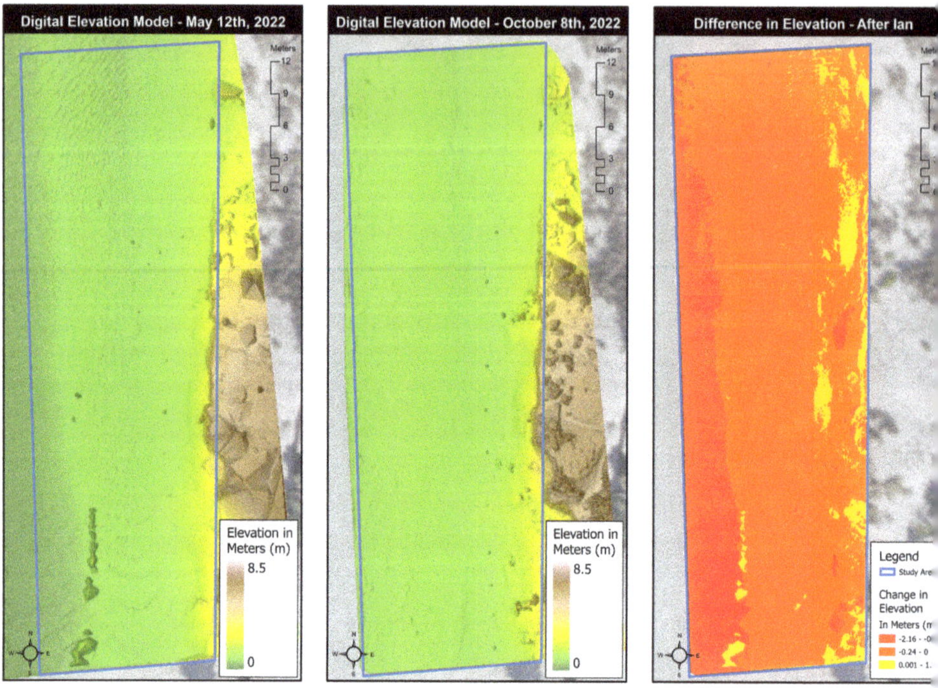

Figure 7.18. DEMs before and after Hurricane Ian, showing a difference in elevation resulting from the loss of 385.6 cubic meters of sand. This loss is difficult to detect without 3D lidar analyses. The orange and red image on the right shows specific areas where beach sand was lost during Hurricane Ian. Map created by Steven Fernandez, University of South Florida.

Table 7.3. Erosion at Egmont Key Before and After Hurricane Ian

Date	Volume in cubic meters (m^3)
May 12, 2022	955.01
October 8, 2022	569.41
Difference	-385.6

Mapping, Modeling, and Visualizing Heritage at Risk at Egmont Key

Egmont Key faces an uncertain future because of interacting environmental and human forces. Rising seas, shifting sands, and human impacts converge to threaten the island's built heritage and natural landscape. Strategically addressing these concerns requires combining physical interventions with digital documentation and spatial modeling to understand risk, prioritize actions, and digitize what can't be saved. Preservation efforts cannot rely solely on reactive measures. The three case studies presented here highlight how high-resolution lidar data and long-term projections reveal the scale and immediacy of threats to both individual structures and the island as a whole. They also demonstrate the benefits and limitations of efforts to stabilize the island, like beach renourishment.

The first case study shows that Battery McIntosh will be inundated by rising seas by 2080 if the NOAA High scenario is realized. Heritage preservation measures like conserving and reinforcing the structure may be useful in the short term, but ultimately the site is likely to suffer irreparable loss. Digital documentation and monitoring should be a key part of heritage management plans moving forward. These findings are the result of an innovative method of analyzing georeferenced 3D terrestrial lidar scans of heritage sites in GIS.

While this analysis provides important insights into the risks posed by sea-level rise, the analysis of Battery McIntosh presented here only addresses one dimension of climate change: sea-level rise. In addition to rising seas, climate change is also contributing to more frequent and intense storms, hurricanes, and flooding events that may exacerbate the threat to Egmont Key's heritage sites. The island's significant and irreplaceable coastal fortifications are particularly susceptible to the increased storm surges and flooding expected in the coming decades. Beyond these natural threats, human activities such as overtourism, vandalism, and the intrusion of roots as a result of vegetation overgrowth pose further threats to the preservation of the island's built heritage. Developing proactive heritage management strategies in the face of the risks outlined here is the focus of Chapter 4.

The second case study adopts an island-wide perspective and shows that Egmont Key is likely to be fully submerged by 2080 if the NOAA High scenario is realized, or by 2120 if the NOAA Intermediate scenario is realized. Beach renourishment provides some stabilization to the dynamic western coast, and slows erosion, but does not completely stop it. Future plans for heritage and tourism development on the island should acknowledge the likelihood that the island will be a remnant of its former self in the coming decades. A key sign to watch for is not just the erosion happening on the western shoreline but the encroachment of waters from the east. The east dune is much lower than the western dune, and when it is crested by rising seas, waters will encroach on the center of the island, gradually flooding heritage sites. Eventually, as water floods the buildings (as visualized in the Battery McIntosh model in Figure 7.11) they will collapse in on themselves and crumble into the sea. Bits of rubble may peek out above the water's surface.

The third case study shows that nature is slowly winning the battle between erosion and beach renourishment. Erosion is perhaps a more immediate threat to the island than sea-level rise, and renourishment—while costly—does help stabilize the shore. As a conservation strategy, it is hampered by cost and the fact that it is tied to the economics of dredging the shipping channel into the Port of Tampa. Ironically, dredging produces the sand artificially placed on Egmont Key's shores and accelerates the currents that wash them back out to sea. Beach renourishment is also no match for hurricanes and strong storms, and even after relatively minor storm events like Hurricane Ian, the island faced a substantial loss of sand. If a Category 5 storm makes landfall in the future, the erosion will be devastating.

Together, the three cases presented in this chapter reveal Egmont Key's vulnerabilities from several perspectives. High-resolution terrestrial lidar data show fine-scale risks to individual structures; island-wide modeling identifies long-term trends; and erosion monitoring illustrates the limits of artificial shoreline stabilization. This uncertain future underlines the importance of digitally recording threatened sites (Chapter 6), engaging in regular monitoring (Chapter 4), and developing inclusive interpretations of history (Chapters 2 and 3) that allow knowledge, memory, and meaning to endure. The multidisciplinary, participatory, and inclusive methods outlined throughout this volume ensure that multiple communities and stakeholders can engage with Egmont Key while it is still here—learning its lessons and creating memories that may outlast the physical island itself.

References Cited

Bailey, P., J. Wheaton, M. Reimer, and J. Brasington. 2020. Geomorphic Change Detection Software (7.5.0). June 18. *Zenodo*. https://doi.org/10.5281/zenodo.7248344.

Bewley, R. H., S. P. Crutchley, and C. A. Shell. 2005. New Light on an Ancient Landscape: LiDAR Survey in the Stonehenge World Heritage Site. *Antiquity* 79(305):636–647. https://doi.org/10.1017/S0003598X00114577.

Conolly, J., and M. Lake. 2006. *Geographical Information Systems in Archaeology*. Cambridge University Press, Cambridge.

Cremons, D. R. 2022. The Future of Lidar in Planetary Science. *Frontiers in Remote Sensing* 3:1–7. https://doi.org/10.3389/frsen.2022.1042460.

Cuca, B., F. Zaina, and D. Tapete. 2023. Monitoring of Damages to Cultural Heritage Across Europe Using Remote Sensing and Earth Observation: Assessment of Scientific and Grey Literature. *Remote Sensing* 15(15): 1–33. https://doi.org/10.3390/rs15153748.

Dawson, Tom, Joanna Hambly, Alice Kelley, William Lees, and Sarah Miller. 2020. Coastal Heritage, Global Climate Change, Public Engagement, and Citizen Science. 2020. *Proceedings of the National Academy of Sciences* 117(15): 8280–8286. https://doi.org/10.1073/pnas.1912246117.

Fatorić, S., and E. Seekamp. 2017. Are Cultural Heritage and Resources Threatened by Climate Change? A Systematic Literature Review. *Climatic Change* 142:227–254. https://doi.org/10.1007/s10584-017-1929-9.

Florida Trust for Historic Preservation. 2017. Florida Trust for Historic Preservation Announces 2017 Florida's 11 to Save at the Florida Preservation Conference. May 19. https://floridatrust.org/wp-content/uploads/2024/07/2017-11-to-Save-press-release.pdf, accessed April 1, 2025.

González-Tennant, Edward. 2016. Recent Directions and Future Developments in Geographic Information Systems for Historical Archaeology. *Historical Archaeology* 50(1): 24–49. https://doi.org/10.1007/BF03377332.

Goyer, G. G., and R. Watson. 1963. The Laser and Its Application to Meteorology. *Bulletin of the American Meteorological Society* 44(9): 564–570.

Guidi, G., and B. D. Frischer. 2020. 3D Digitization of Cultural Heritage. In *3D Imaging, Analysis and Applications*, edited by Y. Liu, N. Pears, P. L. Rosin, and P. Huber, pp. 631–697. Springer, Cham, Switzerland. https://link.springer.com/chapter/10.1007/978-3-030-44070-1_13.

Hoppe, M. K. 2002. Wildlife Flocks to Man-Made Beach at Egmont Key. *Bay Soundings*, Fall. https://baysoundings.com/wildlife-flocks-to-man-made-beach-at-egmont-key/, accessed September 1, 2025.

Ikawa, H. 2023. New Technologies and Disaster Risk Management for Cultural Properties. In Routledge *Handbook on Cultural Heritage and Disaster Risk Management* (pp. 279–288). Routledge.

James, S. R., Jr., C. C. Pearson, and M. C. Krivor. 2006. Historic Assessment, Remote Sensing Survey and Diver Evaluations at Egmont Key, Hillsborough, Florida. Prepared for the US Army Corps of Engineers, Jacksonville District. Panamerican Consultants, Memphis, Tennessee.

Lercari, N., D. Jaffke, A. Campiani, S. Guillem, S., S. McAvoy, G. J. Delgado, A. B. Neeb. 2021. Building Cultural Heritage Resilience Through Remote Sensing: An Integrated Approach Using Multi-Temporal Site Monitoring, Datafication, and Web-GL Visualization. *Remote Sensing* 13(20): 1–24.

Lewis, E. R. 1993. *Seacoast Fortifications of the United States: An Introductory History*. Naval Institute Press, Annapolis.

Maglio, C. K., J. D. Ousley, A. Hershorin, and M. A. Mora. 2015. Tampa Harbor Maintenance Dredging with Egmont Key Beneficial Reuse of High Silt Content Material Using a Traditional Template Versus Cross Shore Swash Zone Placement. *Proceedings of the Western Dredging Association and Texas A&M University for Dredging Studies' "Dredging Summit and Expo 2017,"* pp. 216–226. Houston, Texas.

Mallinson, D., S. Culver, E. Leorri, S. Mitra, R. Mulligan, and S. Riggs. 2018. Barrier Island and Estuarine Co-Evolution in Response to Holocene Climate and Sea-Level Change: Pamlico Sound and the Outer Banks, North Carolina, USA. In *Barrier Dynamics and Response to Changing Climates*, edited by L. Moore and B. Muray, pp. 91–120. Springer International, New York.

Maté-González, Miguel Ángel, Vincenzo Di Pietra, and Marco Piras. 2022. Evaluation of Different LiDAR Technologies for the Documentation of Forgotten Cultural Heritage Under Forest Environments. *Sensors* 22(16): 6314. https://doi.org/10.3390/s22166314.

Mezzino, D., L. Chan, M. Santana Quintero, M. Esponda, S. Lee, A. Min, and M. Pwint. 2017. Built Heritage Documentation and Management: The Bagan Case Study. *ISPRS Annals of the Photogrammetry, Remote Sensing and Spatial Information Sciences* IV-2/W2: 143–150. https://isprs-annals.copernicus.org/articles/IV-2-W2/143/2017/.

Miller, S. E., and E. J. Murray. 2018. Heritage Monitoring Scouts: Engaging the Public to Monitor Sites at Risk Across Florida. *Conservation and Management of Archaeological Sites* 20(4): 234–260. https://doi.org/10.1080/13505033.2018.1516455

Monego, M., A. Menin, M. Fabris, and V. Achilli. 2019. 3D Survey of Sarno Baths (Pompeii) by Integrated Geomatic Methodologies. *Journal of Cultural Heritage* 40 (November–December): 240–246. https://www.sciencedirect.com/science/article/abs/pii/S1296207418305867?via%3Dihub.

National Oceanic and Atmospheric Administration (NOAA). 2020. Historical Surveys (T-Sheets). Electronic document, https://shoreline.noaa.gov/t-sheets.html, accessed April 1, 2025.

Opitz, R., and J. Herrmann. 2018. Recent Trends and Long-Standing Problems in Archaeological Remote Sensing. *Journal of Computer Applications in Archaeology* 1(1): 19–41. https://doi.org/10.5334/jcaa.11.

Orr, Scott Allan, Jenny Richards, and Sandra Fatorić. 2021. Climate Change and Cultural Heritage: A Systematic Literature Review (2016–2020). *Historic Environment: Policy & Practice* 123–4 (3–4): 434–477. https://doi.org/10.1080/17567505.2021.1957264.

Rayne L., B. Rouhani, and J. Lavris Makovics. 2023. Remote Sensing and Disaster Risk Management for Cultural Heritage. In *Managing Disaster Risks to Cultural Heritage: From Risk Preparedness to Recovery for Immovable Heritage*, edited by Bijan Rouhani and Xavier Romão, pp. 114–132. Routledge, London.

Rouhani, Bijan, and Xavier Romão (editors). 2023. *Managing Disaster Risks to Cultural Heritage: From Risk Preparedness to Recovery for Immovable Heritage*. Routledge, London.

Ringle, William M., Tomás Gallareta Negrón, Rossana May Ciau, Kenneth E. Seligson, Juan C. Fernández-Díaz, and David Ortegón Zapata. 2021. LiDAR Survey of Ancient Maya Settlement in the Puuc Region of Yucatán, Mexico. *PLOS ONE* 16(4): e0249314. https://doi.org/10.1371/journal.pone.0249314.

Roberts, T. M., and P. Wang. 2012. Four-Year Performance and Associated Controlling Factors of Several Beach Nourishment Projects Along Three Adjacent Barrier Islands, West-Central Florida, USA. *Coastal Engineering* 70:21–39. https://doi.org/10.1016/j.coastaleng.2012.06.003.

Sesana, E., A. S. Gagnon, C. Ciantelli, J. Cassar, and J. J. Hughes. 2021. Climate Change Impacts on Cultural Heritage: A Literature Review. *WIREs Climate Change* 12(4): 1–29. https://doi.org/10.1002/wcc.710.

Tallon, A. 2014. Divining Proportions in the Information Age. *Architectural Histories* 2(1): 1–14. https://doi.org/10.5334/ah.bo.

Tyler, Z. J. 2016. Morphodynamics of Egmont Key at the Mouth of Tampa Bay: West-Central Florida. MS thesis, Department of Geology, University of South Florida, Tampa. Digital Commons at the University of South Florida. Tampa, Florida.

US Army Corps of Engineers (USACE). 2014. Tampa Harbor Dredging Benefits Egmont Key. September 12. US Army Corps of Engineers, Jacksonville District Website. News Release Archive. Electronic document, https://www.saj.usace.army.mil/Media/News-Releases/Article/497212/tampa-harbor-dredging-benefits-egmont-key/, accessed April 1, 2025.

Vinci, Giacomo, Federica Vanzani, Alessandro Fontana, and Stefano Campana. 2025. LiDAR Applications in Archaeology: A Systematic Review. *Archaeological Prospection* 32(1): 81–101. https://doi.org/10.1002/arp.1931.

Warner-Smith, Alanna L. 2020. Mapping the GIS Landscape: Introducing "Beyond (Within, Through) the Grid." *International Journal of Historical Archaeology* 24(4): 767–779. https://doi.org/10.1007/s10761-019-00527-6.

8

Reflections on the Disappearing Island

LAURA K. HARRISON AND BROOKE HANSEN

Egmont Key has proven to be an unparalleled living learning laboratory to explore issues of heritage at risk, climate change, invisible histories, sustainable tourism, complex land management, and digital heritage methodologies. Our research has involved many students, organizations, and community members and forged a community of practice through workshops, courses, and presentations. The island has become a crucial training ground for the next generation of heritage and sustainability professionals who have taken the lessons learned from our collaborative work and applied it to new contexts. In this way, the Egmont Key Project continues to reverberate beyond the tiny island and its disappearing shores.

The work done at Egmont Key was only possible because of strong collaborations with multiple partners, from nonprofit entities and government agencies to tour operators and conservation organizations. It is our hope that these relationships will continue to manifest positive change for the resiliency of the island and surrounding region in the future. Egmont Key has been an incredible multidisciplinary research site that has something for everyone—from the humanities to the sciences to the general public, there is a story to tell, a challenge to be addressed, and a way to get involved. Egmont Key's unique capacity to connect with so many issues from heritage, climate, and tourism to sustainability and more, propels interdisciplinary, stakeholder, and community collaboration.

Egmont Key continues to be a site of learning as we expand the project into a more comprehensive regional approach to safeguarding Florida's cultural and natural heritage. The island will be interpreted from other locations, including

Fort De Soto, the neighboring seacoast defense built simultaneously with Fort Dade and in view just across the Egmont Channel. As we extend our work from the island to nearby areas linked by heritage, tourism, and sustainability, we will apply the perspectives and methods outlined in this book to other at-risk places.

Egmont Key is everywhere now. The island—though still difficult to visit physically—is now digitized and can be toured virtually. By scanning Egmont Key's iconic heritage sites, we have created an enduring, tangible record of the past that cannot easily be erased. These diverse digital records, which include 3D digital twins, interactive exhibits, GIS visualizations, and virtual reality tours, also capture and memorialize intangible histories that were once overlooked. As a result, the island and its stories will continue to have a digital afterlife, even if the physical lands and sites disappear.

Egmont Key is more than a small island off Florida's Gulf Coast—it is a microcosm of the tensions, challenges, and opportunities inherent in managing heritage, tourism, and sustainability in the face of global environmental change. Across the chapters of this book, a complex picture has emerged of a place where histories of colonization, military conflict, Indigenous resilience, and environmental vulnerabilities intersect. The lessons learned from Egmont Key highlight the island's unique past and endangered present and offer a roadmap for how heritage and tourism professionals can navigate the complexities of stewarding cultural and natural resources in coastal environments.

Retrospective: Reflecting on Egmont Key

What have we learned from this deep dive into Egmont Key? There are important and diverse histories everywhere at risk of disappearing if no one steps forward to record them and ensure they are passed down to future generations. During the course of our research at Egmont Key, we connected with a wide network of scholars, archivists, and history enthusiasts to piece together numerous archival documents and develop a better understanding of the island's fascinating past. In addition to underlining Egmont Key's significant role in US history and connection to well-known figures, this work revealed countless little-known stories. We were delighted to discover the colorful life of Julius Tiedchen, the bugler-turned-baker of Fort Dade, and to read Roberta Moore Cole's firsthand accounts of military target practice and Friday night dances on the island, where her family of lighthouse keepers lived for over 40 years. While we have documented many lesser-known invisible histories, there are many more yet to be told. Future research directions could include the experiences of enslaved people escaping the Civil War and taking refuge at Egmont Key, the lives of women during the Fort Dade period, and more specifics of how Egmont Key was involved in rum-running, to name a few.

The Seminole Tribe of Florida's connection to Egmont Key offers another powerful reminder of why incorporating Indigenous perspectives is such a crucial element of contemporary heritage practice. The island's role as a site of trauma but also resilience during Indian Removal reinforces the need to challenge dominant historical narratives and amplify the stories that have long been silenced. Efforts by the Seminole Tribal Historic Preservation Office (THPO) to preserve this heritage are critical not only for healing and cultural continuity but also to serve as models for decolonizing heritage practices globally. In Chapter 3, Seminoles reflect on the impact of their experiences at Egmont Key and the lasting legacy of these events and figures such as Polly Parker. As sea-level rise threatens the very ground these stories rest upon, digital storytelling and participatory research become lifelines for sustaining memory and visibility.

We approached the Egmont Key Project from interdisciplinary and participatory perspectives to amplify historically marginalized voices and document the threats facing historic sites like Battery McIntosh and landscapes like the fragile western shoreline. The integration of digital heritage tools and methods—such as terrestrial lidar scanning, GIS analysis, and virtual and augmented reality—has allowed us to document structures that may soon be lost forever. More importantly, these tools have promoted education and public engagement, making it possible to share Egmont Key's complex histories with audiences within the Tampa Bay region as well as across the nation and globe.

What have we learned from carrying out a multiyear digital heritage research project about the island? It can be very challenging to navigate the competing agendas and interests of stakeholders, in addition to obtaining research permits and planning how to conduct research on a remote island. Logistics were daunting, from finding passage to the island to securing funding. Timetables were also short—most of our funding and permits were issued for a single year at a time—which hampered our ability to operationalize long-term site documentation and monitoring. On a shoestring budget, we conducted our research at the same time as teaching hands-on lessons and professional development workshops on the island. From the unrelenting sun and swarms of mosquitoes to the challenge of doing digital fieldwork on an island with no

Figure 8.1. The western shore of Egmont Key, where turquoise waters meet a white sand beach. By permission of Laura Harrison.

power or Wi-Fi connectivity, conditions were not always easy (and the lack of restrooms does not help either).

The Egmont Key Project highlights that the loss of physical heritage does not have to mean the end of meaning and memories connected to those places. As climate change reshapes our world, digital heritage methodologies and community engagement offer ways forward and allow us to rethink what heritage means, who it belongs to, and how we safeguard it in an era of uncertainty. The story of Egmont Key is still unfolding. Its legacy lies not just in the structures that remain, but also in the narratives that have been revealed, the knowledge that has been shared, and the partnerships that have been forged. Through collective action, we can ensure that disappearing places continue to speak.

Introspective: Evaluating the Current Moment

Egmont Key is an island of contrasts. Upon first glance, its natural beauty is striking and alluring, with sparkling turquoise waters lapping up against expansive white sand beaches peppered with seashells and colonies of nesting shorebirds (8.1). The brick pathways traversing the interior of the island

Figure 8.2. On the interior of the island, vines and foliage encroach on historic buildings from the Spanish-American War. By permission of Laura Harrison.

feel mysterious and atmospheric, periodically revealing hidden vistas of vine-covered historic buildings, crumbling into foliage that surrounds them (8.2). The sounds of oystercatchers and osprey pierce the air, while gopher tortoises calmly walk by and tend to their burrows, dug into the soft earth. Recreating tourists play and laugh on the beach, enjoying the ample sunshine.

THE TROUBLE WITH TOURISM

Beneath the bucolic veneer there are many issues and pressures that tourists bring, from waste and debris (there are no trash receptacles or bathrooms on the island) to overcrowding one another and the wildlife. Nesting birds get flushed by unthinking tourists and often their dogs chase the birds off shoreline nests with fragile eggs, leaving them open to predators. This occurs despite the island being clearly marked with numerous signs prohibiting dogs. Turtle nests are monitored and marked when they are found, but supervision is not continuous. With the western shore popular for both visitors and turtles, impact on the turtle eggs and hatchlings is inevitable. Solving these problems requires intentional planning and monitoring of tourism sites, as outlined in sustainable tourism approaches and called for by the UN Sustainable Development Goals (SDGs).

A balance needs to be maintained between travelers and ecosystems. Other tourism related issues are compounded by the lack of oversight on the island that leaves heritage structures open to vandalism. Even when there was a resident park ranger present, it often was insufficient for the task at hand. For example, in May 2024, a man landed his helicopter in the refuge, scattering birds and eggs during nesting season, while his wife roamed the beach taking pictures. Egmont Key is a case study, and unfortunately not a unique one, for why sustainable tourism needs to be a guiding framework for addressing tourism destinations that are at risk.

Sustainability in tourism and heritage cannot be achieved in isolation from land management frameworks, community input, and the realities of funding and staffing public lands, an increasingly challenging endeavor. Many of the measures that would have benefited Egmont Key and reduced tourism impact were included in the 2010 Tampa Bay Refuges Comprehensive Conservation Plan (USFWS 2010) but never acted upon. Implementing visitor management is hampered by the layers of organizations with authoritative oversight. The island's position within overlapping jurisdictions—from federal wildlife refuge to state park—mirrors many destinations globally where fragmented governance undermines long-term planning. This complexity highlights the need for cooperation between government, nonprofit, academic, and public stakeholders. Sustained collaboration is a fundamental component of any serious pursuit of sustainability and resilience at a public heritage site.

THE CHALLENGES OF CLIMATE CHANGE

Climate change threatens destinations such as Egmont Key by degrading shorelines, raising urgent questions about protecting heritage at risk. When sites are lost, we lose the tangible anchors of stories that are connected to communities and identities. These stories are fundamental to tourism by providing the interpretive building blocks that allow visitors to understand destinations. To address this imminent loss of cultural heritage, we adopted a geomatics approach integrating lidar and GIS, which enabled a robust risk assessment of the island's heritage under rising sea levels. Simulations and models of projected climate change impacts on cultural heritage—like sea-level rise—provide frameworks for data-driven decision making to safeguard heritage at risk. If we know approximately when and where heritage sites will be lost, such as Battery McIntosh, it can help land managers better direct their limited resources to what is most imperiled. Academic partnerships can be a great resource for this research modeling; incorporating students not only educates them about place, but it also provides them with increasingly in-demand skills for addressing climate change impacts in real-world scenarios.

HURRICANE HAVOC

Egmont Key is a disappearing island. Many of the predictions made in this book—about destruction, disappearance, and erasure—unfortunately were realized in the aftermath of two back-to-back powerful hurricanes that bashed Egmont Key with high waters and strong winds. In late September 2024, Hurricane Helene roared up the Florida Gulf Coast as a Category 4 hurricane bringing with it widespread catastrophic damage and numerous fatalities across the southeastern United States. It was the strongest hurricane on record to strike the west coast of Florida and the deadliest storm the United States had seen since Hurricane Katrina in 2005. It brought a 6–8-ft storm surge to Tampa Bay and inundated Egmont Key. In the days that followed, the retracting water left cars, refrigerators, and massive amounts of wreckage and pollutants floating in Tampa Bay and swirling around Egmont Key. Debris torn from the island during hurricanes added to the material cast out to sea. Much of it was eventually brought back by the waves.

The Tampa Bay Pilots Association village, which had functioned as their center of operations guiding ships into the region since the mid-nineteenth century, was completely destroyed. The buildings were toppled and smashed against one another in a show of force that must have been tremendous to witness. One of the buildings literally disappeared; it was ripped from its foundations, carried off the island's eastern shore, and plunged into the sea. The US Fish and Wildlife Service command center, the Florida Park Service ranger house, and the docks used to access and monitor the island were also destroyed. The island's land managers in effect lost their ability to maintain a presence on the island. After years of intensive, collaborative work on the island, we were devastated to learn of the destruction and loss.

Incredibly, just thirteen days after Hurricane Helene, on October 9, 2024, Hurricane Milton hit Egmont Key as the second-most intense Atlantic hurricane ever recorded over the Gulf of Mexico. The storm reached Category 5 strength and was the strongest tropical cyclone to occur worldwide in 2024. The eyewall landed on Siesta Key, 57 miles south of Egmont Key, as a Category 3 storm with 120 mph gusts. Like Helene, this was not a direct hit on Egmont Key. Milton brought the wind and served as the second of a one-two punch to

Figure 8.3. Golf carts were once a frequent sight on Egmont Key, used by land managers to patrol the island. The 2024 hurricanes left several golf carts in their wake. By permission of Laura Harrison.

the island's infrastructure (what was left of it) and ecosystems. A Pilots' cottage that had withstood Hurricane Helene's storm surge on its stilts was ultimately knocked down by Milton's powerful winds.

On February 14, 2025, we traveled to Egmont Key to assess hurricane damage at the Pilots' Village and conduct new lidar scans to compare with earlier surveys. We went aboard retired Pilot John Timmel's boat with his son Jack Timmel, now manager of the Tampa Bay Pilots Association. Several family members came along as well as journalist Paul Guzzo (Guzzo 2025). Our first sight was the ruined dock; only the pilings remained of this piece of infrastructure so integral to the activities of the Pilots (8.3). The walk through the village was shocking. It was indeed completely destroyed with the interior furnishings of houses washed out to sea and debris everywhere (Figures 8.3, 8.4, and 8.5), some of which was molding in the humid air. Dead gopher tortoises dotted the landscape (8.9), and it was said that almost 50 made their way across the Egmont Channel in harsh conditions and have taken up residence at Fort De Soto Park. As a symbolic statement of what had occurred, a book titled *Mayday* had washed out of a home and lay on the ground among scattered belongings

Figure 8.4. Debris strewn about the Pilots' village in the aftermath of the 2024 hurricane season. By permission of Laura Harrison.

(8.6). The loss of infrastructure on the island forced the Pilots to evacuate their base of operations. They relocated off-site while planning a permanent home, which will likely never be on Egmont Key again.

We pondered how much it would take to clean up such a disaster zone and couldn't imagine the costs and logistics necessary on the remote island that now didn't even have a dock (Figures 8.7, 8.8). The trees along the west coast were stripped of foliage. An attempt to walk up the road to take a look at some of the other areas of the island was thwarted by a 6-ft pile of sticks, palm fronds, and other plant materials that prevented passage to the northern part of the island, where the lighthouse still stood. The Egmont Key Lighthouse weathered both of these storms (as it had many before it, including the 1921 storm that decimated the island) to remain a beacon on the beleaguered island.

The island was closed to visitors shortly after Hurricane Milton and did not reopen until late spring of 2025. Monitoring was difficult after the storms because all docks were destroyed and no habitable structures remained. The Florida Park Service ranger had to leave the island. Despite regular but intermittent trips to the island to check on its status since the reopening, there is no daily or weekly monitoring. USFWS and the Tampa Bay Pilots Association

Figure 8.5. A house in the Pilots' village that was ripped from its foundation and detached from its front steps as a result of Hurricane Helene's powerful storm surge. By permission of Laura Harrison.

Figure 8.6. *Mayday* was embedded within the detritus of the 2024 hurricanes, evoking a call for help. By permission of Brooke Hansen.

Figure 8.7. The ruins of the dock near the Pilots' village after Hurricanes Helene and Milton. By permission of Laura Harrison.

Figure 8.8. A cottage in the Pilots' village, destroyed by Hurricane Helene and Hurricane Milton. By permission of Laura Harrison.

Figure 8.9. There was once a thriving population of gopher tortoises on Egmont Key, but Hurricane Helene and Milton decimated the population. By permission of Laura Harrison.

were able to arrange industrial-scale wreckage removal, focusing primarily on the mountain of debris strewn along the shoreline and the Pilots' Village. Recreational boaters and tourist ferries continue to go the island regardless of the hazards. The days of old in the 1960s and '70s when many boats landed on an unsupervised island leaving piles of beer cans and trash may unfortunately return again unless monitoring can be restored.

Almost a year to the day after Helene, the first major cleanup of the island was organized by numerous community organizations, including Take MAR, the Egmont Key Alliance, Tampa Bay Estuary Program, and Suncoast Aquaventures, among others. Volunteers, including those from the University of South Florida's Sustainable Tourism class, were met with piles of trash, hundreds of beverage cans and bottles, the bedliner of a truck, and over a thousand pounds of twisted and rusted metal. Half of a mannequin wearing navy blue pants was located in the bush by the USF students wondering how he got there and who he was (8.10). We discovered he was an exhibit prop that was originally placed inside of one the buildings adjacent to the lighthouse. He was displayed among other items that spoke to the long history of the US Coast Guard, and he was wearing a Coast Guard uniform and hat. How he washed out of the building and lost his upper half is anyone's guess.

Figure 8.10. USF student volunteers find half a mannequin in the Egmont Key cleanup on September 27, 2025. By permission of Brooke Hansen.

Prospective: Looking Forward

The gravity of destruction, devastation, and loss at Egmont Key in the past and present makes it challenging to predict what lies ahead for the island. It is interesting how this question has been pondered for decades. In 1988, the *Orlando Sentinel* ran an article about the island noting its "wild past" as a prison, a fort, and a refuge and stated that its future is "up for grabs" (Orlando Sentinel 1988). This is especially relevant now as the first quarter of the twenty-first century has come to a close. Egmont Key's histories and ecosystems face great risks in the coming decades, and the island is at a crossroads. If it washes away, will we have done enough to document, preserve, and memorialize its many histories, including those that are lesser known? If the island does wash away, it will survive digitally and in the oral histories and experiences of many, including the Seminole Tribe of Florida. Memories are still held by visitors across decades who have spent time on the island. It is, however, much more difficult to keep intangible heritage alive when the tangible foundations are gone. Additionally, while cultural heritage can live on without the existence of a physical place, this is not the case for the thousands of birds, gopher tortoises, and other species that call the island home. When the island disappears, so do they. There are very few habitats left along the Florida Gulf Coast that have not been swallowed up by development or overrun with tourists.

IMMEDIATE NEEDS AT EGMONT KEY: A NEAR-FUTURE PRAGMATIC AGENDA

The immediate future of Egmont Key involves some pressing priorities: to clean up the wreckage from the hurricanes and ensure land manager presence to monitor and patrol the island, especially in the National Wildlife Refuge area that already had issues with staffing coverage. It is uncertain how the Florida Park Service will reinstate a full-time ranger with no house or dock left for them, and how much of a presence USFWS will be able to maintain after facing massive federal job cuts in 2025. For either of these agencies to have around-the-clock management, staff needs to be allocated and the infrastructure repaired including the dock, suitable housing, and other essential amenities. This is challenging with federal funding cuts across the board affecting agencies that are tied to Egmont Key.

Other immediate issues that need to be addressed include evaluating the impact and damage done to populations of birds and turtles who count on Egmont Key as a nesting and habitation site. The island sustained loss of coastline in the critical area within the National Wildlife Refuge during the hurricanes of 2024. There are multiple barriers for USFWS to evaluate the effects of the storms on the terrestrial and sea turtle populations. They might be unable to carry out yearly turtle nest counts and protections. In the past this work was done in collaboration with Florida Park Service and community groups such as the Egmont Key Alliance, Friends of the Tampa Bay Refuges, and Eckerd College. To resume these ecological-monitoring activities, it is imperative that the island be cleaned up with dangerous debris removed and infrastructure repaired. While we witnessed dead gopher tortoises during our post-hurricane Valentine's Day visit, other interesting accounts assert that some of them washed up at Fort De Soto Park, about 1.6 miles away across the Egmont Channel. As many as 50 tortoises from Egmont have been reported on Pinellas County beaches (some of them had markings as part of prior studies).

Like Egmont Key itself, these reports are mysterious, and it is intriguing to ponder the land-based reptiles being swept out to sea and making it across the turbulent channel in a hurricane event with strong winds and high surf. We applaud their tenacity for surviving this journey.

COLLABORATIONS AND PARTICIPATORY ACTION: A FUTURE ASPIRATIONAL AGENDA

The Egmont Key Project has been guided by participatory approaches and has striven to be inclusive, locally grounded but globally relevant, and to stress the importance of stewarding heritage at risk—both cultural and natural heritage following SDG 11.4 (protecting and preserving natural and cultural heritage). As in the past, the way forward for Egmont Key will involve collaborations of many kinds and participation from key stakeholders. These include nonprofit organizations, Friends groups, government agencies that have a stake on the island (county, state, federal), tourism organizations, and academic institutions and projects like the one we have described in this volume. Will this be enough? Will we be able to implement lessons learned about sustainable land management, interpretation, and heritage conservation? Or will the vision for a sustainable, engaging, inclusive, and thriving island be sidelined because of red tape, a lack of funding, or sheer apathy?

There is some talk among stakeholders, including us, about how we can all come together to make sure that Egmont Key is resurrected to the degree it can be. Fallen-down interpretive signs can be updated and reinstalled. The moldy items in the restored Guardhouse could be removed, and the area and exhibits cleaned with the air-conditioning restored. The gun batteries could be physically conserved and stabilized. The lighthouse could be opened to tourists. New infrastructure, which is required for the land managers to maintain an on-island presence, could bring some innovative sustainable designs that will be more resilient when the next storm comes. Groups that have already worked in the past on turtle nest monitoring and bird counts can continue. Education about Egmont Key can be done—and has been done—off-site. While we have delivered many international presentations about our work on the island, an ideal location for continuous interpretation is at the adjacent Fort De Soto, a county park with millions of annual visitors that already has a small museum not far from the shore where the Egmont Key Lighthouse can clearly be seen.

EGMONT KEY: A BEACON FOR US ALL

The Egmont Key Lighthouse is a vibrant, vivid beacon in Tampa Bay—a landmark that has withstood the battering of many storms while safely guiding ships through tumultuous waters. The structure lends a feeling of permanence to the sandy soils at Egmont Key's north end; its strong brick walls reaching up toward the sky, where its beacon radiates out toward the horizon. The structure sits at the nexus of the past and the future; with deep histories embedded in its aging brick walls that bore witness to many triumphs and tragedies of past centuries. Yet the structure is also fully of the moment, guiding maritime traffic in and out of the busy Port of Tampa in a modern, changing world. After everything, it stands.

The Egmont Key Lighthouse is a symbol of heritage, change, and resilience, all key themes of this book. It serves as a tangible link between the past and the present, yet it also faces an uncertain future with the question of how rising seas, strong storms, and erosion might one day leave it in ruins. It is visually striking to all from a distance, yet closed and inaccessible up close; its timeless design marred with fading paint and rusted iron. In many ways, the lighthouse is a metaphor for Egmont Key itself—a beacon of the bay that raises awareness of the island and its surrounding waters, despite challenges that evolve over the centuries.

We hope this book also serves as a beacon for residents of Tampa Bay and beyond. As the lighthouse is there to protect people, our chapters foretell and warn people of the dangers that lie ahead, and the need for decisive and quick action. This imperative is of the moment—informed by the latest research on climate, sustainability, and heritage. It is also retrospective; informed by history, with an honest assessment of the difficulties the island has faced in terms of management, heritage destruction, and erosion. It is our hope that these perspectives anchor Egmont Key as a sentinel of a changing Tampa Bay and guide readers and community members toward working together to honor history and heritage and face the challenges that lay before us.

References Cited

Guzzo, Paul. 2025. USF Is Digitally Preserving Egmont Key's Historic Harbor Pilot Village. USF Newsroom, March 17, 2025. https://www.usf.edu/news/2025/usf-is-digitally-preserving-egmont-keys-historic-harbor-pilot-village.aspx, accessed June 25, 2025.

Orlando Sentinel. 1988. Island in the Stream: Egmont Key Has Been a Fort, a Refuge, a

Prison. It Has a Wild Past. Its Future Is Up for Grabs. *Orlando Sentinel*, April 24, updated July 29, 2021. https://www.orlandosentinel.com/1988/04/24/island-in-the-stream-egmont-key-has-been-a-fort-a-refuge-a-prison-it-has-a-wild-past-its-future-is-up-for-grabs/, accessed January 15, 2025.

US Fish and Wildlife Service (USFWS). 2010. Comprehensive Conservation Plan: Tampa Bay Refuges. May. Southeast Region, Atlanta, GA. https://iris.fws.gov/APPS/ServCat/Reference/Profile/168154.

Contributors

Alex Fawbush is an archaeologist and digital heritage specialist at the University of South Florida's Access 3D Lab and Institute for Digital Exploration (IDEx). His expertise centers on advanced 3D imaging, lidar processing, and digital preservation. He produces precise point clouds and digital surrogates that support research, teaching, and public engagement. At USF, he works closely with faculty, students, and partners, providing training and consultation in 3D technologies, developing workflows, and contributing to public outreach through demonstrations, lab tours, and digital platforms. His archaeological fieldwork spans Florida and Sicily, including projects with the American Veterans Archaeological Recovery program and Cultural Resource Management (CRM) firms. His publications highlight digital heritage and lidar applications in archaeology and public history. He holds a Master of Arts and a Bachelor of Arts in Anthropology from the University of South Florida, as well as an Associate of Arts degree in Anthropology from Columbia State Community College.

Steven Fernandez is an associate instructor in the Master of Urban and Regional Planning Program at the University of South Florida. His expertise is in geospatial technologies, including GIS, UAS, and Lidar mapping and analysis. Steven has 21 years of experience in the private sector working on site suitability and location analysis for commercial real estate. Those projects were completed for over 250 municipalities in 20 states, 50 of which required fieldwork data collection. He has conducted various terrestrial and aerial lidar projects throughout the Eastern United States, US Virgin Islands, Hawaii, Italy, France, Spain, Armenia, Mexico, and Guatemala. In 2018, he joined the MURP program where he developed four graduate courses that focus on Urban Planning and Lidar applications of GIS. Steven Fernandez has a MA Degree in Geography from the University of South Florida, and a BS from SUNY Oneonta in Geography–Cartography and Remote Sensing.

Brooke Hansen is director of the Hospitality and Tourism Management Program in the Muma College of Business at the University of South Florida.

She serves as an Expert for Hospitality Net's World Panel and as an Academic Affiliate at the Center for Responsible Travel (CREST). Numerous grants, including two from the US Department of State, have her funded research projects on virtualization technologies for cultural heritage tourism, sustainable businesses practices, eco-certifications in tourism, and promoting the UN Sustainable Development Goals. She also works as a consultant with hospitality companies and internationally on sustainable development projects. She is a Fulbright Specialist in Serbia hosted by the University of Belgrade Faculty of Economics working on extended reality applications for tourism. Dr. Hansen is a social scientist and received her PhD from the University of Arizona in Anthropology and her bachelor's degree in psychology from the University of South Florida.

Laura K. Harrison is principal of Archeo Consulting and former director of Access 3D Lab at the University of South Florida. She serves as a City of Tampa Historic Preservation Commissioner and Associate Editor of Studies in Digital Heritage. Her research in digital heritage, archaeology, and museums includes work in Turkey, Greece, Sicily, Malta, Serbia, New York, and Florida, and has been funded by organizations including the National Science Foundation, Archaeological Association of America, National Park Service, and the US Department of State. Dr. Harrison is also the scientific director of Project CLAY (Creative Learning Through Archaeology), an educational outreach startup. A thread that connects her work in heritage and museums is a focus on ethical, applied, and community-driven approaches. She received her PhD and MA from the University at Buffalo and her BA from Ithaca College.

April Min is a genealogist, anthropologist, and attorney who brings more than 25 years of research expertise to her storytelling. As founder of Heritage Discoveries, she specializes in uncovering lost histories through archival, historical, and genealogical research. Her current work also includes forensic genealogy, where she provides heir and estate research, kinship reports, and narrative family histories. Past anthropological and historical research has included topics such as African and Dutch heritage in Curaçao, African American historical figures in Tampa, Florida, and a historical analysis of the evolution of the Pinellas Bayway in St. Petersburg, Florida. Min holds an MA in Applied Anthropology from the University of South Florida, and a JD from the West Virginia University College of Law.

Tina Osceola is the Executive Director of Operations for the Seminole Tribe of Florida's Tribal Historic Preservation Office. She is an enrolled member of the Seminole Tribe of Florida and serves as both the Tribal Historic Preservation Officer and the Director of the program. Osceola has served her Tribe in many capacities, including being appointed an Associate Trial Judge on the first Tribal Court. Osceola is a lifelong resident of Naples, Florida, where she lives with her family. Osceola is a graduate of Rollins College, where she earned a BA in Political Science, and of Nova Southeastern University, where she received a master's degree in public administration.

Richard Sanchez is a lifelong resident of Tampa, Florida, and has been involved in historical research on Tampa Bay and the State of Florida for many years. He spent 17 years volunteering with the State Park Service at Egmont Key and was president of the volunteer organization, the Egmont Key Alliance, for 15 years. He worked in telecommunications for over 30 years before retiring to pursue historical work on Tampa Bay and volunteering with the Tampa Bay History Center and the Tampa Rough Riders where he is on the Historical Committee. He is the author of several books including *Egmont Key: Stories from Eyewitnesses to History*.

Dave Scheidecker is the senior research coordinator for the Seminole Tribe of Florida's Tribal Historic Preservation Office. He has worked on historic and prehistoric archaeological sites in Texas, Ecuador, and Zimbabwe before returning to Florida. Scheidecker has been with the THPO since 2015. He graduated from Florida Atlantic University with a BA in history, and from Texas Tech with a master's degree in anthropology.

Index

www.ingramcontent.com/pod-product-compliance
Lightning Source LLC
LaVergne TN
LVHW060932180926
848329LV00035B/396